LOVELY, HUMAN, TRUE, HEARTFELT: THE LETTERS OF ALINA SZAPOCZNIKOW AND RYSZARD STANISŁAWSKI 1948–1971

BOOKS
N°6
The MUSEUM UNDER CONSTRUCTION book series
We are building a Museum of Modern Art in Warsaw
We are writing a new history of art

LOVELY, HUMAN, TRUE, HEARTFELT: THE LETTERS OF ALINA SZAPOCZNIKOW AND RYSZARD STANISŁAWSKI 1948–1971

EDITED BY AGATA JAKUBOWSKA, KATARZYNA SZOTKOWSKA-BEYLIN
TRANSLATED BY JENNIFER CROFT

MUSEUM OF MODERN ART IN WARSAW 2012

BOOKS
N°6

INTRODUCTION

Alina Szapocznikow (1926–1973) and Ryszard Stanisławski (1921–2000) met in Paris in 1948—they recognized July 14 as the date and later celebrated it as "their anniversary." She came to Paris in the fall of 1947 from Prague, where she had ended up after the end of the Second World War, most likely accompanying Czech women that had been in the concentration camps with her and were subsequently liberated (researchers are not certain which camp was the final site of Szapocznikow's wartime ordeal; the basic information about her childhood and her youth under the Nazi occupation has been placed in the notes to the letters). In Prague she began to sculpt, first working in Otokar Velimski's stonemasonry, then as a student at the Academy of Arts, Architecture and Design in Josef Wagner's studio. The circumstances of her voyage from Czechoslovakia to Paris are unknown. We do know that it occurred in November of 1947, and that Szapocznikow continued her art studies in France, attending classes at the École Nationale Supérieure des Beaux-Arts.

Ryszard Stanisławski, when the war was over, lived for a few months in Warsaw, then in Wrocław, where he enrolled at the University of Technology. Unable to legally transfer to a French university, in the spring of 1946 he fled Poland via the so-called "green border" (illegal crossings through forests or other poorly guarded areas) and spent several months (perhaps an entire year) in the ranks of the First

Polish Armored Division in Meppen (in Lower Saxony). In 1947, he made it to Paris, where he attended a French-language course at the École Supérieure de Préparation et de Perfectionnement des Professeurs de Français à l'Etranger at the Sorbonne. Stanisławski described meeting his future wife as follows:

> It was a coincidence with Alina, I would call it a "Slavic-type coincidence". We met at one of those canteens at Port-Royal [...]. A friend from the Armored Division—[Mieczysław] Szabliński [...], who had come to Paris with me—used to frequent it. He had ended up at the École Nationale Supérieure des Beaux-Arts, and one day he came for lunch with Alina.[1]

The first extant letters from Alina Szapocznikow to Ryszard Stanisławski come from August 1948, thus they were written shortly after they met. The last letter, from September 1971, was written by Szapocznikow a year-and-a-half before she died. The correspondence is not merely a record of their relationship—of their love and then friendship (they divorced in 1958), but also of professional formation and of artistic life. The most emotionally charged letters, as is not surprising, are letters from the first years of their acquaintance. They are moving not only for their intensity of emotion, but also their passion in the description of the world and of the search for a path in life. It becomes clear what most influenced the fate of a whole line of artists and intellectuals, particularly those that lived and worked between Poland and France—and what an enormous influence on the formation of their attitudes and beliefs the western Left had.

In 1951, Szapocznikow and Stanisławski returned to Poland, taking up residence in Warsaw. A year later they were married and adopted a son, Piotr. They started to successfully build their professional positions—she as a sculptor, he as an art historian. During those years, the most intense exchange of letters took place in the summer of 1956—Szapocznikow was in Paris at the time, and Stanisławski in Italy. All of their letters, but these in particular, portray the political and economic context of the activities of Polish artists and intellectuals; they speak, among other things, of the typical difficulties encountered by citizens of the People's Republic of Poland who wished to work outside of Poland as well, or to at least be able to go abroad.

1 Piotr Rypson, *Dwie rozmowy z Ryszardem Stanisławskim* [*Two Conversations with Ryszard Stanisławski*], CSW, Warszawa, 2006, p. 19. This publication accompanying the exhibition "Ryszard Stanisławski: The Open Museum," curated by Agnieszka Szewczyk and Paweł Polit, CSW, Warszawa, 2006 [also available at www.obieg.pl/rozmowy/1391].

The last group of letters between Szapocznikow and Stanisławski—from the beginning of the 1960s up until 1971—has a different quality, as did their relationship. Following their divorce, Alina Szapocznikow lived with graphic artist Roman Cieślewicz (1930–1996), and Ryszard Stanisławski entered into a relationship with art historian Urszula Czartoryska (1934–1998). In 1963, Szapocznikow and Cieślewicz decided to settle in Paris. Szapocznikow and Stanisławski remained friends, as evidenced by the tone of the letters that have been preserved: considerably more laconic, but nonetheless still heartfelt. They are no longer, however, just letters between the two of them—Alina and Roman and Piotr would write to Ryszard and Urszula together. We have elected to maintain the portions of Szapocznikow's letters that have been added to by her second husband and by her son (after leaving Poland, Piotr Stanisławski would write to his father first in Polish, then later in French). In fact, they form a coherent whole, reflecting the evolving nature of the relationship linking our two epistolary heroes. Not a single letter from Ryszard Stanisławski has been preserved from this period, and of the earlier letters there remain just a few. The explanation for this lies in the fact that it was Stanisławski who attempted to conserve all the documents. That he not only always dated his letters, but also noted the dates on which he responded to letters received attests to his meticulousness. Szapocznikow does not appear to have attached the same weight to such things. Stanisławski managed to save a few of the letters he had written to her during the time they shared together, but the later letters are most likely lost.

Two narrative threads predominate in the letters from the 1960s—the first concerns their son Piotr, and the second work-related issues. The changing professional position of Szapocznikow and Stanisławski both is evident. Ryszard Stanisławski was consistently developing his career—he first worked at the State Institute of Art, and then at the Ministry of Art and Culture, as well as for the Desa Bureau of Foreign Trade (the latter a state enterprise charged during the era of People's Republic of Poland with the sales of works of art and antiques). He served in that period as curator of a range of important exhibitions of Polish art abroad. In 1966, he became the director of the Muzeum Sztuki in Łódź (and remained in that position until 1991), building the prestige of that institution not only in Poland but all over the world. His innovative way of thinking about the museum as the institution inspires to this day. Szapocznikow enjoyed a very good period in Poland in the late 1950s and early 60s: she was an artist valued by critics and public alike. She was not able to match this success in France. At the beginning of 1967, she was writing to the painter Wojciech Fangor, whom she had befriended, that Cieślewicz *unfortunately irrationally throws away* [his money] *on financing my art, which, like anything else that is different and interesting, no one here wants* [Wojciech Fangor Archive]. Her situation did improve somewhat later: she had solo shows, took part in several important international projects, and sold some of her work, but it would still be difficult to call hers a great success. But this was to come only 40 years or so after her death.

In Poland, Szapocznikow is an artist that is consistently present, particularly intensively since the exhibitions organized in 1998 by the Zachęta Gallery in Warsaw, the National Museums in Krakow and Wrocław, and the Muzeum Sztuki in Łódź. Outside of Poland, she is being discovered only now. Her work is being shown in international exhibitions (among others at the Museum of Modern Art in New York in 2012), and aquired for the permanent collections of the world's major museums like the Centre Pompidou in Paris and the Tate Modern in London. Her work contains elements that fascinate today's audiences: the trauma of the Holocaust, corporality and sexuality, formal experimentation, departure from classical sculpture and a movement toward "awkward objects"—polyester casts of the body, "photosculptures" out of chewing gum, and conceptual art. In response to the growing interest in her work, in 2011 the Museum of Modern Art in Warsaw published a collection of papers on her work, *Alina Szapocznikow: Awkward Objects*, edited by Agata Jakubowska. We have now undertaken to present material that offers a glimpse both of the distinguished sculptor herself and of Ryszard Stanisławski, an art historian of great significance for Polish culture.

Agata Jakubowska

The correspondence between Alina Szapocznikow and Ryszard Stanisławski is published here for the first time (a modest selection of the letters prepared by Stanisławski was included in the catalogue of the aforementioned exhibitions organized on the occasion of the 25th anniversary of Szapocznikow's death). Here we print every letter written by the couple still extant. They are held in two archives: Szapocznikow's letters from the period of her relationship with Ryszard Stanisławski (here letters 1 to 103) are held by their son, Piotr Stanisławski; those from the 1960s and '70s (letters 104 to 142) were in the Ryszard Stanisławski Archive (now at the Institute of Art of the Polish Academy of Sciences), belonging to Olga Stanisławska, Stanisławski's daughter from his marriage to Urszula Czartoryska.

For permission to publish this correspondence, we wish to extend our heartfelt thanks to the authors' heirs, Olga Stanisławska and Piotr Stanisławski. We thank Wojciech Fangor for allowing us to cite excerpts from his unpublished text, as well as letters sent to him by Alina Szapocznikow. The majority of the supplementary information pertaining to these letters has been taken from the Alina Szapocznikow Archive (National Museum in Krakow, some of it on the website of the Museum of Modern Art in Warsaw: www.artmuseum.pl/archiwa.php) and from the Ryszard Stanisławski Archive (Special Collections at the Institute of Art of the Polish Academy of Sciences'). Jola Gola's publications have been exceptionally valuable, above all her catalogue of sculptures by Szapocznikow (*Katalog rzeźb Aliny Szapocznikow*, National Museum in Krakow, 2001). We also owe a great deal to those willing to share their knowledge—their information enriched the notes in addition to allowing us to correct some errors. We also extend our particular gratitude to Olga Stanisławska and Piotr Stanisławski. We also extend our gratitude to Anna Grabowska-Konwent of the National Museum in Poznań, Professor Marcin Kula of the University of Warsaw's Institute of History, the Czech art historian Tomáš Pospiszyl, Dr. Joanna Sosnowska of the Institute of Art at the Polish Academy of Sciences, Agnieszka Szewczyk of the Museum of the Academy of Fine Arts in Warsaw, as well as Alina Szapocznikow's friends Michelle Zahorska and Adam Leśniewski. We have doubtless not managed to elucidate the entire background relating to the letters, nor to note every error, and would be grateful if any corrections could be directed to the following address: katarzyna.szotkowska@artmuseum.pl.

The person who put together this volume, and the author of its notes, is Agata Jakubowska. Katarzyna Szotkowska-Beylin has been responsible for editing both the correspondence and the notes. Małgorzata Jakubowska transcribed the letters, and Anna Leyk translated fragments written in French. We extend our sincere gratitude to Maria Ofierska for her insights into the book.

Alina Szapocznikow had a unique, dynamic style in Polish, and her quirks and flourishes have in large part been preserved in the English translation. Piotr Stanisławski's "Frenchified" Polish has been rendered as English with a French flavor, and his early adolescent errors in French have been remained. Foreign phrases have been placed in italics, and the writers' emphases have been underlined. Most but not all of the abbreviations common in Polish (such as "f. ex." in lieu of "for example") have been expanded. Errors in proper names have been corrected, and their spelling has been standardized. The few sections of the letters that were crossed-out have been marked; isolated illegible sections have also been noted. Notes from the editors, and the dates established in the course of research have been put in brackets. Notes to the letters have been restricted to persons alive in the twentieth century.

The majority of the photographic reproductions come from the Alina Szapocznikow Archive (belonging to Piotr Stanisławski and located in the National Museum in Krakow). Most of the photographs from that archive are available on the website of the Museum of Modern Art in Warsaw.

Agata Jakubowska, Katarzyna Szotkowska-Beylin

11

THE LETTERS OF ALINA SZAPOCZNIKOW AND RYSZARD STANISŁAWSKI 1948–1971

Champagne
Monday

It was probably good that the train left a little earlier than scheduled. It saved us a few conventional moments of farewells. It itself (the train) was simply overcome, abashed, and... it ran away. And it was only then that something inside me tightened (intensely, I must admit), maybe my stomach, or maybe my heart.
It is extremely beautiful here. These are the same Jura Mountains that stretch from here across Switzerland and Italy.
The village is utterly tiny, 110 inhabitants, beautifully ensconced in a valley. Stone houses and such a lovely little Romanesque church. My hosts' home is a half-destroyed little cottage 3 or 400 years old, but there is 100% freedom and chaos. A little neglected garden and jugs of milk.
By yesterday I was taking full advantage of all the delights of the village. Of the air, the sun, the cool, crystal-clear water of the mountain stream (the Loue). They even had a traditional village celebration here yesterday where the girls were standing on one side, and the boys on the other, as well as different "attractions" like a lottery, ribbons, etc. They played *musettes*, and the company frolicked in the green grass. I couldn't sleep for a long time after, because they kept playing "Pigalle." Besides that I drank two whole liters of milk straight from the cow and am also meticulously devoured by mosquitoes. The latter are the most despicable plague of village life. Rysiu, if you want to save my life and save even just 1 cm^2 of smooth skin, find out at the pharmacy if they don't have something to fight them off and send it right away.
Mosquitos = *moustique* (moo-steek).
Rysiu my darling, it would be extremely lovely here with

you. (It's also possible that with the sweetness of your body you would draw the mosquitoes away from me, and they would find nourishment on your skin.)

There is stone here! If you haven't been to the studio yet, and you're going, tell Ivo to send me chisels and the hammer, that bigger one, right away. Although you don't have to, because I am writing to him anyway. Unless you were to come here on Sunday—then bring it with you.

If you don't want to stay here even one day (because it's all the same train, and you would rest in the long uncomfortable journey), then just write when you're coming, and I'll come by bicycle to Mouchard station, and we'll talk a few minutes. I am filling up the rest of this letter with the understandable things that always come at the end, though we must still be very cautious in these.

Please take care of yourself and kindly recover.

My sweetest Rysiu, Rysieńku

Your Ala

[NOTE IN THE MARGIN:]

Write how business is going?

[POSTSCRIPT ON THE ENVELOPE:]

The violets arrived in one piece

NOTES →[P 290]

Wednesday

Rysiu my darling, I'm so sad about your Sunday letter. It is (and you don't even know this) completely existential. The form of your ideas completely reminds me of Camus' *Étranger*, and actually the whole thing is a little bit like Dygat's *Lake Constance*..That is bad, bad, and a shame for you to have gotten into such a state of nihilism. And the damnedest part is I feel I can do nothing in the face of it.

I never thought that money would get in my way like this and had never before experienced the intense and cruel power of cash. Because in general, you know, I always have "something some way or other," enough even for a rather pleasant life. And there is a lot of selfishness in this sadness. Just a childish I-can't-have-what-I-want. And I want you to be doing well, so that you might leave at least for just a little while, and so that you didn't get into those kinds of states that wind up in a vicious circle of hopelessness.

Besides which I am kicking myself because the money you sent me I rashly spent right away to pay for an excursion to Geneva (I'm going there on Sunday), and you meanwhile are suffocating like that over in Paris.

But I thought that my mom's letters would come, and that you were preparing to leave.

Please, before you do go, send me Mietek's address.

Thank you for the chocolate, that kid you chatted with must be a regular swine. A brat like that going and getting himself those idiotic calling cards printed up (did you see them?) is just too much. His cousin was a fantastic man.

It's so stunning here that I can't describe it to you at all. I ride my bicycle to a little town nearby to pick up the mail and to neighboring villages. A road between the

hills and leafy forests. A truly French landscape. Little stone houses, and there is the scent of honey and all the herbs and grasses that comes off the fields. I am blissful, and my soul is at peace. I would like to roam around with you here.
What really troubles and distresses me is that my hosts (uncommonly good people) kill ants, bees, wasps, even butterflies, without giving it any thought. Yesterday I thought I would burst into tears and run out because they killed a bumblebee, and I so love them, and they did it in such a beastly way. This really pains me.
They have excursions to Switzerland by [ILLEGIBLE] coach from here that are not expensive. If you will be there, I'll come and visit you.
Rysiu, one more request.
Please go and see Mrs. Mantorelle and ask if I haven't gotten any letters from Salska on Dworcowa Street to her address *pour Alena S.* Because my mom wrote to me that she was sending money. If there is something there, send it to me. You can also do it in a letter.
Darling, I am in a hurry, because I have to go to the post office.
I send you a big kiss, and thank you so much for the letters. I pine here, and they give me a lot of joy.

Your Ala

P.S. I just got your third letter, which is wonderful and simple, but which saddened me (Switzerland). I retract everything bad I have written about your letters up until now.
My mom wrote. Big kiss, again

A

Rysiu, don't worry about anything, everything will work out "somehow."
So we shall see each other soon.
Rysiu, you have no idea how much better a person

becomes and how beautiful it is to be in nature.
Remember your treatment.

[NOTES BETWEEN PARAGRAPHS:]
There is a sad emaciated dog here, but he is already very loyal to me, I'm fattening him up.
Wonderful poem.
I'll respond to the other letter in my next letter.
Did you receive my 1st letter?

It's raining, so I can't go yet, and I'm writing you a few lines more.
I want to respond at least briefly to your third letter. It's so lovely, and it brought me so much joy. I'm just so proud of you, the way you write about your future and about Poland. There is quite a bit more to say on that subject. On the other hand, I'm afraid to take on so much responsibility, because Argentina versus being a student here for 2 more years, that's something that will influence your whole life. Rysiu, I can tell from your letter that you're sad and worried about a lot of things. Please decide exactly what you want to do over the break, what kind of job, and then make absolutely sure you get it. I'm sure it will work out. Have faith!!! Please don't worry about anything. If you're going to be in Paris, then at least you'll really recover. And when you have a moment to spare, get out wherever you can, into the woods or the water. Don't be angry at my unjustly cruel remarks, and take care!

Your Ala

NOTES →[P 291]

dimanche

d'abord forgive me for writing in pencil, but they don't even have ink in this dump, and I'm not cycling to [PORT-] Lesney until tomorrow.
Rysiu, I've grown so accustomed to your letters that I'm more and more fond of them. They come regularly like my hosts' *L'Humanité*, the difference being that in the case of *L'Humanité* I have to listen to all the dreadful "délits" that Madame Hélène reads aloud and grows terribly concerned about. I confess I am more concerned about the fate of my correspondent on the Boulevard Raspail. Please, in all seriousness, how are you actually doing? It really wouldn't be the worst thing in the world to go to those Polish country folk, at least you would get out of town and breathe in the wide expanse of the fields. (That cures the nerves wonderfully and does a person so much good.) Naturally considering your injections I would prefer you to find something in Paris, and of course also because you prefer that.
You know, I was thinking you should sell that suit for now, it is lovely, but—I confess now that I am far away, for from a distance I have no fear—I can't stand you in it. Later you can buy yourself something else that fits you. But enough "butting into your affairs."
There are no cliffs here at all like you imagine, they're magnificent hills all covered in grass, and cows graze on their slopes. They have bells on their necks that have this incredibly pure tone, and they walk in a dignified, milky, serious manner, nipping at the fragrant meadows and slowly ringing. These are the French Alps. The purest air, and higher up above the pastures there are vineyards, and above the vineyards forests and shrubs, and it's only when you get up into the clouds that there are really cliffs, but they're far.

I go around half-naked and completely barefoot, caressed by the sun, and the mosquitoes have finally buzzed off (thank you for the ointment).
My friend from Prague wrote that he wants to claim his emigration pass [PASSPORT] and come here and live with me. And suddenly, faced with the real prospect of living with him for good (because that is why he wants to give up his homeland now), I panicked. And... I realized that I don't want that at all. I can say clearly now: I don't love him anymore, I don't love him as a man. But I still can't say clearly: I love you. Because it's one thing to whisper "my darling" into someone's ear. But it's another thing entirely to properly, honestly, clearly know: I love him, this is my man and will be for all time.
What you write about love as an addiction is very true. Mr. S. Dygat wrote about that in his book *Lake Constance.* He writes that "love is a negative feeling, we feel its lack when it is far away from us." You have to read that book if you haven't done it yet. *Les Lettres françaises* is very good, especially the little article about folk art. I think that Poland is the first country where that gets the attention it deserves, and where it gets handled appropriately.
That was also a nice reproduction of the design on glass. I found quite an interesting little case here with little medallions and little crosses. Two of them are actually really lovely. I am sending you one silver Madonna, so that you have something from me "for luck." It might seem a bit paradoxical to you that I am sending you a Madonna, but it is precisely to highlight my full tolerance and love of things that are beautiful.
All right, that's enough for today. I await your letters. But please eschew difficult words, I'm too lazy right now to have to think so much. Besides that, older women are also beautiful, and have nothing to do with flowers. (A woman is a person, not a flower.)
Life is short, is lovely, as long as it can be sincere, true, and strong, not sugary sentimental. Flowers are a mir-

acle of nature and a joy to humanity. Although of course everything is a miracle of nature. The strongest word in your letter is “damned.” It was only then that I really felt how damned much you love me, and you don’t have to be sorry for that.
I’m thinking of returning to Paris in 1 week–10 days. There’s a wonderful dog here that they never feed, and I can’t do anything about it. I would so love to, but I’ll be damned if I can permit myself even that, just think what it would be with a child.
I send you a big kiss

Your Alena

Rysiu, Rysieńku, do you know now?
Kisses,

Ala

[POSTSCRIPT ON THE ENVELOPE:]
We went by barge along the Loue between reeds and the green slopes of the Alps. A heavenly peace and joy settles upon a person. There are blackberry bushes everywhere.

SZAPOCZNIKOW TO STANISŁAWSKI
[AUGUST 12, 1948]
NOTES →[P 292]

Thursday

Rysiu!
I wrote you an idiotic and nonsensical letter yesterday, don't take it too much to heart.
My mom wrote from Lower Silesia, she's on holiday. She sent funds for Mietek's sister. 10 t [THOUSAND].
Rysiu, you madman, write what you want, we'll argue in person, it's much more fun. Baudelaire is the greatest poet in the world.
Stone is the most beautiful material.
Rysiu, Rysieńku! If I want to, one way or another (the thing with my professor), then don't worry, I'm not doing it because of you, or because I'm counting on you or want to become involved with you. I want to live freely and like I like. I want to work and study, that's the most important thing!
I'm actually ashamed to write about the wonders of being here (and they don't even please me as much anymore), when I think about your situation.
I have quite a few Polish papers here. Madame Hélène subscribes to *Kuźnica* and *Odrodzenie* and I have a ton, a ton of things to talk to you about. Scribbling is an idiotic labor. I feel I am more a person "of matter." I hammer a piece of stone, I don't know what will come of it. You know, I have no patience for anything, and the thought of an exam overwhelms me. That's why I would also just like to be in Paris already, to get it over with.
I read a lot here, lying on my back on a green hillside. In French, naturally. Right now I'm reading Gorky's *Cafards*. You know, I've come to the conclusion that the people who say that Dostoyevsky started existentialism and Sartre just dug it up again are actually right. Because in Gorky, too, I have found so much of exactly that heavy Russian philosophy. For example, he ends one of the

novellas, *Le Héros,* like this (proving that the protagonist, who is a threatening or cruel person, is actually the person that is most afraid)—*Je passai près d'un an en prison. Là, je fis connaissance d'une bande de brigands: cela me fit sortir de prison et me valut une pluie d'agents des recherché criminelles. J'ai tué des homes, cela se fait très simplement. Maintenant, je suis moi-même bandit. Je serais aussi bien bourreau. Tout m'est égal.*
Rysiu, please forgive the chaotic nature of my letter. (It's an excess of wide-ranging sensations.) And some that can't be written about.
Please hang in there! Don't go around with that awful spleenful Johnny. It's only 2 more months. So what difference could it possibly make if you just even went to that Polish farm? (You know, I may know of something for the last month for you.)
I would be so glad to hitchhike around with you. But this break is already off somehow. (Maybe Jasio didn't want to go with you because he was remembering "Siena-Marne"?)
Rysiu, you're horrible!
What am I to do with you?
Can it really be true that the only things left to me are kissing and caressing you? Yet I would so like to somehow help you in a "human," "friendly," "manly" way. But that is "somehow." While a kiss is real.

Your Ala

[NOTES IN THE MARGINS:]
this letter makes no sense
Rysiu, how is your recovery going, does your bottom hurt?

Rysiu. Don't forget—I am firstly me. While the people I meet I love, and they love me, which is the loveliest thing life gives me.
God lives in the mountains, while in the mornings,

behind the mist, a barefoot Christ walks in amongst the green slopes.
One would like to shout one's love out, and yet one feels so very humble before all this grandeur of nature's.
Rysiu, kiss me

Your Alina

St. Tropez
Friday

My Darling
—that is, after all, the simplest and truest I can start this missive.
We arrived here yesterday from Avignon, where I saw the pope's first palace. The first buildings containing Christian architecture are still full of their ancient (classical) predecessors.
The landscape here is just about southern, the bright shades of stone, sky blue, a flagrantly sky-blue sky, and the most important thing is the flora I've never seen before. You know, Rysiu, I've been constantly finding in these landscapes those old Gothic paintings of the French, but even more of the Italian, school. Those paintings people say didn't yet possess perspective. And here, as well, the landscape really is lacking in those laws. These cedars, cypresses, and palms, with their perfect, straight lines, seem to be just pasted onto the rocks without any sense of perspective. I don't really know if I am capable of explaining the sensation to you. I've never actually seen these kinds of shapes and lines before, aside from in the paintings I just mentioned.
My comrade had a rough voyage (his long legs are difficult to fit into a narrow compartment). In addition he was suffering from a slight cough and generally did not feel well. I made him tea, gave him medicaments, amused him, and took care of all the ticket and hotel formalities. I essentially simply feel needed, a little like a governess or a "companion." In a way I am happy that our relationship has reached this point "evolutionarily." A point that is "idyllic" on the surface. For a distinguished older gentleman is traveling with his little pupil. (I am drawing quite a lot under his tutelage). But the pupil has great difficulty reining in her explosive tem-

perament, and the pupil sometimes really does get as carried away and sentimental as a pre-teen.
And like a child I gape with open maw at all these miracles and see again how much there is to learn, learning is needed, and I see again what a young, wide road I still have ahead of me. And only in those moments do all the tangled little women's questions and progressions pour out of my mind, all those things that have already worried me so much that I have desired to cast them aside, even brushing aside with them the healthy young shoulder of a young new love. Always, always, and constantly we must begin afresh. Whether that means being an "eternal student" like Maria Skłodowska-Curie or whether that means eternally changing fields of study, or just eternally looking for new things. And that must come of experience.
Yes, but that has nothing to do with anything. We are now in St. Tropez, I am heading to Cannes and to Vallauris, Picasso's little town. Palm trees grow here just as pines would at home, cactuses grow up like great big trees. The sky is <u>sky-blue</u>, and the sea <u>turquoise</u>. Daisies bloom in meadows, even an apple tree I found in bloom. The more beautiful it is, the more pained I am by this powerlessness, by being unable to return all this accumulated love for nature to this man I love, the rightful owner of what nature has given us, creating us as a piece of all of this.
You can't describe these things, because what comes out of it is that sort of postcard that has an enamel sky, but maybe I will bring you a little bit of it on my skin, my lips, and maybe you will kiss it out of me.
Rysiu, if in your room this letter from the sunny seaside seems to you to be a parody, then know that in that very little room one could live moments 100 × sunnier, seasides of 100 times more joy.
I know. (I know from experience)

Your A

[NOTES IN THE MARGINS:]

That "handful of your observations" clenched up into a fist and struck the table: I know you are right, and I do really 100% recognize that. Unfortunately I am not always able to employ reason.

But neither are you, and Aristotle himself said, "I can't always be Aristotle." So Rysiu I kiss you here, for I truly miss you.

We have to experience this together. But really Rysiu the Baltic is better without chauvinism. It is healthier, mightier, and mine, close and mine. I love the Baltic × 1000000 just like all this

NOTES →[P 293]

Paris Saturday the 9th
4 p.m.

Rysiu
You might or might not be back by the time I finish writing this, I don't know if we will see each other again.
That doesn't matter, this "hunger" to see one another and to be together won't be slaked for now in any case.
Nevertheless here I am, and nevertheless I want to say something to you.
We met under the most ordinary, banal circumstances, or so it would appear from the outside—and in the most unusual, most intricate ones on the inside, where the soul resides. I don't know if the time will really come for me to be able to offer you up all this warmth, all these words that now make me swell to bursting. Or if instead the years will go by, and I will feel your footsteps ever so near me, always. But I know that it is you (perhaps without you even participating) that allowed me the blindness to bravely open my eyes and honestly slam the door shut on one chapter of my life. You released me. *L'amour nouvelle chasse l'ancienne*.
Now the time is coming where matters must be taken care of. Inward, "technical" matters. Matters in which no "pangs of the heart" have any say.
Time, honesty, strength, honor, humanity are needed.
I don't know how I will find you after this. I don't know if you will say "come here!" to me, I don't know if I will say "come" to you.
But before me there lies a free, clear, young, clean road.
What are you doing now, Rysiu?
I received a letter from Irka from Poland, and she writes that things are getting worse and worse there. My God, why? There are strikes in France. People are in pain everywhere, ~~damn~~ fury and sadness oppress me, and a sense of injustice and untruth.

All matters inside me are bad.
Shall we, too, Rysiu, complain?

A.

Write if you want
atelier address
Ivo wants to buy your military clothing.

Alina

[A CROSSED-OUT POSTSCRIPT AND NEXT TO IT A NOTE:]

here I had written that my professor is a noble man, but that doesn't matter.

7.
SZAPOCZNIKOW TO STANISŁAWSKI
[NOTE LEFT IN HIS ROOM, 1948]

Good morning boys!
Rysiu, I need John's army attire. Cash in hand. I'll come for it with 1000 fr. on Sunday evening around 6 or 7. You should be able to get it ready by then.
Please, it's really important.
You have horrible pencils!
If you aren't going to be at home, put it in Vincenz's room, and I'll just take it. Thank you.
Have you and Mietek signed up for school? I would like to kiss you, but that's probably for later.
For now be well and as always more paper Y

Alina

6$^{\underline{40}}$ in the evening

Rysiu
There's a little package for you in Miecio's room. Don't be mad, it's my mom's fault. Eat to her health.
If you happen upon a comb in Miecio's room, return it to me.
Be well
Yours always

thesameAlina

[NOTES IN THE MARGINS:]
Is Miecio back yet?
I'm leaving the bed the way I found it

A

Kiss.

SZAPOCZNIKOW TO STANISŁAWSKI
[NOTE LEFT IN HIS ROOM, 1948]

Rysiu, I'm so sorry that I forgot to give you these notes this morning, but I believe you should still receive them before dinner time. Get that blue sheet of paper to me, would you, and I'll buy you a new writing pad.
The belt cost 150, I think you'll like it.
I hope I see you at dinner, I'm reading something very interesting I'd like to talk with you about.
Thank God I don't believe in ghosts because I would be miserable alone in the atelier.

Your Alina

10.

SZAPOCZNIKOW TO STANISŁAWSKI
[NOTE LEFT IN HIS ROOM, 1948]

9^{20} o'clock

Good evening, Rysiu.
Are you very tired, my dearest?
I woke up with a slightly heavy head, though with joy in my heart. I mean, the general state +– evens out, to a normal capacity for thinking.
Rysiu, I feel like you might be partly right, after all, talking about the logic of life. (Despite this I don't regret a single senseless thing I've done thus far.) In the future, however, I will aim to mend my ways.
The Gauguin print I'm looking at is beautiful, and it soothes me.
I believe that with shared effort we will be able to be sensible and attempt to lend to life at least a little of the profound harmony that exists at the very least in that painting.

If I'm not back by 8^{45} p.m., and if you're not too tired and you feel like it, come.

Your Alina

11.

SZAPOCZNIKOW TO STANISŁAWSKI

POSTCARD, [NOVEMBER 4, 1948]

NOTES →[P 293]

Thursday 12 noon

The concierge woman didn't give me your letter until this morning, at which point yesterday's plans were irrelevant. Besides that, I think we both need to be consistent and wait until Sunday, although it is very hard for me. And I want to and have to talk to you. Apart from our matters, one other thing ails me.

Rysiu, please come tomorrow (Friday) evening to Crillon to Dr. Russak's house. I will be there at around 7. So we will see each other (this has nothing to do [CROSSED-OUT])
A heartfelt kiss

Your Alina

NOTES →[P 294]

Łódź
Thursday

Rysiu, my darling.
I arrived this morning. I just sent the packages, which they promised me would still get there by tomorrow.
I have such a muddle of impressions that I really cannot manage to come to any sort of definitive conclusion.
The sight of you in the "departing" window, then the journey, in the company of a Polish priest from Corsica and a Russian civilian emigré now returning home (a citizen of the USSR). Then Prague, and I am cold, sad, hungry, and then the Polish consulate and now leaving on a Polish train. Later a conversation with the conductor, who is "against," and the civilian, who is "pro." I was proud of the train, of the elegance of the conductor's manner, of the Polish customs officials and their Polish peaked caps.
The trip to Łódź in a 2nd-class compartment with 3 gentlemen, of whom one (electr. eng.) talked about neckties, vodka, about his life as a "man of the world," while the 2 others conversed in muffled voices about the improvement of the day nursery at their factory and about the better medical care for the women who work there that they needed to organize.
Łódź—I am proud of its riches, people are disheartened.
Greetings from my mom.
And suddenly I am so tired. I will write a letter to your father, as well. Forgive me, Ryś, this awful light blue paper, but it's all I've got.
And I miss you so much, Rysiu, would we could share every little sensation. I turn around and say, "Look at that, Ryszard." And in the semidarkness of the compartment I caressed my shoulder in order to ferret out the shape that you discovered there. It was your hands that discovered me, and beneath them my body takes on a reason for being.

I was crossing a white plain, outside there was a dry, sharp wind, the gals' breath billowed out from beneath the scarves they were wrapped up in, the fellows were clapping their arms against their sides, and even the horses breathed out white steam. And above the white snow the sun rose completely pink or the sky did, and it looked just exactly like the cheap kitsch they sell.
It's completely light out by 7 a.m. here. We are closer to the sunrise.
Rysieńku, at least write to me, because I need you so much. And I'm accruing so many kisses inside that I don't know if you'll be able to bear it?!?
Ryś, kiss me, just because you want to.
Is it cold there, too. How are you handling it?
Are you not cold at night? Please take care of yourself.
Mietek's sister wrote that she will be in Łódź for the holidays, so she is going to come over.
I am sending the card.
How is Mietek?
Describe your holidays to me.
Be well and take care. I'll write you a more ordered letter. I await at least a written kiss from you. I.e., I await a letter.
Describe everything. Did you get the metro home?
What about Chaleriere? the meter? the sun?

Your Alina

My mom sends her regards.

[NOTE IN THE MARGIN:]
Here I feel like I would like to give everyone a big hug just for being so Polish (do you know what I mean now?)

NOTES →[P 294]

Łódź
Saturday evening
Christmas Day

You can't imagine, Ryś, how much I wanted last night, on Christmas Eve, the evening you were so afraid of in Paris, for you to be here with me, and how sad and pining I was that we were not spending it together. People going for their "Christmas Eve fish", the mood on the street one of excitement. I was going to the restaurant down Piotrkowska with my mom when we heard a burst of joyful exclamations (all in Polish), and all around us people kissed one another, hugged each other, and wished each other well. Everything Polish is like that, in Poland and on the whole in a state of well-being. An overview of them "looks" impressive: people really are almost all of them nicely, even elegantly and richly, dressed. The ragged children and the unfortunate scraggly uniforms of men demobilized have all disappeared somewhere. The shops are full and... people are buying. Even the ones (and maybe especially the ones) that complain the most. And they complain as per usual and diversely. Like the old doctors saying that they know how it's going to look, all the same...
And the workers that... "You know, doctor, so many children, all the things to get, and how am I going to buy the little buggers their shoes on these wages."
And students, admittedly the future, work, free higher education, but... if they send somebody abroad, it's only the ones on the inside, etc., etc., we've heard it all before. Though even Mietek (the student dandy, "the beaut") "must admit." It's actually more like he doesn't admit, though, when he tells me all about that "exam pork," about American jazz at the Club, about organizations based on something other than what those "idiot" collaborators base theirs on. Because in fact they have everything here. Rysiu, really, <u>all</u> the good books are

getting published here, whether they're by Albert Camus or Vera Panova.
Although people really are afraid to talk about the currency, about the war, about anti-government movements, but... they all yammer on somehow nonetheless. And really in Polish Ryś and life is lived in Polish here. I breathe like a fish in water and... cry. Is this ho-hum feminine mawkishness? But of course, I am a woman (Are you aware?) And Władek bathes Andrzej and combs his hair, gives him his necktie, and the little one is proud he's like his dad.
While Adam sits with Krysia "at theirs" under the Christmas tree (for that matter that couple is 100% activist in the leftist youth organizations). With them it's all Polish, all the way, they go to Zakopane, they gather, and they build, Polishly. I can't quite figure out how to describe it to you.
They opened up a film school here sort of like how it is in Paris. The best Italian and French directors have came here, because in fact they're communists, and in their countries they don't have anything to do, while Poland provides them with terrific living conditions. And they brought in their wonderful Western craft along with them. Once more Poland is a bridge between East and West.
Rysiu, there is a need, a need for good people here, people of your profession don't exist here. But those people must know that you have to work within a state and for a state where there is a great constructive and revolutionary social transformation taking place. Rysiu I'm sorry I'm writing chaotically and so messily, but the force of sensations mixes me up a bit, and besides it is late now, and I am very sleepy.
But I had to speak with you a little bit, because suddenly I was so strongly reminded of our moonlit night in the atelier. That is no doubt sufficient, and I will say no more on it. I think you know we have to get through this bad time, I think you know the way we'll live. Our home in

Poland, and us, us together always as close as that night, when we were bluish-white and drowned in the moonlight and in the pleasure of us. Us Ryś—us both in us.

I'm sending you Wiech because on the other side you have little notes on the visual arts in Poland. There's also an exhibit of Dunikowski in Warsaw, and I'm thinking of going in a week.
I already wrote to your father. If Mietek sends you money, then I would ask you to please not buy anything for me, but instead 450 gr = 9 pelotes of black wool, normal weight, for my mom for a sweater, and send it to me, please. But first and foremost look after yourself. I'm just so ashamed to live here in such a state of well-being when I think of you.
Rysiu, write to me about everything. Remember, hang in there bravely, in any case I believe in your convictions (that they are sincere).
I haven't dared for the time being to tell my mom about anything, [...] because it would be too great a blow for her, when after all she knows that I love you and that we live together (she puts all her romantic faith in you, which I perpetuate and am afraid to destroy). [...]. Rysiu, at this point I sometimes really know that you will be my life's companion. Ryś, there is enough room here for the caresses of all our nights and days. I send you them

Alina

NOTES →[P 295]

Friday 7.I.49 again
in Łódź after returning
from Zakopane

Rysiu!
I feel as though I have sent you two letters full of "moaning and groaning," without any definite thought or remark. Meanwhile many things have become clear to me, become certain, and there are oh so many things I yearn to talk with you about.
We arrived today, and all at once I found all of your much-anticipated letters. So much emotion and joy did they give me that once more into my "ordered" mind they ushered chaos, because once again I wish to respond to everything you said all at once, to agree, to kiss, or to object and to "fight it out." These letters are much more beautiful and individual than the ones you wrote before, like when I was in the Jura Mountains. Or maybe I am simply incapable of critical thinking when it comes to you now? because... I'm falling more and more in love (idiotic phrase), and from a distance I'm making you out to be this ideal figure molded out of the clay of my imagination? God, 5 more weeks!
However, before I forget, first, matters of business.
1.) I am sending the receipt for the 8 thousand sent for Gabriela Zimnoch. This is a contribution from my mom to our "Italian" money.
2.) In the next few days you should receive a package from some former patient of my mot----her's, her last name is apparently Kantor. Eat to my health on your birthday, it should have candies (caramels), honey cake, and melted butter.
3.) I gave your address for the shoes they're supposed to send me from America, they may get there before you move, but I think you should be able to work that out with the concierge woman, because I have no address in Paris, after all. (for now).

4.) I don't know why I haven't gotten a response from your father. He hasn't even written to let me know whether he received the packages. He also hasn't responded to my letter informing him of my arrival and asking him to figure out how I might be able to get in touch with one of you in person. Maybe he is busy and will still respond.
5.) I will go and see Alina, because on Tuesday I'm heading to Warsaw, I'm going to see an exhibit of all of Dunikowski's works and will try to get lilies of the valley.

Saturday

I quit writing yesterday because I was sleepy.
And today I didn't have a letter from either you or from your father. It hurts my feelings because he hasn't even written to say he got the packages, but I think he did, because I did all that monkey business when I sent them (Express, registered, etc.). I did get a package from you in perfect condition. Thank you. The lipstick is too dark, but it's still a pretty shade, I'm using it for now. My color is called *clair*, I only found out when I got here.
If you do pass by there, get me that Ritz *clair* and if it isn't too much trouble, send 450 gr = 9 pelotes of that black wool, it's really good. Combined that will be a 1-pound package. Obviously only if it's really no trouble! Also thanks so much for the Lustres and Comte Plessix. How do you know that he was the one that was in Poland? In any case enough about things that don't matter.
You can't imagine how happy you made me with that little "golden year." It has the name Rachel on 15 janvier.
It was packed in Zakopane like it never was before the war. I spent some time with a group of students/scouts from Gdańsk. They had come for 170 zlotys from Gdańsk to Zakopane and were paying 0–150 zlotys per day, and they had at their disposal horse-drawn carriages and skis. They are healthy, happy people, and

they surprised me endlessly (I had evidently become unaccustomed) with their good manners, "chivalry" etc. But I was most surprised when one young man, dancing with me in this dancing hole called Morskie Oko and on learning that I'd come from Paris, said, "Well, I personally would rather to go to Moscow, they must have really great things there"—That wasn't even one of my scouts, it was just an ordinary "guy" on holiday, on his own or his daddy's dime.

I think that it used to be hard to find someone who would say those kinds of things and with such sincere enthusiasm. People, young people have changed a lot. They're all onward and upward, proud of their new organizations, libraries etc., and they have the youthful zeal. They have changed, but they remain so familiar to me, so 100% Polish. As they go about singing, trying to pick up girls, "tooting their own horns," drinking etc. I could just go and give them all big hugs. They have no idea. I was in a church right as they were holding the highlander carols (on the feast of the Three Kings).

Lovely folk costumes and haughty, happy looks. Everything per "tradishun," and after that, carriages drawn by two horses, with lots of bells and colors, went off to the taverns. Rysiu, here in Poland there is a whole depth of creativity, it's chock-full of it. There were a few that are now at rest in their village cemeteries. A few great, forgotten ones, Dr. Chałubiński, the architect Witkiewicz, many, many; what an incredibly happy life they must have led. Because the nation here is wealthy in spirit, healthy, and full of poetry. But we shall discuss all and sundry.

In my train compartment Zakopane–Warszawa I saw women so humbly and poorly elegant that it was only with their actual beauty that they inspired respect.

The train was wonderfully equipped, quiet, excellent service, additional charge to the 3rd-class ticket of 500 zlotys to get a sleeper.

Good posters at the station, even that "Wash your fruit before you eat it" (remember how horrible it was before the war?) very artistic.
Łódź is ugly as usual, but I went across the Freedom Square, there were droshkies, people returning from work, some ragamuffin kid latched onto a droshky, someone yelled, "Get outta here," "Hey, Wacek, get a move on," then a policeman, "What the hell do you mean, you don't wish to." And of course the whole evening was like that, of course we've talked about this so many times. Such is Poland.
People from Warsaw have inculcated a little "big-city culture" into Łódź (although now they are slowly running back off to Warsaw). There are really lovely (by Łódź standards) places to go, great publishing houses etc. But not once in all of Poland have I seen a single reproduction of anything. In the windows for decoration alongside the really wonderfully published (really graphically great books) *Crusaders* by Zofia Kossak there are hideous cheap prints of flowers or angels with golden hair. Hideous.
I'm happy that Ewa Olszewska is in Paris. I remember her perfectly, she studied under Prof. Pokorny, I couldn't keep seeing her because in those days I was constantly going off to Poland. Pokorny is a good professor, but a terrible "lyricist." And she has in her work that Slavic lyricism, and it's very feminine. I saw a little sculpture called *Warsaw.* Lots of attributes—like broken wheels, bricks, children crying, pots, helmets, etc. The consulate in Prague was very taken with it (especially Mr. Maryško) and bought it, so I would imagine it was with that backing that she got a passport. I'm very happy, because Paris will do her good, and there will be at least one person who is good, kind, and serious from "our line of work." Please tell her I said hello. All the more so because the conditions in Prague are so tough. Really, I actually feel awful for them. My mom invited "Uncle" to

come to us for a week at least to "eat his fill." I doubt he'll get a passport, but I would like to pay back my material debt to him that way, and then in the quiet and malice of my heart be able to say—Take a look, Czechs, at our Poland. This is an unjust "desire," because I've done nothing so far, after all, to deserve this lovely Poland, except perhaps in feeling for it.

I sleep here in such a clean, white bed, everything around me is clean, nothing gets dusty, it's warm, and the window is open, there are flowers and velvety house shoes. But I can't fall asleep. I'll be damned if I can sleep. After all that filth at the atelier I dreamed of such a rest! Rysiu, I miss your head on my shoulder, I miss your arm, which would ever so delicately cause my breasts, my sides, my thighs to fall asleep, I miss your kisses. It's terrible—it's actually a physical pain. I lie down stretch out and try to think that it's today that you bathe "second" and that you'll be in soon, cool from the water, and you'll open the shades and stretch out next to me. You know, I'm a little afraid, or I was afraid of the thought of giving up "my" side. It had even occurred to me to "live as neighbors," but I'm so happy that it was you that finally brought it up. And that dispelled my doubts. Rysiu, we understand each other like a couple of people. We are a couple of people and we can cohabitate in a human way. Definitely! You have my wholehearted <u>yes</u>, and I am happy that I will be coming to <u>our house</u>. Rysiu, I want for everything to be good with us and believe it will be. And I know that we will never be lonely again.

As for the atelier, I would be very, very happy if you could find anything at all. A mad desire and need to work is gathering within me, and really I must finally be <u>definitively</u> done with the Ivo-Lustre "pack." Come what may. You can take any steps necessary, if you need to borrow money for it, do, because I will have something like 50–60 for that purpose. This is the first step, while the rest we bear within ourselves and in our work.

I believe and joy makes me swell to bursting.
The man's head by Matisse and the fruit like ripe breasts are lovely, thank you.
Send the *Lettres*.
Rysiu be happy and well
it was your name day, after all, and it's about to be your birthday, and those are my wishes to you.

Your A.

I drew a dozen or two [SELF-PORTRAITS→], with minimal variations, but they won't fit into this letter.
Rysiu, it's good that you wrote me what you did about good people. I do believe in them. They are undoubtedly good. And I am happy that I believe that and want to always go on believing.
I thought about how you know that as I was standing in the valley, as the outline of the Giewont massif emerged from out of the fog. And they didn't see it, because they were hurrying to dinner and saying, "What are you doing over there?", "What are you gaping at, come on." I was alone, but I thought how you knew that. You know what the painting holds beyond the perfect harmony of colors and the composition, you know what is contained in any of Matisse's brushstrokes or in the darkness (not the holiday lighting) of a church. Rysiu, I think you have to write more. You know. It's good that you wrote about those good people, because then, standing before the Giewont massif, I recalled moments of our life and your words, which were sometimes not what the French call "fine," and I felt the chill of doubt. But now I know. Rysiu, golden Rysieńku, my darling. Our hard, firm life shall not be "fine," but shall rather be "finesse."
My mom is really getting into her sixties now and her little middle-class habits. We sometimes have a falling-out, I can't stand her constant solicitude and her other petit-bourgeois foibles. Sometimes I would strangle her

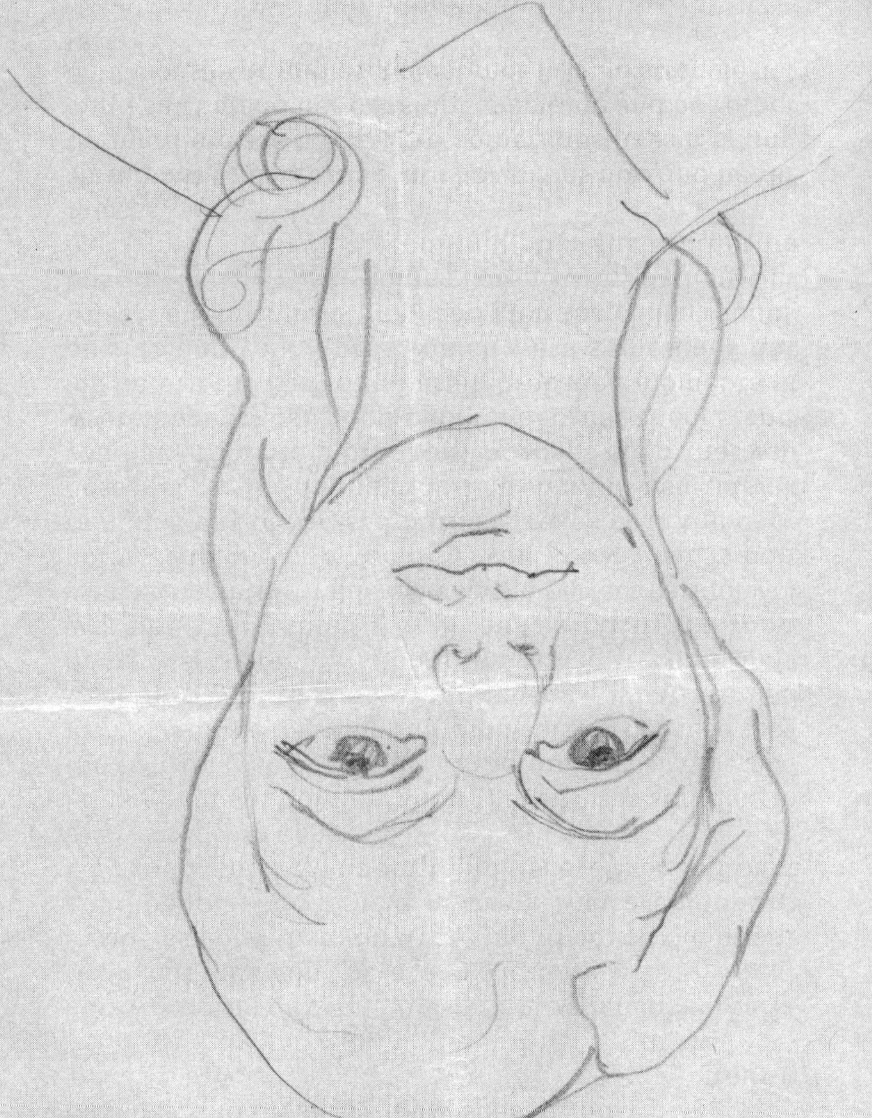

Rysiu bądź zdrów i szczęśliwy
przecież kwiatki imieniny a będziemy mieć
urodziny to nie życzenia. Twoja R

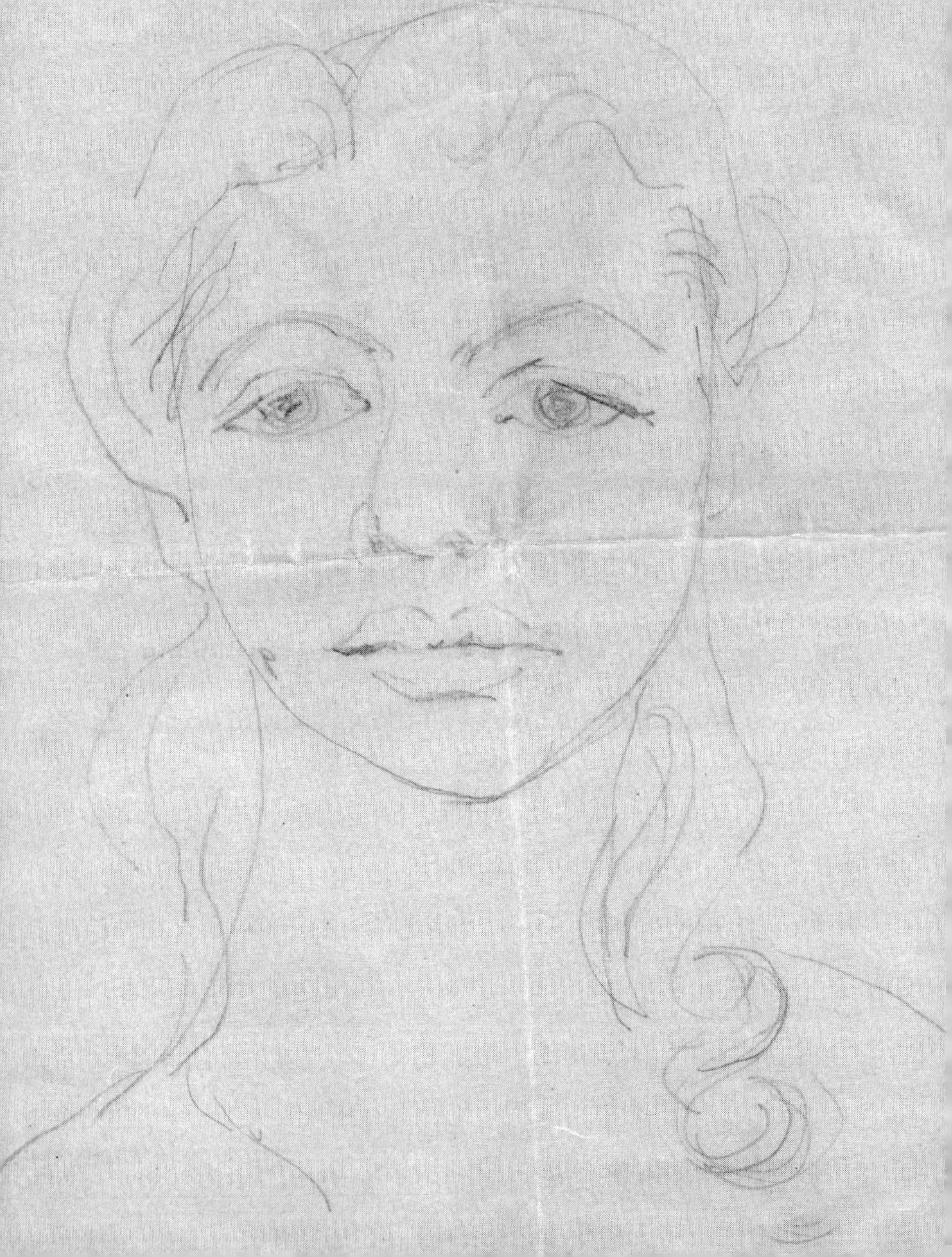

in anger and then weep for having killed my nearest and dearest. There remains indifferent cohabitation, tolerance, and understanding, in order to be able to live together in a single world. It's a good thing that both of us are satisfied with the great love that exists between mother and child.
Ah, Rysiu I've gone on and on, would that you would have enough patience to read it all. I swear that in the future I will be brief. Because after all that's the most important thing, that it's not visibly written, but that it's always nagging at your brain, heart, and all of your nerves. Write to me!
Please try to get both [CROSSED-OUT], it's the only effective means. Write that you are healthy!!! They gave me my papers. Write if you received the newspaper and the book. I wanted to write you a different letter altogether, but this is what came out.
I kiss you so lightly "out of flawlessness" and so forcefully "just because."

Your Alina

[NOTES IN THE MARGINS:]
I heard on the radio that there is an influenza epidemic in Paris.
I beg you, Rysiu, for the love of all that is sacred, do not get sick.
Be careful, I am terribly anxious.

SZAPOCZNIKOW TO STANISŁAWSKI

[JANUARY 1949]

NOTES →[P 296]

Rysiu, please go to this address:—M. Bercholc, 37 Rue David d'Angers, Paris 19^{em}. Ask Mrs. Kantorowicz to bring a package to your address for "the little daughter of Dr. Szapocznikowa." Obviously only if she hasn't already taken care of it. Eat what's in it.
I saw the movie *Ballad of Siberia* (USSR).
Everyone is delighted with it, my mom and your dad, young and old, intelligent and simple people.
I think we are very corrupted by the West.
My mom sends her heartfelt greetings.
I kiss you

Alina

Łódź
Monday 10.I.

Ryś
Today the letter from your father came, he hadn't written before because he thought we were still in Zakopane. The letter is full of "Gracious lady" and other courtesies, so much so that I got the jitters. Me, a gracious lady? I immediately called up 25 Sompolno Kolskie and heard a voice so kind and sincere that I can't wait for Friday, when your father comes to Łódź, and I can see him and talk to him in person. We talked for a few minutes, he was moved, he wanted to "make the most of such an occasion," and there was absolutely no convincing him that I would come to his neighborhood, that "boarded-up world." He wanted to come without any further delay, but when he called after receiving my letter from Łódź, we were already gone. So till Friday!!??
Yesterday I went by taxi to Pabianice, which is the same distance from Łódź as from [PORTE] d'Orléans to you [ON] bld. Raspail. Incredible sensations. The village is as small as the back of your hand. And one Pabianicean, Witek Berlikowski, is in Paris, he studies mechanics and last year he visited his old burg on a consular passport and apparently called all the young ladies *mignonne*!!
My visit also stunned the town, and people would come up to me and say, are you, by any chance, "that one"?
And Rysiu, I am beginning to miss Paris. It's such a particular feeling, which will no doubt ever be done away with in any town. Paris has its microbe, that germ that eats deep into a fresh organism.
But it's only now, Rysiu, that I am looking around, considering, comparing. I meet with this mass of people from different milieux and different attitudes. I spent my time happy or bored in intelligent discussions or in idle twaddle, but all of this gives me—learning.

Fortunately the quantity of activity and social and folk truths always have an influence. Of course. Like the shimmering circles in a broth. Sometimes thin, but always with a particular weight and gold. Ryszard, you wrote that you are beginning to hate those bankrupt bourgeois. That is bad. Alphonse Daudet, whom I am reading now, and who is so wonderful, tying together all the simplicity and all the refinement of sweet France, and who makes me miss it so, writes: *Hatred is the anger of the weak*. You are not weak at all. You can afford to get angry. Get angry and really tear things down.
Rysiu, Rysieńku. I believe in you and swore I wouldn't harass you with rebukes in my letters, but please, take care of your health, because they keep going on here about the tough situation and the flu running rampant in Paris. And remember about your teeth, about no alcohol etc. You know! Don't be angry I'm reminding you. Ryszard remember, I want to always live with you. Good night, kiss me

A.

[NOTES IN THE MARGINS:]

What about the atelier? Work? Classes? Write me.
I'm going to Warsaw tomorrow and will kiss you from there

Your Alina

17.
SZAPOCZNIKOW TO STANISŁAWSKI
[JANUARY 11, 1949]
NOTES →[P 297]

Tuesday
morning

Rysieńku
A card came from you with such a lovely portrait, so sad for me, though. Rysiu, I am terribly anxious and only now realizing that you are now everything to me, and I can't allow the thought that you might be ill. Rysiu, plain and simple—you are now the person closest to me, I have you, I believe in you morally and materially—Rysiu, you are everything to me.
Please, Ryś.
Take care of yourself!
Do not go around with a fever.
Maybe you would go to the Cité and lie down?
Ooph and of course now you are there by yourself. I feel guilty for every comfort I have here!
Rysiu, I am tormented by helplessness.
Write to me this minute to tell me how you are feeling.
Please
Be well!!!
Do not send any "fashions" or any idiocies of the kind.
Thank you for *Arts*, it brought me great, great joy. We'll talk.
Rysiu, spend all the money and don't feel any of your...
Be well. Write
In 3–4 weeks I'll be with you.

Your
Alina

[NOTE ON THE ENVELOPE:]
I've already bought *Polish Folk Art*. It's lovely—I'll send it.
A

NOTES →[P 297]

Łódź
Thursday

Have you lost your mind or what, Ryszard, that you don't write? It's utterly incomprehensible, surely you know how anxious I get about the flu running rampant all over Paris. Write at once and tell me exactly how you are feeling?!
I was in Warsaw yesterday. Rysiu, we will only live in Warsaw! It is so—[DRAWING OF THUMBS UP]
I spent the whole day at the museum. An exhibition of the French book, an exhibition of Hungarian art, the Polish Gothic (all exhibits from Silesia with the great stamp of German art), it was very painful to me when in the face of the Madonna I saw a Gretchen. I longed terribly, to the point of tears, for the little French angel with the broad forehead and the fine features full of sweetness. Then Dunikowski.—He is bad! The critics write that he's the Polish Rodin, but even Rodin it is possible not to like. While the term is apt: that same mass of works, that same fierce expression, even similar themes. But he lacks one thing.—Humility, the humility of really great things. Look at Maillol, at Romanesque things, at Egypt at the end, look at Braque, Matisse (in all his splendor), read Daudet and others. Against the hymns of praise from all the critics I am not afraid to repeat: Dunikowski is no great man. (Ooph, how difficult it is to be one!). A lot of his things are actually frighteningly *morbides*! To the point of abomination and disgust. It's very reminiscent of Mietek's "divine spark," "inspiration," etc. Anyway, we'll talk.
Then I went to Alina's and was late for my train back. I delivered the lilies of the valley to her.
Alina looks very gaunt, and that was what struck me first. She is extremely beautiful, but with her gauntness she gives the impression of possessing an unearthly beauty,

she simply has nothing feminine in her lovely face—no warmth, nothing one could kiss. And yet one would wish to lightly brush or pet her all over without touching her anywhere. I see now that your description of her (remembering her kisses) was perfect.

We were terribly sorry that I had to hurry to catch my train, for after the first moments of slight discomfort we were bound by a thread of genuine affinity. Alina told me a lot about your family and you. Mietek is not here. I'll explain when I get there. I am very happy, because even she is for it, and she would be delighted and suggests we come to Warsaw.

I think that you would find you had a lot more in common with her these days than you do with Mietek. Alina has been sick and has a lot of work, which is why she also complains that in matters of "art" she has become very dull. Nevertheless she has a greater treasure than news "from the world of art"—she possesses great subtlety and a delicacy of the soul that even you, Rysiu, are sometimes lacking. Rysiu, I pine, and yet on the other hand I am actually afraid to return. Are you really as I imagine you to be now?

Rysiu, please write how you are doing. You see how foolishly and intensely I become attached to people and, Rysiu, I am so terribly anxious about you. You are my man, after all.

Rysiu, I kiss you
Kiss me back

Your Alina

Write how you are getting along
How is your health?

19.
STANISŁAWSKI TO SZAPOCZNIKOW
JANUARY 17, 1949
NOTES →[P 298]

The library, 17.I.1949
Monday

Idols!—always Idols! Today's morning post brought me your letter and an announcement cut out of the newspaper. I read everything a moment ago, and I think I found traces of lipstick on the envelope. That is too much and unnecessary. I am writing in pencil as I did not bring along any other paper—which after all is not the most important thing. Good are your words in your letter, and darling.

Ala, do not get discouraged by anything, especially not by minutiae, everything will be good, because we want it to be. In the meantime you no doubt received my last letter and saw my father. That he should have called you "gracious lady" should not surprise you. It's tradition and history that have spoken through my father. Tradition is immeasurably valuable and ought not to be destroyed. Our life, I mean yours and mine, has completely departed from the "customs" associated with tradition—and that is not good. Despite the fact that we live in a new, revolutionary world, we do not have the right to forget some things associated with the old world. As to which things—we will talk when you come. I think you must sense, too, what I do. And Aluś, please, do not let yourself get carried away by impulses and by the senseless enthusiasm that beats out from your letters as you speak of "the new world" and social transformations. We are with them wholeheartedly, but from this it does not follow that we should completely lose our critical distance from ourselves. Enthusiasm is fine, and I understand that in you, but what isn't fine is to let enthusiasm cause you to take leave of your senses.

This new generation is not at all "onward and upward," as you describe it, and that gentleman who prefers Moscow to Paris (Zakopane) is no doubt a very fine "gentleman," but I judge that Moscow would disappoint somewhat, if he is a European. Poles always preferred, as history shows, to go to Paris. And no social transformation will affect that. Aluś, keep your eyes open wider, and don't get carried away by "cheap" enthusiasm. That makes no sense whatsoever. "Costly" enthusiasm, i.e., real enthusiasm, would not permit your return to Paris, were it to capture you completely for the cause in Poland.

Try to get information out of the right and the left. More "from the right." After all, that will neither change our socialist worldview nor, and even less so, have any impact on our goals. Between worldview and politics there is a mad difference. How can you reconcile what you write with the fact that 140,000 functionaries from the Department of Security and the police were killed at the hands of that enthused (onward, upward) group of youth? (As reported by Warsaw radio.) That obviously cannot frighten us, quite the opposite, <u>it will add spirit</u>—so let us both be sincere, let us appraise the situation as it is—at least between the two of us. That is very important, and I should have already written to you about it long ago. Lacking self-criticism—you can make the worst impression, I'm not talking about the authorities, for there you would enjoy the highest opinion. Compare the Germans and their psyche. We are not like that. We know how to fight for a cause, without necessarily giving up our own thinking and common sense if we do not wish to become a horde, in contradistinction to a people of culture.

The things I am writing to you now are just glimmers of a longer conversation. <u>I'm convinced you understand me</u>, otherwise it's not worth talking. I was struck in your previous, long letter by the manner in which you speak of your mother. That is one of the symptoms of the disappearance of "tradition" I mentioned. One can write in that way about someone whom one loves but has no respect for. Do not forget that your Mother is the only

Person in the world that can be your most treasured possession. You and I can be together without limit, giving ourselves over to it completely, with dedication, and the utmost love, but do not forget that <u>the love of your mother comes before all that</u>. It is a love of another kind. Aluś, you <u>cannot</u> write about your mother like that!!!
<u>[4 CROSSED-OUT LINES]</u>
There is no stronger bond than that between mother and child. Do not get angry with me, Aluś, for writing to you like this, but after all who else could, if not me, I love you and—you know already. I'm stopping for now because it's 5 p.m. and class. By the by—Alusieńka—I send you a kiss.

I'm writing after class. That is not, my dearest, preaching, I mean all those thoughts that I summarily transcribed, following from the assumption that we ought to tell each other everything. Alusieńko mine, I want you to understand, I discovered a lot of love in your last letter. Alu, is it really so? My yearning for your return knows no bounds. I've never felt anything like this before. I'm reading *Marysieńka* and am delighted, as always, by Boy. You write that you received *Arts*—I put in the latest issue of *Tricots* on sweaters inside it, did you not get it? Maybe they took it out—that would be a shame. I sent wool the same day as I sent the card, but not by air. You should be getting it around now in any case. Besides I sent the new issue of *Arts* last week. Don't send me newspapers, because Teresa, my sister, does that. I received today a whole bundle of the latest: *Przekrój*, *Odrodzenie*, *Kuźnica*, *Przegląd Artystyczny*, *Tygodnik Powszechny*. In *Przekrój* there was quite a <u>good</u> article by Margul. That chap has a vivid imagination, and his style's not bad.
I'm learning quite a lot and going to classes. For the time being I am not attempting to write anything, but the time will come for me to begin. Aluś, when will you

return? My father no doubt asked you about the publishers I am interested in, since I asked him to do so. I don't need anything in particular. If I could, I would just ask for a subscription to *Przegląd Artystyczny*. An annual subscription is 440 zlotys, and then possibly *Odrodzenie* or *Kuźnica*, but that's more hypothetical—nothing will take effect until after the move, when I will finally give you a permanent address. I am still looking for a room. I found something but not the kind of thing that's needed. This week I ought to be able to yield something concrete. We'll see.

If you were up to it—don't forget at some point to perhaps make contacts that might come in handy.

Mr. Berlikowski—from Pabianice, the one you mention is precisely the one that was taking pictures at the "ball" (at Legendre's). I know him, of course. Paris is so small. In the first days of February there will be the grand elegant ball of the Association of Polish Students for the 25th anniversary of the organization's existence. That ball will take place in that grand, elegant room of the French Ministry on the Place St. Augustin. Besides that other festivities: folk dances, choirs etc. Thus far I have yet to take part in any.

Alusieńka mine, you can't even begin to imagine how much I look forward to your arrival. Your hands, your mouth, and your hair—everything that Baudelaire wrote is nothing in comparison with what I am feeling. If I had as much strength for my studies, there would be no obstacle I could not overcome. I feel that my strength increases in direct proportion to my feelings, and I am happy about that and cannot wait.

The sweetest caresses are not sweet enough in comparison with the ones I send you now.

Your Ryszard

[NOTE:]
(Abstraction)
(but real)

My sincerest regards to your mother, and if 15.I. was her name day, wish her a happy one from me.

R

Don't forget to bring with you the smell of the forest, because I am looking forward to that smell just as much as I am looking forward to seeing you—(being a madman).
IDOLS! ҰҰҰҰҰ
But that a bit later

20.

STANISŁAWSKI TO SZAPOCZNIKOW

JANUARY 18, 1949

NOTES →[P 299]

Tuesday, 18.I.1949

Aluś my darling,
This morning I again received your letter like a kiss. I tore open the envelope of my letter of yesterday and am slipping in this little sheet of paper, for it doesn't matter if it's small or large—what I want to write wouldn't fit on even the largest paper. Thank you for everything, Aluś mine. For getting the lily of the valley, and for Alina, too. I've written about Dunikowski, so you know. Your observations on Alina are interesting. She is "subtle"—you're right. Regarding my subtlety, which you call into question (all right)—we'll talk. Aluś, please do not "imagine" me—I'm sure I'm not how you are imagining me to be. If we act on good faith, we can each become as the other imagines us. I really shouldn't send you the letter written in pencil, I really should leave these matters for when we "talk everything over"—but what the devil—"a man's word is his word." I'm certain that when you do come back, we won't know what to talk about, where to begin. It's usually like that.
ALUŚ—DO NOT LOSE FAITH.
Chin up! Don't be afraid of returning to Paris. We will take our holiday in Italy, after all.
In Italy—can you imagine?
Don't be surprised that I haven't written in a few days. That was due to technical problems, not to influenza. I scoff at all influenzas. The devil leaves the wicked alone. Teresa sent me a collection of Ildefons' poetry. Very intoxicated and very good. It's a completely different kind of poetry. Not the French poetry we are used to and in which everything tends to "revolve" around love—and *amour*. This is quite typical of all French art.

It's almost 2 p.m., and I must quickly run to class—so until the next letter.
Kisses, Alina!

Your R.

February 7 is my father's name day—he would be inordinately pleased if you would send him a card. I, too, would be pleased.

21.
SZAPOCZNIKOW TO STANISŁAWSKI
[JANUARY 1949]
NOTES →[P 299]

I can't quite remember now if your name day is on the 7th, and your birthday on the 20th, or vice-versa, (the name Ryszard is not on my calendar). Nevertheless you are over the hill, and I would like for you to have a few nice books, and also for the things I wrote in my inscription there by the date to come true.

Alina

Tomorrow I am sending a long letter.

NOTES →[P 299]

20.I.
THESE ARE MY WISHES FOR YOU
28 = 3rd CROSS ALREADY

[DRAWING→]

Now for your father. I'm going to go step by step, because I don't at all know how to describe it. He was here on Friday, and we chatted from 10 o'clock in the morning to 3 p.m. without stopping. He was standing so close to me that I really felt like sincerely kissing him, though I lacked the courage. Please send him a kiss from me. We talked about everything and I asked about everything you asked me to. Your father knows you perfectly and... he really fears for you. I reassured him and set his mind at ease as best I could, I do think deep down he believes in you and expects a great deal of you. Regarding your article and many other things he expressed the same opinion that I had, to the point that it really surprised me. He was terribly afraid that that transformation of yours (a new subject of study, new views, etc.) might be just superficial, might be the result of being under my "spell," but because he has many concerns along those lines (just like my mother's), I managed to persuade him along with her that what has taken place in you is definitive this time and independent of anyone. He extended a very heartfelt invitation to come to Poznań and arranged with O. + T. + B, but I'm afraid I won't be able to take advantage of his offer. Besides, I have a terrible cold.

Just two days after he left I wanted terribly to call up Sompolno, just to chat with him a bit. We struck such a chord with each other. If you didn't exist, I could fall in love with him. This way I love him too, but as your father. Rysiu, after the 30th of this mth. address letters to:

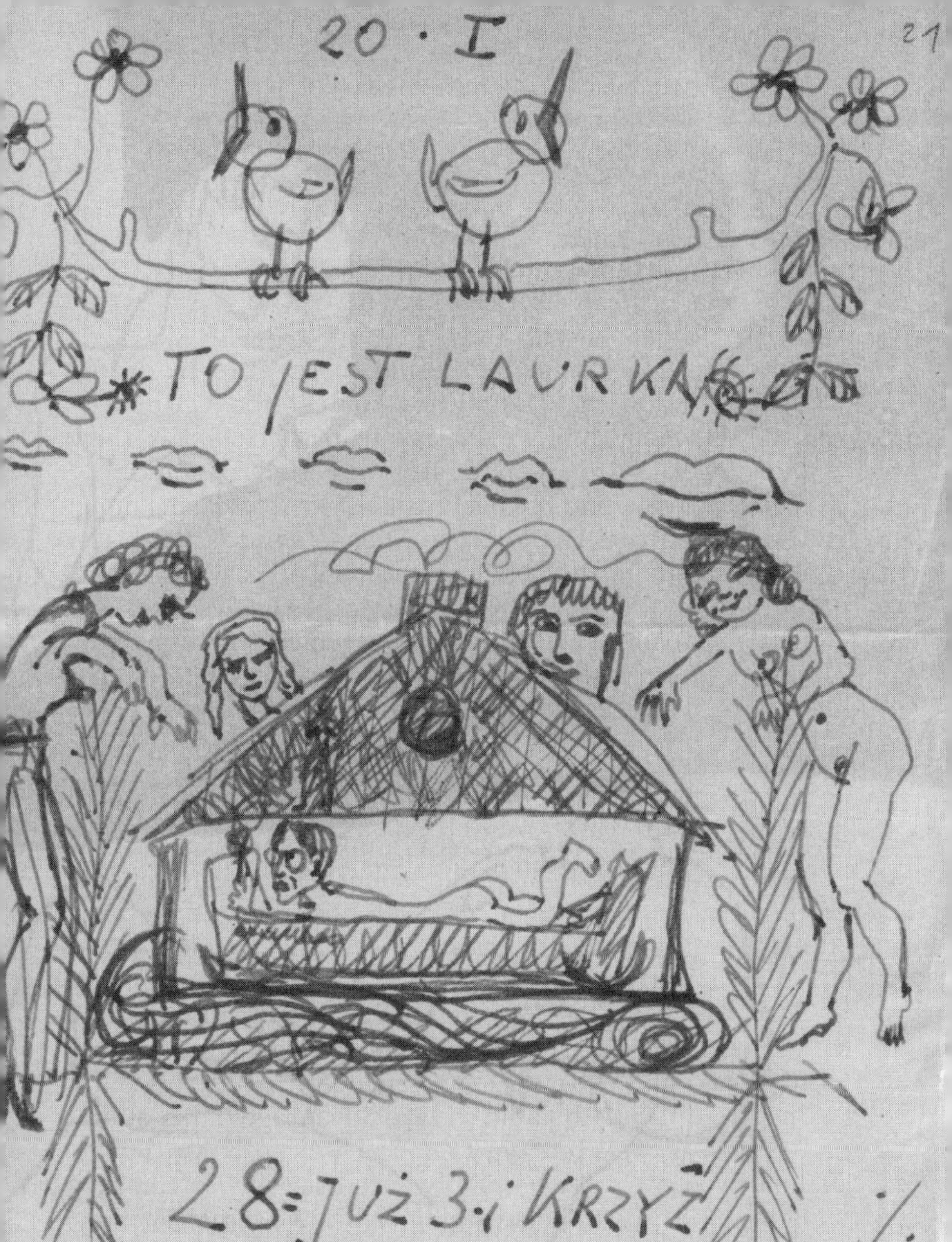
20 · I
TO JEST LAURKA
28 = JUŻ 3-i KRZYŻ

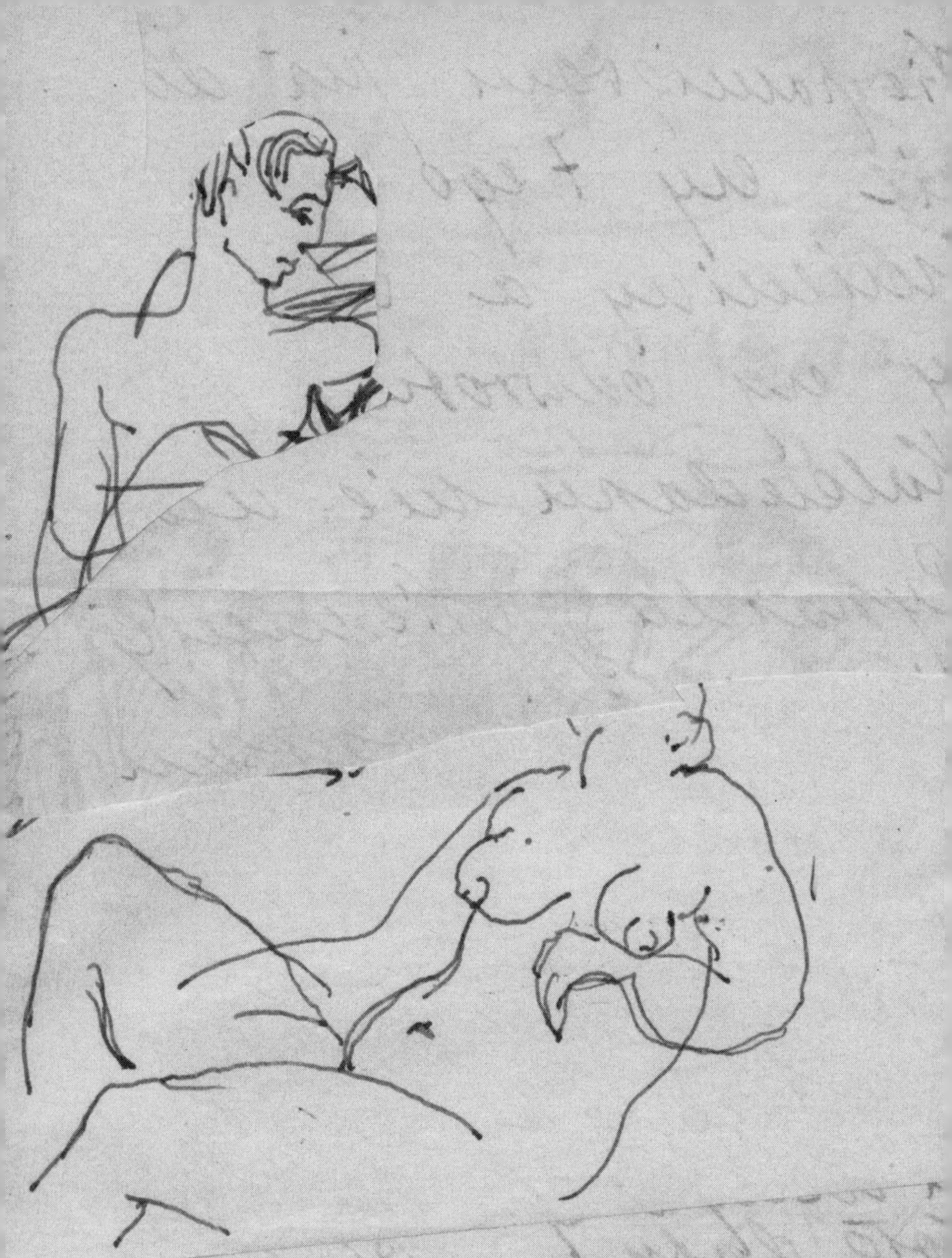

A. Šapočniková Praha XII, Dyková 15. C.S.R. But write me back here again. Concretely.
You could make a living if you wanted to and were able to write a little something for the people here. More detailed information when I see you.
Just 2–3 weeks left. Write to me.
Kiss

Alina

23.
SZAPOCZNIKOW TO STANISŁAWSKI
[JANUARY 25, 1949]
NOTES →[P 300]

Łódź
Tuesday

Rysiu my dear!
It's getting so hard to start writing because I'm already feeling so-called *"righ-za feeber"* and although I'm not actually going to see you for another 2 weeks, still I am already setting aside most things for when we can really "talk it all over." Thus the matter of "blind enthusiasm," not even remotely as blind as you say, the issue of publishers, contacts etc.
Anyway you know, Rysiu, I've discovered that the written word has become a more serious thing in terms of accountability. Behold, it becomes black (or rather blue) on white, and one necessarily feels it weighing distinctly on one's conscience. As you know, it doesn't come easily to me to live in a consistent, responsible etc. way. (But isn't such impulsive lightness absolutely marvelous??) But that is just the foam, with the real beverage underneath. That is also why all the conclusions you drew from my thoughts on my mom make no sense whatsoever. Of course even you want sometimes to strangle me, and I you, and just in general. Besides, at the beginning it was hard for me to transition into a life in which someone was always worrying about me, asking when I would be back, where I was going, etc. I had gotten unused to that, and my "freedom" at times actually despaired of its existence. My mom is working now. Lots of hours per day, and I am swept up again now by despair when I think about our impending separation and about how she will be alone and I... She is really a wonderful woman. I'm not able to write about what I am experiencing with regard to my mother, and perhaps because of that, in order to conceal things that are too delicate, I cover them up with harsh words. Besides, Rysiu, lately I've been reading Brandys' *Invincible*

City (a story about Warsaw). After a lot of books by French writers... And it occurred to me that the antagonism and misunderstandings that take place between us come primarily from a single source. You simply look at certain things still in such a nice, cultured, polite way, as it ought to be, in fact, and maybe sometimes I envy you that. But the difference lies in the fact that during your formative years, over the last ten years, you did not go through that baptism of despair, all of that, <u>all of that</u> did not vanish all those times without a trace, as happened for me in the ghettos and the camps. I'm sorry, Ryś, I'm ashamed by this, you know how I can't stand, am repulsed by those people who reproach themselves or "praise" themselves for the years of suffering that they endured. But you have to understand me, you I have told already, and maybe I will later be capable of telling you everything from those times, but in this case it's a very crucial thing. Because you were no doubt going through <u>a lot</u> then, you were living better or worse, you loved, you got married, you wanted (or didn't) to start a family. But your ideas didn't change as fundamentally as mine did, so that instead of "nice, cultured, polite" what was left was "lovely, human, true, heartfelt." Maybe at some point we will talk.
I've lost the desire to write.
I read André Maurois' *Climats*. Terrific, but I'm now wondering what the point is in doing that (writing), that rummaging around in your self, in <u>your</u> most delicate, intimate feelings, and those most delicate, intimate feelings, while the author conducts those "autopsies" on people whose contact with all of life is mediated by butlers and maids.
Witkiewicz however was an architect, or there was an architect Witkiewicz in Zakopane.
I miss you physically, sensuously, with every nerve and every cell, so much so that it is becoming unbearable. The senses are also those delicate elves that desire "<u>only</u>" to see, to gently caress, and to feel a presence nearby.

I am arriving 6.II. or 7.II. If you don't find a room by then, then please arrange anything at all for me in some little hotel, even just for the first 2 nights, so that I have someplace to go (not too expensive).
Please don't underline so many words in your letters, because I just get disoriented, don't use so many foreign words, and don't write in such boggy little writing. (Did you get bogged down again?)
Write a lot, write that you love me, at least that. Ah, how I yearn for your caresses. Rysieńku.
My mom sends her greetings

Your Alina

24.

STANISŁAWSKI TO SZAPOCZNIKOW

JANUARY 31, 1949

NOTES →[P 301]

Paris, 31.I.1949

Aluś my dearest,
After many, many days, I finally received your dear letter, and I am coming to the conclusion that our correspondence is almost completely pointless. Between one letter and another a considerable amount of time goes by, at least two weeks, and in the meantime I receive another letter from you, and the same for you from me, and there is a confusion of ideas that comes out of it. I regret that I wrote to you about your mom and other matters instead of leaving them for when we "talk it all over." I should only write that I love you—to the point of complete madness, and that I can't wait for your arrival. The closer it gets to when we will see each other, the more I miss you. I can't focus on anything and even studying—I get caught up in thinking about you. I know, Alina, that I am completely bound up with you. Aside from the caresses that I miss like a child—I await you, you, because I can't manage on my own. This is a sort of *maladie*, but I can't do anything about it, and I am very happy that it is that way, that I can love you so madly. Alina, I'm not actually capable of writing what I feel. It is so strong that it's impossible to capture it in words. Sometimes I'm even afraid of my feelings.
Ala, I don't know if I will be able to be as good to you as I would like. Ala, dearest, you know everything. No words are necessary here.
Today is Monday, and I think that it must only be a week at most before we will see each other. A room like the one we talked about I have not found. I did everything I could—I'll tell you when you return. Tomorrow or the day after I am moving out and into a hotel, and we will live there together until we find something. Maybe something will come up soon, since I've already put all

the search machinery in motion. Even in terms of hotels it is insanely hard to find something for a price that *à la longue* would be feasible for us. Keep hopeful, Alina, that everything will be good, we have to be together, I can't imagine it any other way. I will think about work, maybe something will come up, I will try to get started with writing—but first I must have you. I await you so, Alina My darling Alina,

Your Ryszard

You don't give an exact date of arrival, so starting on 5.II. I will go out to the Gare de l'Est, unless I receive a letter from you in the meantime.
My regards to your uncle.

25.

SZAPOCZNIKOW TO STANISŁAWSKI

[FEBRUARY 4, 1949]

NOTES →[P 301]

Friday Praha

Rysieńku

Two letters from you were awaiting me here, I mean, one letter, and one addendum. You did well in writing me.

I won't write to you any more, because I am terribly tired from the trip. I arrived in Prague yesterday, I have loads of luggage, and I spent the whole journey on top of the radiator, so even today I'm still a little dazed and fearful of the rest of the journey. And I would like to already be there and to be telling you about it all.

Rysiu, I'm coming on the Orient Express either on Monday (most likely) or on Tuesday morning meaning I am leaving here either Sunday or, if I don't make it, Monday morning.

If you don't have class, then come, because I don't know where to go from the station.

If you don't have time, I'll leave my luggage at the *consigne*, and you can just come to the atelier in the afternoon, I'll wait for you there.

I don't even have the strength to kiss you, so I will just nestle into you now

A.

NOTES →[P 301]

Rysiu mine
I'm lying in this clean bed and thinking to myself how strange it all is. It is simply not possible that after nights like those there came a bright day with flowers on the tables, with comfort and a smile. Sometimes this life here seems unreal. And unreal precisely because it's purely corporeal. As though a human contained only flesh and organs. Then how is it possible that I am and you. Maybe I am just imagining that you are there? Maybe it really is just flesh and organs. In any case I think that to arrive at conclusions like these I am already going crazy. However, to be going crazy means that there is something there that can go crazy, something other than flesh.
Rysiek, I love you.
I want for that me to be shared by both of us. And for us to be one. And I want a lot of other things with you, but not here in the hospital.
I cuddle you and kiss you

A.

My darling Ryszard!
Today again we were not alone, and yet I held up so well! It's so hot and stinks so badly that I'm already losing the will to live! (though that strong instinct is of course always there). Rysiu! I end up bearing you a little grudge that sometimes you can't be just a little bit understanding with me. And you say I haven't even been through all that much yet. But I have only that one hour to complain a bit. And sometimes during the day I am so weak. But I also know that once we are finally together we will be able to appreciate it. For that matter we have always taken full advantage of our time.
I am tired now, so I give you as big a kiss as I can.
Yours always

Alina

hospital 2 octobre 49

Rysieńku my Alusieńku
Rysieńku golden, darling
The pen writes beautifully, it's just that I lie wrong, and from this position the letters come out crooked. That is not worthy of such a pen.
There are some things that torment, that come to mind only at certain dark hours of the night, things that in the light of day one doesn't even dare to say. What else to write. Later you will read this while I am not beside you. That's probably the same feeling that bids us whisper certain confessions, even though of course no one is listening, and sometimes it's easier to speak at dusk. Do you want to correspond with me like this, Rysiu? I've wanted to write to you for a long time—it's one more way to get to know one another deeper—but ordinary laziness, no—more what you call "old age," that lack of enthusiasm that so often sentences the most beautiful thoughts to death. This now "grown-up" criticalness that doesn't allow many things to be carried out simply out of the fear that it might not be good enough, worthy enough, etc. It's the same in order to create something in art, you have to have the courage of a child, because there, too, nothing is definitely good, you just have to be brave enough to carry out even the impossiblest, most preposterous thing that arises in your mind and heart.
Just don't look at "what people will say," "how it's going to look etc.," just consistently tell the truth, seek out without blinders what is truly breeding in your heart.
A great pen—how it writes. The problem is the thoughts —how miserable they are. When I was 17 I wrote in a little yellow book. It said "The apple trees are blooming. Oh! I am so lovely. Ooph! I am so unhappy, so happy,

oppressed, depressed, how I wish for freedom! How I wish to get out of here." Etc. Etc. Me, me, me. But right beside me there was life, lovely, desired, anticipated. And now I want to get out of here—out of the hospital, out of this illness, but life is no longer there beside me, just on the other side of the wires. Life is here, this itself is life.

I'm beginning to write dumb banalities.

But I wanted to write you that all of this is actually senseless. Even if it's very, very painful, one still forgets afterwards, and trying to remember or share "with someone" is idiocy. What matters is the moment itself. And of such moments there are millions, and like beads make up a necklace that we alone wear, one that adorns (or disfigures) only us. Everyone has beads of their own and is alone with them, and can neither give way, nor give away, nor share it (the bead—the moment). The moment when a good dish melts in your mouth! The moment when at the sight of you I am overcome by emotion—and a different moment when there is nothing, just an atmosphere of peace, and a different moment when there is terrible anxiety, "because of what will be."

In the night I was thinking that there is no reason to puff up and convince myself that in spite of all the material-physical shortcomings, we live better and deeper than other people. Everyone lives to his own measure. If we really feel things more intensely, then those others feel things just the same, "deep down," at most they are shallower or deeper. But every person feels to the depth of his heart.

[DRAWING OF 2 SCHEMATIC FIGURES: ONE LOWER AND ONE HIGHER, WITH "VERTICAL" INDICATED, AND THE NOTE:]

The vertical is longer, but down to the knees of both.

I wanted to write you, too, what I like about you, and what I don't. That may be of interest to you. Write me too.

Malować się powinno, człowie- II
ka i jego czynności. Powinno
się malować dobrze. Bo źle na-
lowany obraz niech tam sobie
będzie „realizmem soc." jest złym
obrazem. Przykład tego odkrycia
filozoficznego w grafic[illegible]

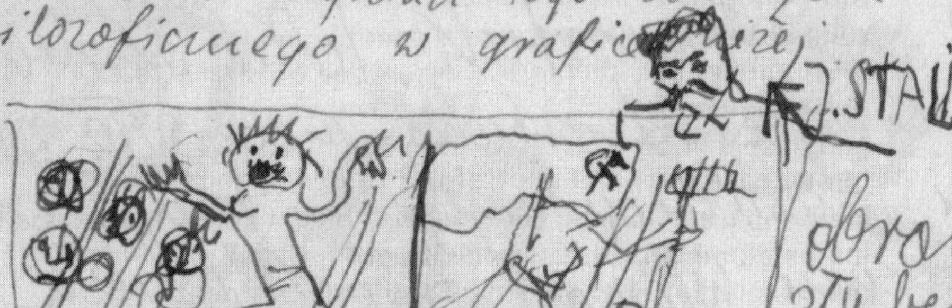

obraz
zły bez
koloru
i kreski

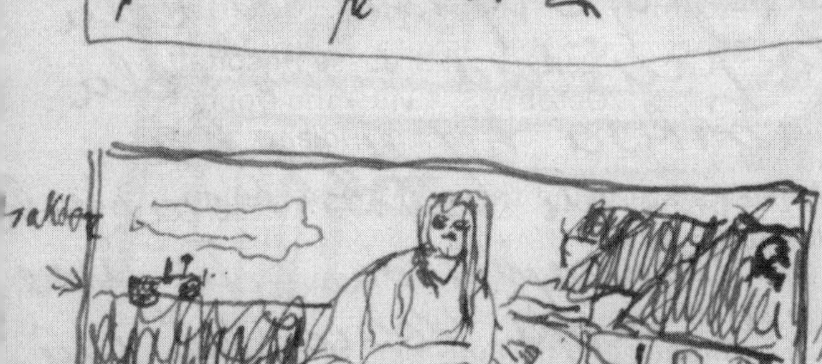

obraz
doskonały
prawda społ
wielkość
kolor
kompozycja
symbol
partyjność

I like
Your years of boyhood and youth.
Your plans for the future.
Your boyishness. Your stories.
Your vivacity, precision, intelligence, and lack of haste.
Resourcelessness.

I don't like
Your journalistic exploits and intentions.
Your verbiage, "gushing" over the past.
Your unfounded "somehow" plans and groundless hopes.
Resourcelessness.

In any case perhaps a lot of the things in these catalogues are inaccurate, a lot might still change. A lot are inconsistent, but it is precisely inconsistently and for no reason that I like some and dislike others.
And actually the ones I don't like don't really offend me or even bother me.

I

Paris, Paul Brousse Hospital,
October 3, 1949 Anno Domini,
4 *post meridiem*

different thoughts are flying through my head and I can't always handle it

II
One ought to paint man and his activities. One ought to paint <u>well</u>. Because a badly painted picture—let there be a "socialist realism"—is a bad picture. Example of this philosophical discovery in the illustration below

[←DRAWING]

J. STALIN
bad picture with no color and garish

[←DRAWING]

tractor
excellent picture
work, peace
greatness
color
composition
symbol
party loyalty

III

The family, that is, the state cell that the state really likes in its entirety, composed of various pieces. These pieces have to really hold together acc. to the state. But if there is a war, then they shatter into individual pieces with the goal of working for the state, that is, the goal of defending the state, that is, the goal of killing other pieces of family-cells of foreigners. That is clear. I want my state cell to have 5 pieces. Me + Rysiek = 2 + 1 Krzysztof + 1 Rachel + 1 unknown = 5. And for it to always be together.
No blue ink I substitute gray ink

[DRAWING→]

IV

Here a lunch is occurring, and after lunch or dinner the other joys of life. Illustrated next to it.
hors d'œuvre
lobster in mayonnaise
œuvres
baked chicken
pork loin
tender steak
Wiener schnitzel or something else
légumes
carrot with peas
salads etc.

rasem. [Brak farby —
drukarskiej kol. niebieskie-
go zastąpiłyś farbą naro-

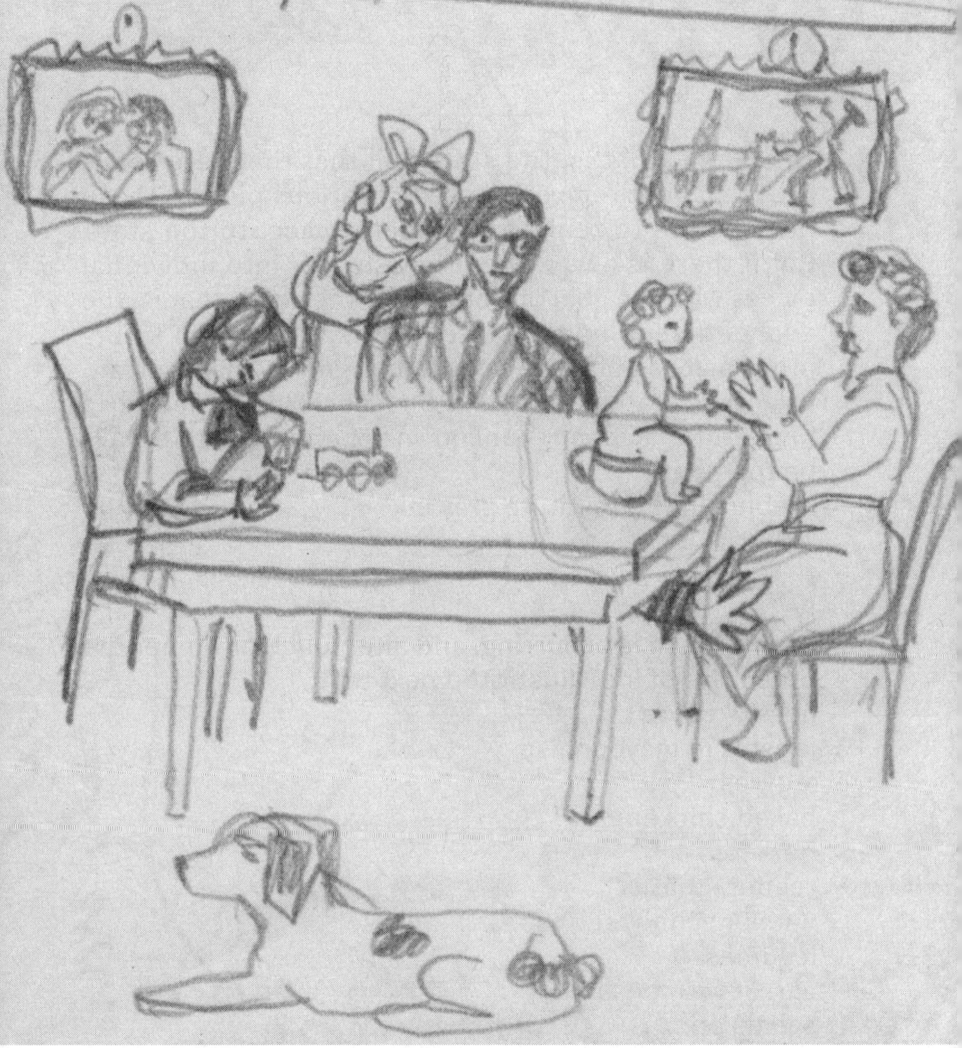

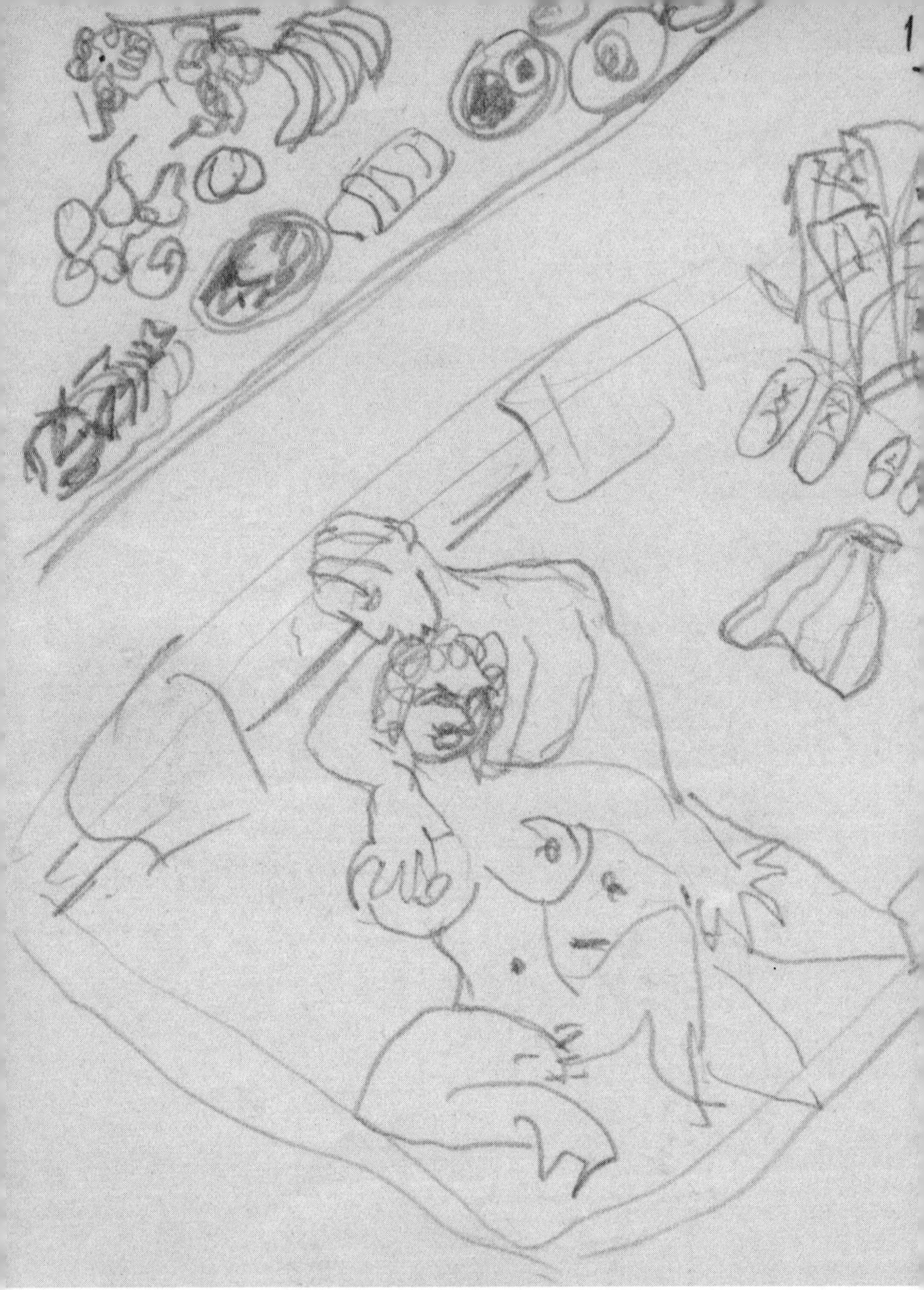

desserts
gruyère camembert cakes fruits
everything Ist class

appropriate beverages the whole time

[←DRAWING]

Table of Contents

I	introduction p. 1 and ½
II	art p. 2
III	cell, i.e. family p. 2 and ½
	illustration p. 3
IV	joy of life p. 3 and ½ + p. 4

[DRAWING]

printer's mark

29.
SZAPOCZNIKOW TO STANISŁAWSKI
POSTCARD, [OCTOBER 6, 1949]

Rysieńku
I don't understand what happened. You were supposed to come at noon.
I waited for you all day and am terribly, terribly anxious. You didn't have anything you had to do that would have prevented you.
So there is one thing that is troubling me, and I can't stop thinking about it even for a second: you're not ill??? I am helpless. But I of course cannot believe that you would have left me in such a state of uncertainty for some trifling reason. So what happened?

My one and only Rysieńku!
One and only, really, because that is precisely the basis of my great weakness, my great affection, that you are everything to me. Not only a lover and a brother, and a son, but in addition you bring my life from the outside into the hospital. Paris and the museum, the atelier and the gardens, and the bus, and the hotels, and the whole motion of life that overflows into the distance. Because you have to traverse the suburbs and change buses and get off where our objects of interest are.
While in the morning it's back to hospital life, which has the smell of ether and disinfection, and of disinfected filth. And everything is white and aquamarine. Even I am light blue (also an insipid color), and nearby there are very red, almost glowing little roses, and you are there again, Rysieńku. I would like to find words here that would be full of colorful shades in order to write to you about love. But it's difficult to look for them here, and it is after all poor to reward with words what to fulfill otherwise is impossible. Rysiu Rysieńku, my dear, my golden one.
When will I cradle you, and when will I kiss you kissily so quiet, in the dark, aquamarine night-time room. Because I still haven't kissed you in the shade of the forest or in the sunshine of the grass. But I know what the nights and the mornings are like when we intertwine so tightly, I know when you bathe in the evening and come to me cold. How your heart beats in excitement, and mine too. And I love to soap up all of you, and my hands in the soap slide down you in the shower. We laugh amongst ourselves.
I won't write more, because these words spoil everything. They're so bad that I'm actually ashamed at what

they do to the images that I see and feel.
I nestle all of me into you.
Rysieńku, Rysiu, golden, dear

Paul Brus [BROUSSE]
Hospital 17.X.49

Rysiu, write me something, anything, so that I could at least, while you are not here, see your words. Have something tangible, real from you. Because when you leave and this hospital atmosphere closes in on me once more—I am helpless and so frightfully strangely alone that I lose touch with all of my surroundings. With the whole of my life before the illness, and I sink into a completely barren void. I am afraid of suffocating in it, so I cling desperately to your images from my memory. Because that's what's closest to reality—images. When I think about my sculptures, it's mostly about what I've done—it's already lived, swept off into a corner as a thing that's been done and forgotten. I no longer love it. And yet what I am thinking of doing in the future is of course at most a topic or picture of a form suffusing my thoughts. Only you are real, I love you intensely and only. Of course nothing in my current life is unworthy of love. And I love you with all the love I still possess, that I can afford.

And your eyes, your hands are distinct in my lonely thoughts. Not only distinct, but in the lonely hospital nights your hands embrace me, your eyes gaze at me, your lips kiss me. You hold me to you so that I feel close and to chase away those stupid, tormenting thoughts. Thoughts of illness and of loneliness... The body slowly begins to have a reason for being that begins to be fulfilled, my sides that become round again, and my breasts heavy. Because you come to caress them and take pleasure from them. Rysiek, there are hours when it seems so real that you are beside me, that I feel your smooth skin and in sheer perversity I cannot restrain myself from some barb about the imperfection of your thighs or about a hair that is somewhere it shouldn't be.

And I feel you as I remember you next to me. Warm, close, nestling into me with your restless smooth and skinny body. So very restless that your hands wander over me, your head tickles me with its hair, your legs open my thighs, until at last exhausted we nestle into each other in a joyful sleep. A sleep preceded by a brief laugh over nothing, over liberation, over joy. And I think that then in that sleep comes the thing that is supposed to be love. Because I never really saw exactly what love looked like, so I think that it must come to us while we are asleep.

But here I wake up and you're not next to me. And I pine terribly.

Rysiek—life, love, work, activities are all one. When I wake up, I don't find any of that beside me or within me. Thus by a natural instinct of self-defense, a desire for life, I defend myself. I search and cling tightly to—at least the memories, so as not to drown, and what so smothers me, what drags me down into the depths of death, is yearning, I think, isn't it? Because it hurts so much that you're not here. I miss you so much, Rysiu, at least just write to me. Just a line or two for me to have when you go.

Your Alina

NOTES →[P 302]

25.X.49 l'hôpital

Rysiu Rysieńku
I wanted to do a sculpture of a nurse. Without any of what typically surrounds it, like "devotion," "sensitivity," "gentleness" etc. That is all a bunch of very romantic dead weight. These women that care for the sick are professionals as in any other sector of life. They spent 8 hours at their workplace and return to their family and their personal activities and entertainments. Nonetheless, and as in other walks of life, their occupation has impressed its specific character on their entire person. Sometimes this character is strong and truly lovely. Healthily there echoes from the wards of the sick and exhausted their springy step, their eternally energetic legs and strong, often supportive arms. Such a figure, which would join all the qualities of the nurse-woman caring for the sick, a figure symbolizing and typifying the nurse, is a really lovely theme. But... in order for the figure to be representative, it has to depict the nurse in some movement characteristic of her as she does her work. And there is where sculpture robs the nurse of her gravity. Movement destroys monumental dignity. A sculpture of a person in motion ceases to be a sculpture. And this is also why, I think, that same difficulty may arise in all socialist art. Sculpted people shown at work have to have an exceptionally unschematic form, the artist has to limit himself exceptionally in his means of expression and simplify the composition in order to emphasize the dignity of the work, in order for the activity itself to reach the viewer's consciousness, and, basically, in order not to mess up the specifics, that is, of the activity. That is why in Romanesque and Egyptian art we can see the activities of the craftsmen so clearly, and the little sculpted figure is like an embodiment of the entire craft.

But all speculations in one's head are crap, it's only when you start to compose that you see what makes sense and what doesn't, and you destroy and redo as needed until the image corresponds to the felt truth. Rysieńku, this was supposed to be a letter to you, but what am I supposed to write to you? I could at most caress you in embraces.

A.

Paris
Friday

Ryszard! Rysiu, Rysieńku
Please take me away from here. I am asking you as seriously, and it is as important as when at the beginning of our holiday I asked you, "Take me to the forest, to the meadows." And with just the same sadness I ask you. I know at the same time that I have to stay here for a while longer, and I know why. So that is precisely why I don't want to go on about this anymore, and why I am writing, so as not to keep bringing up a topic that has been unfurled too many times. But don't forget, and don't take my plea lightly. This is important. Where there will be peaceful nights and quiet, and an open window, and where I will sit back in a big comfortable chair, without so many strangers, and where I will return to health. For the moral and physical health of our life. For I so want to live!
I never knew that dying was so difficult. In the camp people dropped like flies. They didn't have time to be dying for long. A woman at the other end of this ward was in agony all night before she kicked the bucket. Actually I don't even think it was her anymore, because those terrible sounds and howls had already ceased to be human, and in the darkness they begat all of the most terrible (the ones it seemed I had forgotten) nightmares from the camps and of that miserable, inhuman, wartime life. While around me other women I didn't know (how cruelly, inhumanly unknown to me) talked about her indifferently (!) with complete indifference, like it was just nothing at all. They coughed, complained of colic, vomited, and whined that they couldn't sleep because of it. And from that darkness full of nightmares the stray words of living people did reach me, but there was not a single human soul. While at

least in the camp—there were human souls that allowed you to survive and believe.
I am boundlessly sad. That word cropped up despite being so banal because it was sadness that I saw without the slightest horizon of further desire, without limit.
I was supposed to write a "treatise" on why you have to do everything first of all "for yourself." But I will tell you only short and sweet. I'm telling this to you.
It's the same with every creation as it is with a kiss, which—when it's not "of one's own free will"—holds no value for the recipient. Of your own free will and for your own joy and happiness is how we must fulfil every work and create every thing, in order that it have (and only then will it have) true value for others. We must have love for what we create.
If a soldier goes into battle not with enthusiasm but only out of obligation, he is a bad soldier.
If a farmer, doctor, gardener, or sculptor does not enjoy and is not excited by his work, he is bad at his profession. And a worker is best and most productive when he loves his workshop and works at it with joy.
There are some disciplines that can't be exercised "for others" and not for oneself (to cheer or convince another). That is why it is said that "love is selfishness," because for the loved one it is only real and palpable when the one loving genuinely wants the loved one for himself. But I think at certain moments of love that me and you begin to merge into one, and that it is one. Wanting for you (health, for example), I want it-yours for myself, and wanting it for myself, I want it for you, in any case it's now one.

NOTES →[P 302]

6 in the evening
evening siesta (when it
comes down to it, the
whole day here is siestas)

The moment itself I always experience "dramatically," and there's nothing I can do to avoid it. In spite of my best intentions it always turns out that way. So I am sorry and please make peace with your fate of being burdened with such an awful creature as me. Meanwhile you no doubt are already sprouting angel's wings (check above your shoulder blade.)
When I went back, afternoon tea was already waiting for me (coffee with milk, very good bread with jam, peaches), they gave me a napkin, a place at the table with my own drawer etc. The room is lovely, clean, a radio and around 20 young women in the establishment. 3 maids, a nurse, etc. My suitcase had already been taken up to the second floor. A big room, very warm, an enormous window before the bed. 2 beds, but for the time being I am here alone. Fever 2 × per day, siestas by the open window, beyond the window... before the window... a really lovely pine tree of abstract forms, past that a long view of the grounds and the spruces. Clean. In the hall a cabinet, each of us has her own key. (Each of us has her own cabinet.) A bathing room where everyone has her own sink (hot and cold water) and her own bidet. Peace, rest! Very narrow bed, <u>non</u>hospital atmosphere, more like a girls' boarding house. Necessary to sleep by an open window.
My room is basically empty (just a bed and a little table), but not poor, nor bare because... the window, lovely, charming, distinguished, rich, close, beloved, and friendly.
Please bring or send me:
2 little spades from Julek. A package of white plasticine. The little board from in front of the window (if the sparrows have shat on it, it will have to be washed), 2 pink

garters (so that I don't have to wear a belt), your gray pants, a roll of toilet paper. Something good and interesting and French to read (borrow something from Hanka or from someone at the canteen), a Czech-French dictionary, 6 *pelotes* of gray wool, the lightest gray, *couleur d'argent*, normal-weight wool, quality ≈ 100 fr. *pelote*. There are moments here when one must *tricoter* (the radio is on, you're sitting in the dining room and—staring). I forgot to give you those remaining 3 thou. So buy the wool when I send it to you.

To Pacanowska go in two days, because I am sending her a letter now, too. I'm writing to her from us, i.e., you and me. So she will leave it with her hostess when she goes out. Write me a line every day. What are you sending to your mom, dad, etc? The *facteur* is much anticipated here and greeted with a general squeal. There is a parlor and a piano. I think I will be cured here!

I don't want to kiss you, because I'll burst into tears, so I just snuggle up to your warm body. Take care of yourself and eat lots!!!

YOUR Alina

Thursday

My Rysieńku
I got your letter, the date of which I did not like at all: Tuesday (12$^{\underline{30}}$ a. m.). I don't want to nag you, but that does also fall under the heading of "self-improvement," overcoming those habits that ruin your health! (Ah, how very intelligently I wrote that, when all we're talking about is going to sleep and getting up earlier.) You don't have to hurry too terribly much with the spades, I am so enchanted by the air here that I literally don't know what is happening to me, and I can't do anything yet. Apparently that is a normal phenomenon here, hence the first week of siesta takes place in your room, instead of in a deckchair in the garden. But by the wide-open window. Night, too, is spent by a wide-open window. I put "is spent" because there is no way to sleep, so sharp is the air. I now understand why they said to bring a hot-water bottle and a blanket. Some of the girls equipped themselves with goose-down duvets, and they make out much better that way. Last night I slept in your khaki shirt over my nightgown and beneath such a mountain of things that it felt heavy, and I only fell asleep toward morning. But these are silly things that will pass, and one gets used them to after a couple of days.
The grounds are very beautiful, if small, but beyond the low enclosure there is the forest again, and all around you see nothing but trees. The food is fairly simple, but for now it more than suffices, plainer perhaps than in the hospital, but quite tasty. In fact the conditions are excellent and the repose complete, but far from being a real sanitarium, however, or a deluxe or ½ deluxe *pension*. For example, there are no parlor games whatsoever, not even checkers, no books at all, and the girls

are shrill and uninteresting. Apart from no intellectual level whatsoever, they lack even the primitive individuality of "children of the people." Age range 16 to 25 (only one is 25). Secretaries, stenographers, behold the little geeselets on the marriage market now. Tomorrow they are supposed to seat me at the table where the one student eats, but even she appears quite ho-hum (medicine).

Next to mine is the nurse's room. She can be distinguished by the fact that she wears a white apron and calls us in to lie down. She only actually nurses her little dog, who just had her *mamelle* surgery; she wraps an elastic bandage around her stomach and takes her out for walks. Besides, she is an older lady suffering from love-sickness for the art of painting, being herself a painter. She would be Cézanne if it weren't for these stupid duties she has to perform to earn a living. She was terribly pleased to learn that there was a "stud. de Beaux-Arts" here and promptly displayed for me her works in pastel. Red sails on a green sea and red apples on a green tablecloth, etc. I pronounced a judgment ridden with hypocrisy.

The biggest event of the day is the mail carrier. He brings either squeals of delight or disappointed faces. He was kind to me today—he brought a letter from you. I'm yammering on, but down to business. I don't think the thing with Mencel is any good, because if someone from the BIB is replacing Potisz. now, then that's it, that substitute could last for a while, they won't be in any hurry. Mr. M. is in no hurry, he is not obligated to be in one as you are. I'm not sure you will get an answer from Warsaw, either, because they probably haven't even gone to them, they're probably just stalling to try and get better information on you. I don't know if they would have gotten any information that would be satisfactory, because they may be very suspicious, and Heniuś is also a swine. Definitely try as soon as possible to talk to Mencel and talk to him sincerely, too, making your situation clear to him and getting him to tell you whether in his (Mencel's) opinion you should wait or not. Make sure he understands that waiting means you risk being hungry and losing your health. That is, after all, the worst of it. Remember last year's waiting from Wednesday to Monday etc.? But Rysiek, don't worry. Just hang in there, because I am writing all of this in fear for your already depleted health.

What you write about things that are vulgar is only partly true. I have come to the conclusion that all things, those we have neglected and those we have given a lot of thought to, are equally necessary, and if even one were missing the rest would limp. Feeling, intellect, beauty, health, money, work, etc. There are no "less important" ones.

This letter somehow turned out awkward, I wanted to speak to you otherwise. These days will pass, I guess, somehow.

I'm not writing that our days and nights are going to be restored, because in fact I believe that other, new, fuller and lovelier nights will come in their stead. I hope I will get completely well here.

Ryś, Rysieńku you are my dear, my darling, my love. I often feel that you are really always with me. I kiss you and snuggle up to you

Your Alina

[NOTE:]

Out of the money from Pac. please give some immediately to the Weisses and Pappé.

36.
SZAPOCZNIKOW TO STANISŁAWSKI
[DECEMBER 1949]
NOTES →[P 304]

Rysiu.
The girl brought me 2 packages from you and the news that you had phoned, but the workers were laying down linoleum, so she couldn't get through to call me, she was blocked, damn it. For the parcel I thank you.
It's great you bought *Paul and Manon*. With respect to *Women and Dolls* (I saw that title in Polish somewhere), I'm not holding my breath, from the images and the period (1896) I fear it may be pure sap.
Time now passes perfectly. In the breaks between siestas, I draw. The little Denise came to me, embarrassed that she would like to have a likeness of herself. She has a little body, but full and "sprightly." She agreed to pose without her clothes. I gave her one sketch and... all of them want to pose. Only now do I see how out of practice my hand was, and how good it will do me to draw for ½ an hour every day. Or more than my hand—my eyes. It's so difficult for me to really realize what I've seen. Compare proportions etc. This requires a mind intensely straining and really becomes work. The question of my glasses is also becoming a burning one. I see worse and worse (it's already been a year since I was supposed to get new ones), this really tires me and interferes with my work. I would need so much to have a pair of proper lenses that I could wear so that I could give my eyes a rest.
You can't even imagine how much good the rest here is doing me, how peaceful I feel, and almost happy in this regular life in the fresh air. Rest and the absence of cares, only now am I experiencing all the great human feelings and only now out of passed cares and pains can I create. It's proximity to nature that works so soothingly. I finished the sketch of the pilot, he has a lot of human

truth in him. Because he doesn't wear the dust of the city. With fear I think of the days when you would say to me, "go on, lie down, rest." While I wasn't in a state to do anything, and at night I would cry out of exhaustion, because your words lacked the backing of peace and fresh air. I'm simply afraid that once more those nasty days will envelop us. And if I can't work, then I can't live, and our feelings will also somehow get crammed in between the dirty sheets and the pots and pans.

Even here, in the preventorium, there are intense "class frictions" and class differences. I'm here and attempting not to step out of my role as witness and observer. Class markers are: a nicer sweater, richer parents, way of speaking etc.

I don't belong to the class that dips bread in coffee and then drips it all over their tattered sweaters. However, their reasons for being, which they vivaciously defend, their strong and healthy hatred is so lovely in its purity of the primitive, that I stand wholeheartedly with them. And I lament that I can't hate sufficiently (because not organically and with disgust) the well-mannered hypocritical little ladies.

I received a lovely letter from Bedo. He's to turn in a plan for a relief near the "springs of love" in "Francbad." He writes of his work and of Prague.

Is it sentimental weakness that I think about Oldo and swimming in the spring in the overflowing Vltava, about Zdeněk and the little winding streets of Mala Strana, the green light of the gas lanterns and his room packed with sculptures, where we put on that record from *Cyrano de Bergerac* 100 × and where Ježerský would recite us poetry. I think about the assistant at the gypsum plaster place, who had blue eyes, spoke little, and was so boundlessly good. Good is a label that doesn't mean much, but nor can many people just be called good and have that be that. Slavically good. You know? It was really there that I came of age. And thence my *trésor* for

my future work. And that I was a foreigner among them, and Polish thinking gave me the necessary distance, I could draw on it for my "works."
And now I think about Prague, or maybe about my youth, and I think about Polish people and broad fields, about my mom, and this I think is that shattered heart that doesn't scab over and heal, which is why it exudes (pus and blood), because otherwise, like any other obstructed wound, it hurts. It will probably never heal, because for us it will have been torn there, by Paris. But for an operation, though in that case I will lose that heart in its integrity. From the pus and blood from a shattered heart one must shape art.

[NOTE IN THE MARGIN:]

sorry about that ink smudge, I don't know how that happened

[IN THE BACKGROUND A DELICATE PENCIL SKETCH OF A SEATED FIGURE]

SZAPOCZNIKOW TO STANISŁAWSKI

[DECEMBER 1949]

NOTES →[P 305]

My Rysieńku!

You know, as soon as I returned to my room and saw the things you had brought me, I realized what a moronic situation this really is. You yourself exhausted, skinny, lacking in everything, while here I am stuffing my face, doing nothing, and getting fat. These delicacies have completely ceased to cheer me. I have to treat this stuffing my face like medicine, but when I think of you, that you, too, could lose your health, I am gripped by terror. After all fatigue is the first pre-sickness symptom. And if you don't have your health, then everything else is down the drain, and there's no point left. You're probably the only one who understands what I'm talking about. Rysiu, Rysieńku, if we are still to be happy together at some stage (after all this is our hope and almost our only reason for being and for the struggles of today), then don't forget yourself, and eat. If it's to be only for me, and it's not enough for you, then I don't want it at all. I've written all of this a bit in the tone of my mom, but believe me when I say that it really makes my hackles rise. I think that maybe that day job would actually be better for you, and healthier. With a certain self-discipline, it could be made to work alongside the École du Louvre. Write to me to tell me how that's looking.

Could you please talk to Lipiński for me and tell him about my inventiveness and facility for drawing and show him these 3 little drawings that I am sending now. Explain, too, to what end they were done (that third one is the sketch of one of the girls for a portrait, in a letter I can only send such scraps). I would really like for him to take some illustration from me. Maybe for some newspaper or journal. I could do it easily, and with my being sick it would be a great help in terms both of finances and morale. Maybe they need something for something, I'd be happy to do it, though I can't do any woodcuts or anything in metal here, but I can, however, do whatever they need in pencil or ink. He could just give me the theme and the format and so forth and the specs. You don't need to tell him anything about my sculpting. But do give him an idea of my idiotic—illness and situation. In fact, you can read him this. Just so that I can earn a little for my treatment or even just for glasses, the lack of which I am feeling more and more, and so that I can take some joy from being good for something. Let me know what he says immediately. They can take and use these drawings wherever they have a place for them.

[NOTE IN THE MARGIN:]
tell him I have drawings that are better than these ones

I was thinking about those Egyptian women, that this current fad for *œil à la biche* also very likely comes from them, and although so artificial in stone or bronze, that coquette was all right, and so on.
I'm curious to know what "bright idea" you'll come up with?!
Did you see the doctor? You can't imagine how much I would like to be with you and healthy. In such [CUT OFF]

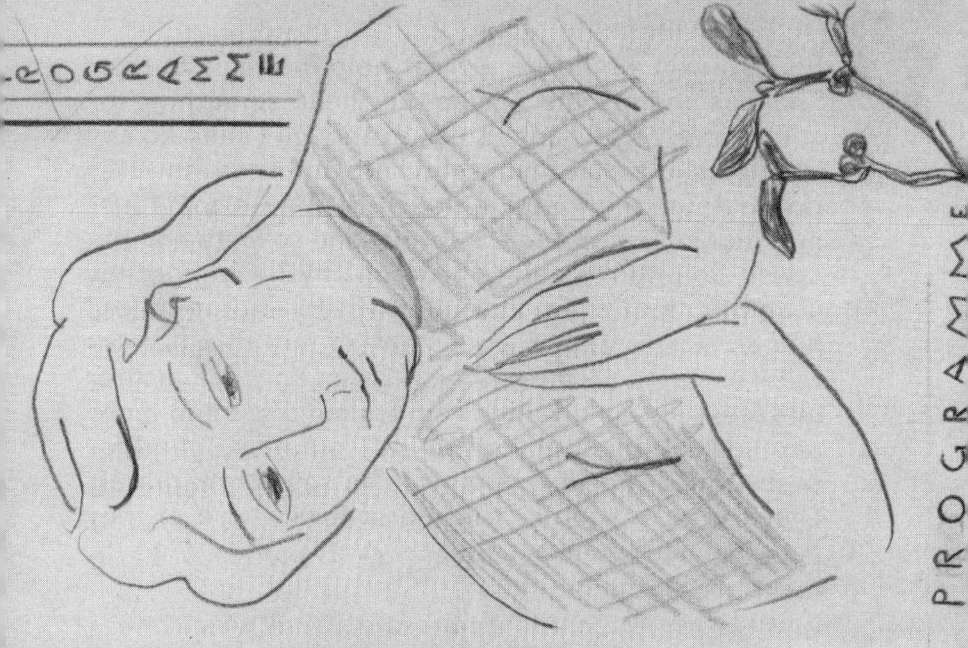

bjaw. A jak zdrowia nie ma to wszystko
inne jest do luftu, wogóle nie ma
sensu. Rozumiesz mnie chyba sam
co mi chodzi. Rysiu, Ryszeńku jeśli
ęcie kiedyś mamy być razem szczę-
śliwi (a przecież to nasza nadzieja i jedy-
na prawie racja bytu i dalszych zma-
gań) to pamiętaj o sobie i odżywiaj
się. Jeśli ma być tylko dla mnie
dla ciebie nie starczy, to nie chcę
cale. To wszystko napisałam trochę
łowie mojej mamy ale wierz mi, że
jak mnie trafia. Myślę, że może ta
dzienna praca jednak lepsza będzie dla

I'm terribly glad, Rysiu, that you were here, we didn't talk about what we wanted to talk about, but that is the way it is, and it's probably for the best. About the weather, about trivial things, and then about overly serious matters, but the important thing is that you are here. We know about the other stuff anyway, and chatting is moronic.
You smile uncrookedly! You made me happy with that tooth. Material proof that all the burning questions ultimately get resolved. I'm lying down by the open window. I'm happy that you also feel how lovely it can be in nature, in the landscape etc.
I am sending you cards. I marked in pencil which one is for whom. Do a nice job erasing that before putting them into an envelope. I'm sending a few, too, to use as you wish, where I've written "whoever you want." The propped-up little angel is pretty.
I'm sending ones for Vautre and Roland with their addresses, since you don't have them, and just my name, because you don't know them.
Good *Action*. It uplifted me and my communist spirits. (!?!?)
Are you doing nothing other than preparing gifts for Christmas Eve? I'm thinking of your academic work? and classes. Write.
Kiss, kiss

Alina

Call me!
Write if you got in all right, etc.
The chicken wings were extraordinary and right after dinner I ate them all up with gusto.

Forgive me for writing in pencil, but I can't write with that pen anymore lying down, and it's so hard to read after.
Rysiu, don't come to get me on Saturday. We are allowed to go on our own. So it's a waste of time and money. I'll go along with the others. I'll be home at around 10 in the morning on Saturday.
In case I forget, please have ready by then: 1°) rubber soles and 2 pairs of heels for women's shoes size 6, that is [SKETCH OF THE SOLE] like that, not pointed ones, because in those fur ones they're completely worn out now, and another pair also needs heels. I'll affix them at home over the holidays. 2°) From the atelier 2 brushes (a thin one and a thick one), buy 1 pound of good gypsum plaster *à modeler* and ask at the dyer's shop where you can buy *fil pour couper la forme* that is a piece ~ 1 ½ meter thin as a thread, but strong. And get a saw for making plinths out of wooden boards. 3°) My sheer nylons are hanging in the wardrobe, they have 2 small runs, please give them to the laundress to mend, I want them to be ready for the holidays, it's just a little thing for 20 fr.
Your Czech-Egyptian-Polish-financial letter with illustrations came just now. For me please set aside money for:
—Mietek's debt, (if he asks for it in francs, 9), for 2 doctors (for you and for me, 4), for glasses for me (8, combination lenses ~ 6 thousand), clothes for you (20), for the tailor (10), and shoes (5) for me.
Yet another hierarchy.
I had the nightmare again. This time you starved to death in the hospital. Mietek was at your funeral. I saw everything so clearly, and felt it so intensely, that when I woke up it was with enormous relief that I discovered it was just a dream. This, too, may be a good omen in the end.
I'm sending a clipping from *Action* about a competition. Please get the details!

The rest in person and with my whole body, because it's already Wednesday afternoon.
Kiss, kiss

Alina yours

libám tě milý jak jen dovedu

Paříž 19 prosince pondělí
tvojě češtiná je špatna.

39.

SZAPOCZNIKOW TO STANISŁAWSKI

[DECEMBER 30, 1949]

NOTES →[P 305]

Rysieńku!
Please think up something, anything.
Can it really be possible that because of stupid money, because of a stupid fifteen grand or so I am here? With this gang of morally and sexually underdeveloped and spoiled little lady idiots? And that I can't even get out into the sunshine even for a little bit, I snivel in this damp and fog.
Rysiu, I know I will get better, just send me into the sunshine for one month.
Without that any assurance of love has as little weight as the paper it is written on!!
Maybe the consulate would lend me something or through Mencel with the aid of the Polish Red Cross. I'll make them a lovely Chopin afterwards, and give them some other sculpture, if I can't pay back the money in any other way.
It's an outrage, I would be able to work, just let them help me just a little bit now to regain my health. 50–60 thousand or so.
Do what you can.

Alina

Or tell that consul that I'll give it back when he comes from Poland.

Alina

Ask Russak for me, or read him this letter.
And take care of the package from Poland.

[NOTES ON THE ENVELOPE:]

Out with capitalism, long live the peoples' republics.

Here, even including the doctor, what you don't pay for stinks.

"while into the telephone through the receiver tears..."
(*An Unremarkable Story*, J. Tuwim)

40.
SZAPOCZNIKOW TO STANISŁAWSKI
JANUARY 9, 1950
NOTES →[P 305]

1/9/50
9.1.50 Monday

freedom, home!
Thou art like good health!
I never knew till now
How precious,
Till I lost thee

I wrote a letter to Artur. Let me know if I should write to Kott (as we discussed) regarding your work, possibly packages from Poland? I don't want to do that without settling it with you. I do, however, want to do everything in my power this week to make sure I don't have any regrets later.
Yesterday was an idiotic afternoon. But everything (including demanding money) issues from the fact that I want to stay with you at all costs.
But I am actually starting to seriously come around to the idea of a trip out to Poland. That might even be better. Because as for my work, what is it I am looking for here? More normally, systematically, better I will be able to work at home instead of abroad. And the sooner I start, the better my chances are of settling in there. If in 2–3 more years we meet again, "freely (in our hearts)," you will at least have a ready apartment in me. If we don't meet, then clearly that was how it had to be, and maybe it's better that we end it earlier and at the "height of adoration" than for us to have to part with regrets. I confess that I am now beginning to be happy, little by little, about my trip out to my mom's. It's the end of the Paris chapter, but after all it is also the beginning of another. Maybe more wonderful?!
All of the "scenes" between us issue from the most ordinary thing in the world—that we love each other like the most primitive individuals. All of the symptoms we

don't want to admit to exist—we are both jealous over each and every blink of our partner's. We both cloak our moves in the noble "it's for your own good." But in reality we want to have our "other half" only and exclusively to ourselves. We both want our partner to be lovely, wise, valued and esteemed, because our partner is "ours." It's the simplest thing in the world: you want to provide for your woman, and I want to be taken care of by you. You want to be the father of our children, and I their mother. We cloak that in fairy tales full of hypocrisy, but in the end it's good that it's that and nothing else. And so it shall be!
I can't get over how little I was in your arms yesterday, and that you didn't feel me up at all.
Hugs

Alina

41.

SZAPOCZNIKOW TO STANISŁAWSKI
[JANUARY 1950]
[ADDED TO THE BLANK SIDES OF THE LETTERS FROM HER MOTHER FROM DECEMBER 23, 1949 AND JANUARY 7, 1950]
NOTES →[P 306]

Rysiu
I got the 2 letters and the 500 fr. Thank you. Especially for the letters, because I am less lonely because of them. I am sending you a letter from my mom for you to know what a dear she is and how she thinks of us. And it also has information about the *pardessus*, I don't think there's much to get worked up over in it! Maybe it's better that the issue is becoming clear: I am ill, for the time being I can't work. If you are not going to be able to keep me and support me, I have to go to Poland. I'm even a little bit happy (as much as I can be given everything), because the years when my mom might be able to spend joyful moments with me are rapidly passing. I am robbing her of those years, and here she is approaching genuine old age. We still have "our lives ahead of us." Do we not? I feel a little like I'm already "away." To be continued on a fresh piece of paper.
I got a long list from Roland. I don't know why I am so ill-used and why there is such injustice in the world that impotent blockheads are sculpting stunning models while I lie in this empty room as in a coffin. For it's so cold, gray, lonely. I also received three letters from my mom. In the first she asks whether there is medical care, good food and company etc. To all of these questions the answer is no, so I prefer to pass them over in silence. The next two letters I am sending you because they contain words for you as well, and you'll have the information about the money, when she'll be able to send it etc. I am genuinely moved by her words, because in them I do see my mom, such a dear and so simple, unpretentious, and so full of love. Let us be grateful to her. I am curious, too, what the "little miracle" might be that the dear old lady has thought up.

Probably my greatest sin was leaving her alone.
You and I were scared of parting, of never meeting again (when I was to go to Poland for my treatment). I think that was a mistake. The situation now is 100 × worse. I can't think about the past, because that's weakness, stupidity, hiding one's head in the sand etc. The present moment is not a life at all, and can't be counted as such. The future? Will I find you again after this, and you me? Will we meet again, as we once did, in Mietek's room on Raspail? Doubtful!

SZAPOCZNIKOW TO STANISŁAWSKI
[JANUARY 1950]

Rysieńku
I got your letter where you give your two reasons for my decision. So the first ("that I don't want you for obvious reasons") is idiotic, there's no question of that whatsoever, I feel we have said enough on the subject. The second one, on the other hand, is 100% true. Long story short: I have lost all patience. I'm happy you've understood me, and I think that there is nothing strange about that.
Today I was sorry I had sent you such a scathing, rude letter yesterday putting everything in such terribly material terms. But I will make this little confession to you: it's the first time in my life that I've come up against such an insurmountable difficulty. And for the first time I've realized that everything is predicated on filthy mammon—on money. I forced myself to think about our circumstances objectively, although in my heart I would much rather nestle into you and not think about anything.
Rysiek, do not forget that I will be exactly as unhappy without you as you will be alone. That it is harder and sadder for me to think about us separating than it is for you.
I would so like for you to somehow relieve me of this mental burden, for there to be no more worries or regrets, for it to be possible to be with you for good. But how can I not rebel, since I am far from you, can't do anything, am sick as a dog, and in my mind have a dark outlook. Our self-preservation instinct teaches us to protect ourselves, and thence issues my decision.
You don't need to write to me about competing for positions, about work here etc. I would like to stay regardless of all that, even if just for you. But how? Ryś,

this should not surprise you. I have really gotten quite ill. And I really don't see any other way out in the face of this financial helplessness—besides leaving. And it will even be easier financially for you, too. But yours always

Ala

NOTES →[P 306]

Thursday

Rysieńku
Your long-anticipated letter finally came, and in spite of my *cure de silence* I am writing you back. First regarding the more burning questions, i.e., transferring out of here.
I can't remember the name of the lady from the Cité, but at the *service médical*, first right as you go in through the big gate to the "Cité" (across from the Cité metro and the P.C. bus station). On the first floor, hallway on the left, second door on the left (first is to the bathroom). There are three desks in the room. This woman sits opposite the door at the main, largest desk. She is a *mademoiselle* about 30–35 years old, good-looking, with symmetrical features, very black hair with a part in the middle, and was wearing a blue blouse.
her coiffure [DRAWING OF A HEAD-PROFILE AND EN FACE]
They are open in the morning 9–10–11.
Go straight to her, please, right away, and say something along these lines: *Il y a quelques semaines était chez vous Mademoiselle une jeune sculpteur* (here show that paper from Niclausse) *de part de Melle Desjobert.*
Elle est maintenant en Jouy-en-Josas. Vous avez dit à elle que si on aurait besoin d'un autre sanatorium on pouvait faire les démarches. Alors cette demoiselle a reçu une convocation de la préfecture pour aller dans une sana près de la Rochelle. Elle était chez son docteur qui a trouvé le climat d'océan très bien pour son cas (tuberculose des ovaires). (I talked to her for a long time about my illness, and back then she expressed great feminine sympathy with regard to children, those organs, etc.) *Mais une fois envoyée par votre institution elle ne peut pas profiter les autres de prefecture j ai parlé déjà d'elle avec Melle Desjobert, mais sont des finances e.t.c. Je viens alors vous demander si vous ne pouvez faire "prise en charge" pour elle dans*

une autre maison qui convient pour sa maladie. You could also show the address that you got from Henio. Rysiek, I have to be healthy finally now!!! I think that that woman will be of great help, she was extraordinarily kind to me and full of respect.

As for your working, I would emphatically like for you to get something as soon as possible. If you were working, I could go home right now and take care of this sanatorium stuff myself, it's just a matter of going back and forth a few times, after all. And really, on both moral and physical grounds, I will not undertake such a precarious life of borrowing around from different people and neighbors, which has always caused me great anxiety and humiliation. Even were I not sick at all. With respect to your studies, you do not really dedicate, on average, more than 3 hours a day to them, so working wouldn't really stand in your way. For a variety of serious reasons I would really like for you be working now, and I fear you are not trying hard enough (or maybe you're just not going about it right?). Maybe Elsner, as an artist, would say something on your behalf?
Did you see Mrs. Głogowska at the museum?
I received 5 letters today, among them one from the lady Lustre that was sincere, nonsensical, a frenzy of her faith in Communism. Please go and thank them and maybe congratulate them, etc. Do not neglect those correct courtesies that make you. Also remember the [CROSSED-OUT] socks, barber!
I have a similar Axentowicz card from my mom.
I can't write lying down.
Yesterday I pined so in the night.
My body is acquiring plenitude and vitality, and the only things that are missing are your hands that seek the little lump on my breast and caress my thighs. Lately at home I was simply too tired by the late hour to reach the pinnacle of joy! Your caresses tired me at times

with their healthy persistence. Rysieńku! These nights now I miss your head on my breasts so much, and everything in me strains and opens up for you. My body, childishly, disapprovingly, simply refuses to understand that your hands are not drifting over it. Rysiu, it is actually frightening how much it has to be you by my side, and only you. And I can't sleep at all without you. And can't do anything. I will say this to you on Sunday.
I have not gotten my period, I don't know what that means?!
Please bring me French books, good literature. Your humanities friends from the canteen will no doubt have things and lend them to you (Hanka). Also bring me 1 jar of strawberry or other jam from Turpin and 1 liter of ordinary red wine. Nothing else, maybe 1 bar of chocolate and 2 pounds of apples. But do not borrow any more money. Just don't buy things. Maybe Hanka can pay you back, because it's just after the first, and she has gotten paid?
Also please write to Artur immediately and ask how our deal is going, because he can't just not let us know. Write that instead of the sun treatment I need, they stuck me in here. And if I had money, I would already be healthy by now. Rysieńku, kiss, kiss, kiss

Alina

[NOTES IN THE MARGINS:]
Service „prise en charge sanatorium"
excuse mes fautes!
it's a shame my Bethlehem didn't work out. The photographs made me happy, thanks.
The photographs are good, but neither technically nor artistically, just sentimentally.

NOTES →[P 307]

Thursday

Although the days are long, seemingly endless, I haven't been writing you because I was awaiting news from Dr. Monsaingeon. But nothing came, which means I'm staying. I don't know if I should grieve this—don't know if he's even asked M[elle] Desjobert about transferring me to another preventorium with sun.

I feel sick (my stomach hurts).

From constantly lying around my muscles are slackening, and the worst part is that all this time has been wasted. Yet I have the strong sense that a month of sun and absolute peace (without the shrieking violence of these idiotic girls, and of the Sunday excitement) and <u>good</u> food would put me right back on my feet, without any doctors.

I know my organism (*résistance*), which has already coped with so many *incroyable* difficulties. That is what I want and have needed for months now, since even before my illness, when I was beginning to feel tired and said, "Let's find the quiet of the forest." Well, why go on.

It's a complete flop because you can't get any decent food in here! At the beginning I thought that it just seemed that way to me after the hospital, and that I would get used to it. Besides I knew there was nothing I could do about it. But today some of the other girls actually wanted to draw up a petition because they're hungry. Always the same soup and the same little slice of boiled meat, 2 × a day. 2 × a day 2 pieces of bread with a little butter. Since Monday the bread has been served with margarine.

They <u>never</u> give us: wine, cheese, eggs, or meat rare, which I so need (ah, gone are the days of Monsaingeon's steaks and the gallons of milk at the Paul Brousse!)

I am so vexed by the fog and the cold, I want fresh air

and sunshine! Why do so many people that are strong as oxen and don't need it go up into the Alps to make the time they feel stands still fly! My time is running, and I can't catch up with it. Five lovely years got away from me as I waited for liberation. 5 dear months of that priceless freedom got away from me awaiting my health. Anyway what is the point of sniveling? Let us be realistic. I was supposed to stay here as long as it suited me, no, so I do not have to waste time and let it tax my nerves. If I had 30–40 thousand, I would go to an ordinary *pension* in the mountains, like to Pierre's family's, I would eat well and come back healthy. And if I had even just a guaranteed 500 fr. per day, it would be better to wait at home to be transferred by Melle Desjobert and eat well, and I think we would be strong enough to establish a regular routine for sleeping and getting up. And I would be able to start working sooner. I'm ready to let them operate, anything just to be done with it! I must work, because I know how, and I am bursting at the seams with it.
I don't even know how to kiss you anymore, because even that art requires practice—and joy. There is no joy here. I only want to cuddle up to you, and my head wants to be pet and answers to the caresses of your dear hands. We'll decide on Sunday

Ala

[AT THE BOTTOM A SMALL SELF-PORTRAIT IN PENCIL; IN THE BACKGROUND A PENCIL SKETCH, A SELF-PORTRAIT WITH FLOWER]

I am doing programs for these little idiots. Bring me: a package of cotton, 2 slices of ham, 4 hard-boiled eggs, a jar of mayonnaise. A piece of gruyère.
Do not bring sweets!
That is all, please bring books if you can!!!
Envelopes!!

[DRAWINGS IN PENCIL: A LITTLE FLOWER AND A LITTLE BOY-ANGEL, AND ON THE REVERSE A PRAYING WOMAN AND A PORTRAIT]

Tuesday

I cannot prevail upon myself and am writing. I think about you all the time now, and <u>only now</u> am I thinking about you.
I traverse the streets and regions I traversed with you and so so close beside you. You may now be sitting in that room of "ours," and I know that I should be comforting you and keeping your spirits up. However, not that I wish to complain, but I am going through hell here. Hell of a sort I do not even remotely know how to write about.
Rysiu, Rysieńku, you're becoming more than a man to me ("off with her head!"). You are the person closest to me, the person I would want to seek shelter in. I am doing horribly, horribly badly.
Your Alina
Do we have enough patience and strength?

What are you doing?

If you can, please bring the camera on Sunday. Also bring an empty bag and a net bag, perhaps, that way we can take some of the things that I don't absolutely need, so that later it won't be so hard to lug everything out at once. We can just have dinner together on Sunday.
Kiss, kiss

A.

And on Sunday I will kiss and rekiss and bekiss and counterkiss you, too.

47.

SZAPOCZNIKOW TO STANISŁAWSKI

POSTCARD FROM PRAGUE, [MAY 26, 1950]

NOTES →[P 307]

Friday

Rysieńku
The Frenchman was sleeping, the German didn't say anything. The road went on and on, but everything went well. Prague is lovely, but the men are horrible, I think constantly of you, my darling.
I'm going to my mom tomorrow, write what you are doing, and everything.

Alina

[NOTE IN THE MARGIN:]
the roses wilted and smell

NOTES →[P 307]

Łódź 28.V.50

Mine!
I am with my mom in Łódź now, the weather has taken a little turn for the worse, Łódź has gotten good-looking, I was driven by a driver who just came back from France ½ a year ago. The women are prettier than in Prague, but uglier than in Paris. In Prague the sculptors' workshops are all fully given over to monuments. Bedo is really doing very lovely things and roused my respect and I'm terribly sad that I cannot do anything so lovely myself. My mother gave a terrible cry, "Alunia!!!" from the window, because not knowing what day I would come—she was on the lookout and listening for it every morning. It's a holiday today (Whitsun), and I won't call your father until tomorrow, but I've already written to Kachu and am going there. The house is in very bad shape, the door creaks out for oil, the water drips from the tap but doesn't work in the W.C. etc., I'll have to take a little initiative and do some of it myself. My mom has really turned into an old lady, her features and her body have changed, and I am still having to get used to the idea of her actually being my mom. It pains me that she doesn't know who Degas is, for example, and other things, and it's hard for me to talk to her. I'm curious about your father. Rysieńku, how tired I am, and my "eggs" hurt, no one can care for me and encompass me with such feeling as you. If you haven't already cast it, please throw that figure out. It's very weak and not worth casting. I'll do a better thing in that stone. Please do just destroy that figure.
They are "crazy about, ooh, ah" those little things that I brought, and I myself inspire oohs and ahs!
I'm sending you a sample, but I don't like it much. Write if I should send it, and say that it's instead of what they may have kept of mine, or look for something else,

although I doubt I'll find something better. Or just send it, say it's from your father, and be done with it? The wool is 100%. Despite that, I'm very happy I didn't take it. Deal with this as you think best. Ryś, I really miss you. Are you taking care of yourself? What about money? Have you been to the restorer's? Definitely work at whatever you can find, not only because of finances and morale, but just in general. Maybe out of doors, on a tractor, or as a driver. It's important! Will relate details. Are you going to Crillon?
I kiss you Rysieńku my darling you.

Your Alina

Bonjour pour Mme Honoré and the others.

SZAPOCZNIKOW TO STANISŁAWSKI

MAY 31, 1950

NOTES →[P 308]

31.V.50

Rysieńku, I haven't written for a couple of days because I wanted to let you know once I had spoken to your father. I talked to him (on the telephone) just yesterday, because he is spending Whitsun in Poznań. We talked just a few minutes, during which time your father asked me about the results of the exam and other things to which I vowed to respond in person. Because I am very likely setting off in 1 week for the coast, your father will take a look at his schedule and telephone in the next few days to let me know what day he will come.

The last 2 days I was very busy reorganizing my mom's apartment, which has become more comfortable and nicer and more modern.

I also talked to Adam, whose version of things is exactly the opposite of everyone else's here. Apparently they've done a lot of squares in Łódź, torn down a lot of ugly things, and put up lovely stores with state goods.

I ask you expressly <u>not</u> to cast that figure with the child. I need to do completely different things. And that one is exceptionally poor. Please say hello to the Lerendus from me and from my mom. I'll write to them in the next few days. Did you remember the exhibition of young sculptors? I am also eagerly awaiting confirmation that you took care of that debt. Has Hanka come back yet? I met a couple of her friends here, almost all of them married, with children, owners of apartments, living proper, "grown-up" lives. I bought Mayakovsky's *Poems*, a lovely edition, cloth-bound—300 zlotys. Unfortunately the photographs did not turn out well (the reproductions you were doing recently of my things). I am sending you, however, a few of the old ones that hadn't been printed. I am eagerly awaiting news from you and the photographs of Ginette. After the fumes and the noise of Paris, the Łódź air seems so fresh, and I feel very good. My great wish is for you to settle down somewhere in the provinces and work there, because it might possibly be for the long term. Fresh air is needed to replenish strength. I forgot to buy vitamin D3, so if you can, send me 2 ampoules, and also dark glasses, because my mom doesn't have any, either, so I am going to give her mine.

I really miss you, because I have no one with whom I can share sensations. And in these spacious rooms we could respire more amply, and there would be fewer little things to muck up our feelings.

I am now reading in French a lovely book by Balzac called *Mémoires de deux jeunes mariées*. That man was truly a genius. And how subtle their sensitive culture is.

Rysiu think of yourself

and... our children.

Also send me *Art s. t. p. et si tu peux* (from *pouvoir*).

I'm waiting to hear back about the material I sent a sample of. Send it or change it?

kiss kiss

Alina

Enough for today, because my mom is going out to drop the letter. She sends her greetings.

I will keep thinking, because evening and night are long and lonely without you. I feel in you that faithful friendship that is impossible to replace. My man

[NOTE IN THE MARGIN:]

Did you finish the Ehrenburg?

NOTES →[P 309]

Monday
Łódź 12.VI.50

My Rysieńku!
I returned yesterday from Warsaw, and so much presses from beneath my pen that a letter is probably not enough. Anyway it's worth nothing whatsoever, because I have to see you, talk with you, so you can hear me and at the same time hold me to you. And you know that sensations experienced individually become mere dry facts, observations lacking that essential seasoning (salt or pepper). Life. So, telegraphically:
I was in Warsaw for 2 and ½ days. I dealt with the things for Jerzy. His mother was crying and gave me his first little baby shirt. Editor K. already has the official consent of the Ministry of Foreign Affairs for him, it's just a matter of implementation. In any case, he'll consider a number of things as scheduled, write, and pass them along to me, and then we'll speak in Sopot, where he's also going to be spending his vacation. I also saw Ważyk. At the Ministry of Art and Culture. At the Academy of Fine Arts and at the Museum. I found out a lot, but actually there are lots of bureaucratic paths open to me leading to the High Road of Work. It is a very wide road. Then I went on my own to masonry workshops. There's one in the city center where they supply the hands and feet and noses for the figures in the parks and—as usual in the one opposite the Powązki Cemetery I found lots of things of interest to me. I took samples of the stone. People uncommonly obliging. Workers sympathetic, and there is even a shack—excellent, brick, with overhead light, just missing a floor. Everything in bloom and in blossom. All that remains is to get to work. The cemetery is lovely, lush and verdant.
I stayed with a cousin of mine whose husband (a conceited fell-low) I had a series of talks. He does not agree

with your father, like many people, and especially young ones. But, in spite of everything, I am beginning the share portions of your father's opinion, just from a different point.

They're developing Mokotów. Alina is wearing a golden bun and has a truly noble egg of a head [SKETCH OF A FACE WITH A BUN]. Maciej looks like a Warsaw-Western dandy and has a slight stutter. Both sweet and in love with Warsaw. They completely disagree with your father, but more because they like your company. Like lots of people—people have expressed their sympathy for you 100 times over. Especially Mr. Wnuk the father, with whom I drank mead and who is 100% from Warsaw with a mentality somewhere between a carriage-driver and a surgeon that is temporarily binding books.

Warsaw is impressive and darling. Nowy Świat is completely new and Krakowskie Przedmieście, Muranów, the East-West Expressway, the Theater, all of it revealing itself to me in the uncanny illumination of the setting sun, totally unlike Paris. The air here and the colors are somehow more violent, barbaric, not so idyllically harmonious as they are in Paris. The sun burned like the tongues of red-yellow fire in the windows, blindingly dazzled from the eye-sockets of the ruins, warmed the color of the still new houses *sans* patina of any sort. Because the houses in Warsaw are lovely, historically reconstructed little palaces, with even French windows. Everything reminds me a bit of a theater set—because it's in that style, and new, as if fresh out of the box. I had an extraordinary sensation in a cathedral being rebuilt, covered on the outside and on the inside with a net for the scaffolding, and in the side chapel an evening service and a choir of children's voices. The types, of the people and the children, inspire me enormously, and I would love to sculpt them, ask them to pose, and I feel here I might create something real. They put a tradeswoman done by a young woman sculptor on Mariensztat Square. Nice head, but the height of ignorance with regard to the material, and a total absence of composition. Her legs grow out of the hen she's holding.

My mom confessed that she wrote you letters during my absence. Were they not absurd? Because she and your father both kept on about this "uncertain life" without a monthly paycheck. Don't worry, Ryś, after all we will always get by "somehow." I believe again, because I feel very good. Even the exhausting trip to Warsaw did not wear me out. Though probably the best proof of my health is—my dreams, in which you so often occupy an unambiguous place.

Alina is studying diligently, she's now quite taken with syphilis and co-organizing an anti- campaign. It turns out that this illness has become significantly less prevalent in Poland, and the eradication is being carried out by means of investigatory methods (who?, when?, with whom?, from whom?) and the police. Alina told me about it all with the excitement of a college kid. And I listened excitedly, too, as she enumerated the terrible and unexpected consequences of the disease. Here they consider the sole effective means to be penicillin—naturally in the primary stage.

I'm happy the material is good. Your father also thought it was ideal for the country and practical in terms of color, it was ten feet. Are you getting up early? Have you been to see the Lustres? Are you making sure to forget nothing—food, bathing, Crillon etc.?

[NOTES:]

What about the job for you?
What about the young sculptors' exhibition?
I forgot to give your father the chocolate, but I will be in Poznań from Sopot and will take it to your siblings.
He was delighted with the liqueur.

Write! Write!
You can start writing to Kachu's address: Witomińska 37a, because here everyone is leaving for vacation, and the house is going to be shut up

[NOTE:]

I send greetings and heartfelt good wishes.
I'm in a dreadful hurry to get to work

Mother

51.

SZAPOCZNIKOW TO STANISŁAWSKI

JUNE 16, 1950

NOTES →[P 310]

Łódź 16.VI.50

My dear, darling Rysieńku.
I am happy that we are finally leaving tomorrow, because I truly am properly tired of the city again. And especially frustrated by this dichotomy of not knowing when and how I am going to see you. I would like to be close to you again, to talk everything over—but above all I would like to finally arrive at a point where I won't have to think about everything and rack my brains about the future. Where I will get some peace. I would so like to be able to depend on you, to know you will take care of everything. I know it's a weakness, and a passing weakness. I know I couldn't live like all those women that aren't afraid of life just because... they have a man around them that thinks and works on their behalf. You know that that is not my nature. But, to be honest—sometimes I do envy them that life. Maybe it's just that I am tired, or maybe it's some idiotic "latent femininity?" Or maybe it's these bad examples I unfortunately keep encountering in this bourgeois milieu. Yesterday I went to see Prof. Sowiński—he's the best gynecologist here and a specialist in the illness I went through. It is an illness that is much more common here than in France, in fact. He's even published a paper about it. It turns out that I was very dangerously ill, because before (streptomycin) such such cases tended to end in death. But the latent tuberculosis must have been in my organs for many years. He said the bacteria are still there, but encysted, that I can do absolutely anything—except ever neglect myself, that means good nutrition and frequent rest. For neglect could bring about another acute crisis. He was, however, reassuring to my mother, who considers you her benefactor and the *sauveur* of her child etc., to the point of repeated exclamation points of gratitude.

I however am very sad, because Prof. Sowiński told me that there is almost no chance of being a mother after such an illness—because of how the tubes are blocked, and in my case a purge would mean another inflammation.
We've already talked about this more than once and made plans for our future life, so there is no sense in going over it again. But you yourself are aware of what that life will look like, and I don't know if there is any sense in my being with you. What will "grow" out of me. And given this excess of *sensibilité* that I possess, how do I maintain my equilibrium, when no one will ever call me "mom," and I will never be able to play with a soft little body smelling of milk? But what is the use of getting upset! I don't at all know when these two months will finally end, and I'm afraid of their ending, because what will happen to my mom? The problem remains as it was—unresolved. You resolve it.
Write to me please <u>at this address</u> (Wólczańska 4 apt. 5), because the housekeeper is staying and will forward my letters—and I don't know if I will always be in touch with Kachu. Write to me often, Rysiu. You know what those letters mean. Of course I would like to be by your side as usual, share every decision you make with you and experience every event with you.
Do you have a shelf in your room now? I'm sending you that UCP(B) history today. Who have you been seeing? What is that whole gang from the canteen doing: what are their plans for the summer? Is Charlie still acting like a madman? I have so much to talk to you about that I can't write. And at the thought that I might not see you again my heart goes numb. Rysieńku, maybe all the stupid things I've written you to this point are the result of this anxiety. But let's hope that everything will be all right, and that then—you will forgive me.
Write to me about even the littlest things. Don't forget. You are always with me. I send you a kiss.

Rysiu, why have I not had a letter from you in a week.
Two months is a long time. We should never part again—
Your Alina

[NOTE:]

Dear Ryszard, there's not much room, but I send you lots and lots of heartfelt wishes. Please do not worry, Alunia is not feeling so bad, [ILLEGIBLE]
A well-wishing mother

NOTES →[P 311]

[THE FIRST PART OF THE LETTER IS MISSING]

We came from Łódź by plane, I convinced my mom with the argument that if we were going to die—we should do it together. Whereas now I wouldn't want to travel any other way. I spent 1½ hour in the company of a young engineer who had graduated from Gdańsk and said to say hello to Łępicki—he was a classmate. His name is Wiktorko, he's currently working in Łódź on the building of the waterworks earning over 50 thousand.

Today Kachu and I are going to write a letter to Porębski in Warsaw. (Apparently he knew you). Regarding you. He works somewhere in some art research institute—or for it. I would like for him to write regarding concrete preparations being made for you to get a position. But you really have to present your exam results, and it would even be good if you had your diploma. You could of course do that here. But you absolutely pass this year's exams. Those are concrete facts, and that is the effort you are going to have to make. No enthusiastic exclamation marks will help. Why have you not written me what's going on with Ginette's patina? I am very much in favor of the patination.

Use the address A. S. c/o Ms. Mizerna, ul. Obotrytów 50, Sopot, but take into account that a letter takes ~ 7 days, and we'll be here until the 15th. Then I'm going to be flying to Poznań, and around the 20th to Prague. Unfortunately, there is no way whatsoever to extend my ticket. But I'm happy because I've already begun to think about my return and about work. I miss you, and time seems longer and longer. And I have so, so many things I need to talk to you about. Think over my letters very carefully, please, and read them attentively.

Look for work, Rysiu, wherever you can, just so that you can earn a living, don't think that some physical labor while you are in transition will degrade you.
Ryś, I think I will kiss you to death when I see you. After all this to think that I will see you again—and I'm already thinking about work.—Our shared work. Write me! Do you pine as I do? Probably not—it's so lovely in Paris. What do you do all day? Write!
Just one more month, and we won't need paper kisses anymore.

Alina

[NOTES:]

My mom says hello.
Are you going to Crillon!!!!!!
That watch needs to be gotten back from the pawn shop because my mom wants to give it to that cousin from Palestine when he comes, it's his wife's, and my father bought it from him when they didn't have enough for their ticket. My mom doesn't know that it's been pawned.

NOTES →[P 311]

[THE FIRST PART OF THE LETTER IS MISSING]

Gustaw comforts me with the proverb: *Pas de nouvelles, bonnes nouvelles*. Yet I don't need comforting. I would even say that people should not be allowed to comfort me. It's just Gaston and his father in the boutique. The mother-in-law and her mother went off to Sables.

If only I knew that you were receiving my letters. In any case this is probably the last one I will write to you in response to silence. After that I will just wait, because there's no point in writing into the void.

Today is the twenty-sixth. In two weeks it will be July 14. *Quatorze Juillet*. Without you.

When I think about you— [CROSSED-OUT]

Do you know, Alino, what your silence is?

Ryszard

The photographs of the shepherd are done

[...] Gaston powiemu mnie przysłowiem: Pas de nouvelles – bonnes nouvelles. A mnie powiemać nie trzeba. Powiedziałbym nawet, że mnie wspominać nie wolno. Gaston jest sam z ojcem w butiku. Fesiowie z wnukiem wyjechały do Sables. [...]chym je [illegible], czy ty choć otrzymujesz moje listy. Zresztą to chyba ostatni już list do ciebie [bez] odpowiedzi na milczenie. Później będę tylko [mil]czał, bo nie ma sensu pisać w próżnię.
Dziś już dwudziesty ósmy. Za dwa tygodnie będzie 14 lipiec. Quatorze Juillet. Bez ciebie. [B]ez myśli o tym – ~~[illegible]~~.
Czy Ty wiesz, Alinko, czym jest Twoje milczenie.

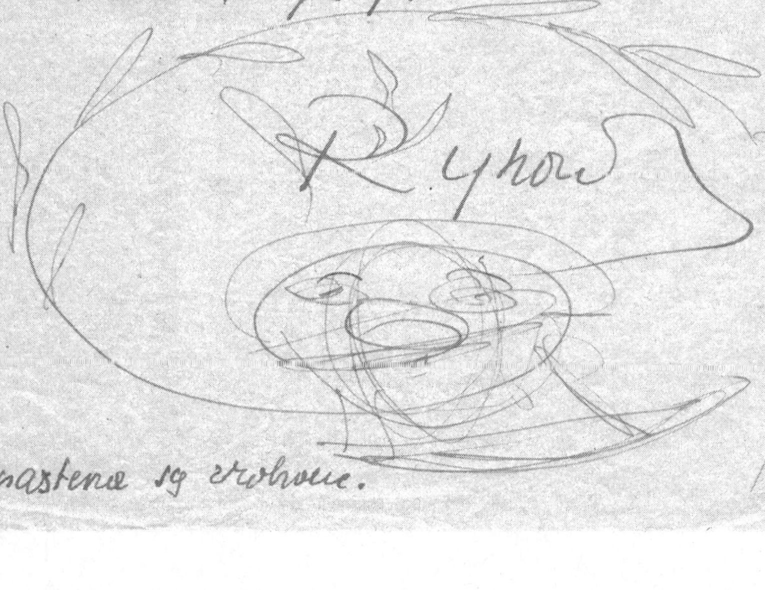

Życie [illegible] się zrobiło.

54.

SZAPOCZNIKOW TO STANISŁAWSKI
POSTCARD, *THE BEACH AT JASTRZĘBIA GÓRA*, [JUNE 26, 1950]
NOTES →[P 311]

Sopot Obotrytów 50

I haven't had a letter from you in a week. What are you doing Rysiu? I am now strong and healthy. I am seeing a number of artists from the Sopot circle. After many conversations I agree with your last letter (that one with the poem), so it must be, in spite of everything. And: you will kiss me to death—that already makes me happy.
Your

Alina

[SKETCHES IN PEN: SELF-PORTRAIT, EYES, LITTLE FLOWERS]

Sopot 26.VI.50

My Darling! Darling
Rysieńku, today I was forwarded three of your letters from Łódź that had been sent express, and now I don't understand at all. I've written you so many letters. Have you not received them?!?
Ryszard, you have no right to think and write that way! After all I think about you all the time, I—at least it would seem so—really love you. And that is a great, very great thing. One way or another, I think about life only with you and make plans only for our shared future.
There are a lot of things that I am not writing about because I still don't have crystal-clear ideas, and besides there is such a mass of them that I would rather just tell you about them. It won't be long. Rysieńku, I can't write at all on those days and nights when I pine so much that I can't think about anything, and nothing makes me happy without you there. It's lovely here, I am resting, getting better, marveling at things—but it is pallid without you. After all I've gotten so used to having everything in place—to immediately share with you and have you near me.
I'm also surprised you haven't heard from your father, because he swore to me he would write to you right away. I gave ten feet for Płoci., which I already wrote you. I really don't know anymore. Maybe there is censorship now, and they're holding up these letters?
Kott wrote to me, they're with Putrament at a writers' summit in Warsaw, and he got my address from Ważyk.
Rysiu, I am already happy about your decision, even now, although I confess I experienced many moments of anxiety.
We have work awaiting us here. That is the loveliest thing life can give a person. Not to a person—to a couple of people.

Rysiek, by now for me it's like you and I are one, and so very one, and always one. I'm going to stop, because I want to go to the post office right away.
Ryś, please write that it's okay, that we will be together, that you love as I do.
Yesterday I was at a competition of teams from the Service to Poland brigades. It was lovely.
I kiss, kiss all of you
mine.

Alina

[LITTLE PORTRAIT IN SOFT PENCIL: A GIRL WITH BRAIDS]

56.
SZAPOCZNIKOW TO STANISŁAWSKI
TELEGRAM, [JUNE 27, 1950]

HEALTHY KISS ALINA

57.
SZAPOCZNIKOW TO STANISŁAWSKI
JUNE 28, 1950
NOTES →[P 312]

Sopot 28.VI.50

Rysiu,
It's raining, so I'm thinking about work. You know Rysiek, I need to get a *chez moi* together somewhere already, someplace that will be "for good." I have to find something—it's just that the time comes when a person creatively grows into that, and now I feel that in those conditions I could really do something genuine. Because up until now I have feared that kind of independence, and I knew that I still needed to work under the supervision of a professor and in a shared atelier with others, to watch what they do, to see how certain formal matters should and should not be handled. Up until now I have done nothing at all of substance. Each thing had some concept, some "something," but on the whole, none of it was of any value. And that is precisely the first and the last and the greatest and the most important reason that inclines me to decide to return definitively to Poland. Here I will be able to work! It's not a question of exhibitions in Paris. (We know what those are like.) What it is about is a good chunk of good work. Yesterday my mom and I were in Gdynia, because the M/s *Batory* was sailing. It is a lovely vessel, and with what pride people looked on. —It's ours, Polish.
Then we went out to sea on the S/s *Maiden of the Sea*. It is a lovely and large luxury excursion craft. The whole way I chatted with two sailors. One from Warsaw, the other from Włocławek, both of them just these super kids. Pleased with their maritime life. They taught me a lot—"Well, there's no place like home." And they asked me to the dance floor on board. You know, there is that Polish "fad." You know I don't much like that kind of Polish "buffoonery" or "overdoing it," but I feel at home here, and this is not that kind of puffed up lordly Polishness, but

rather an honest Polishness, flowing from the folk. We ought to bring our experience here and treat those kinds of things profoundly, with love, and truly—not superficially like Stryjeńska, but transforming them into beautiful art.
I've already written to you about the little girls with the braids and about those old country women in kerchiefs that inspire me here.
You remember how lovely French landscapes are—how we raved about them, and Kachu, too. Wheareas now he is in Kashubia and asserts that only there is one able to paint something. *Nota bene* I was looking here in Sopot at their school exhibition—feeble things, while Kachu did a sketch for a seven-meter fresco called *Parade*—exceedingly feeble. One must work, work—even 10 hours a day. To the point that I grow frightened when I think about my deficiencies in drawing!
By now you must have gotten my completely hysterical letters from Łódź. I'm sorry—but I was in terrible company and was terrified by the thought that I might not see you again. You've probably also received my letters and the telegram from here. I wanted to also telegraph "I love you," but I was embarrassed before the telegraphist. Though there were two young people sitting holding each other on the boat—I was jealous that you weren't there.
Write to me, Rysiu, what you've been doing all these days. You don't write anything about yourself?!
Please go to rue de Châteaudun and take a look, there's an organization there called *Tourisme et Travail*, it's an agency of *L'Humanité*, you can get extremely cheap trips all over France there for different periods of time. There might be something that would work for us, check it out, or sign us up if you find something.
I'm currently reading the UCP(B). One must know and study this. The style alone! Try to write something that

could be printed here before your return. You have the time, after all. And how is the French going?
By the time you get this letter I will be with you in just 14 days. I think it's going to be a lovely holiday.
July 14 is coming up—14 *juillet*. Our anniversary. Although it's just and already two years, and a year since I got sick. It's as though, Rysiu, I have known you my entire life. For have we not been reborn—healthy, both me and you. Health!
Ryś, remember that on the nights of the 13 and 14th [OF JULY], when no doubt Paris will be so lovely and colorful from the rockets—I will be standing beside you with all my heart.
I kiss you Darling

Alina

NOTES →[P 313]

Sopot 29.VI.50
Feast of Saints Peter
and Paul and the mail
is not running

Rysiu
I haven't written you yet about how lovely it is here. We really must come here together. The sea, though not azure-baby blue, has hundreds of gray tones, from silver through celadon all the way up to the dark-menacing color of a beer bottle. It is always cool and unfriendly here, yet so dignified is its beauty. My mom and I are staying well out of town, completely surrounded by real peasant life. Beyond the house are knolls, fields, the forest. The children go and gather blueberries, wild strawberries—they are already on their summer break here. The children have really lovely preschools and little gardens, they already know all about many laws of nature and inventions of man. Meanwhile the old woman (our host's mother) tells me excitedly about a spell, about a sorceress that had taken the form of a mouse and cast a spell on her daughter, and about working "for his lordship." I had no idea that until so recently the folk population was so backward and so exploited. It's really true that no political system does as much for people (as much for man) as ours does.
I'm actually writing this letter to see if I might buy something for Simone Lerendu made of amber, because basically I don't know what I could bring them from here. The vodka is bad and can't be taken out of the country. Maybe a bottle of mead? But I don't know if I can get a good bottle of that, either—and I don't want to take them junk. Would she like an amber necklace—like the one I have? Would a brooch be enough? Write me back about this as soon as you can so that I get it before we leave here—15.VII. Our ambassador is here in Warsaw for the writers' summit. I wrote back to Kott at the summit address and asked him if he could take

advantage of the occasion and speak to him about you. Why do you not write me anything of yourself: what you're doing, whether you are taking care of yourself, of your health?! What are you eating? Are you studying at least a little? Thanks for *Arts*. I'm buying *L'Humanité*, *Les Lettres françaises*, *Avant Garde*, *Peuples Amis*, etc. In even the littlest towns they have a "Book Club" where you can get the international democratic press.

Rysieńku mine, soon you will kiss up my seaside suntan, and I'm thinking of you, and I kiss you. Write! Write!

Alina

[NOTES:]

Write back right away about the presents.

My mom always tells me to tell you hello, and I always forget. She will write you back herself in the coming days.

59.

SZAPOCZNIKOW TO STANISŁAWSKI
POSTCARD, *VIEW OF A BALTIC BEACH*,
JULY 4, 1950

4.VII.50

Rysieńku!
I've written a whole lot of letters, in exchange for which I receive anxious telegrams. I'm going to try writing a postcard. But what of the problems I brought up? I am healthy and worry only about you, and work, and our life together. Better to go over everything in person. I await a letter from you. I will kiss you lots [JULY] 23, darling. Darling.

Your A.

SZAPOCZNIKOW TO STANISŁAWSKI

TELEGRAM, [JULY 5, 1950]

WHY ARE YOU NOT RESPONDING TO THE MANY LETTERS =ALINA SOPOT OBOTRYTÓW 50

NOTES →[P 313]

Wednesday, 5.7.50

Aluś my dearest,
This morning I received a telegram from you: "Why are you not responding to the many, many letters." You know, Ali, I don't even know what to answer to that. Since June 5 I have received one single letter from you, and that was last Monday. I wrote you back immediately. Aside from that I sent a whole host of letters into the void, not knowing at all what was going on with you. All of them were written to your Łódź address, and all of them were filled with question marks and anxiety. Maybe you will find them at home when you get back. I also sent your mother a birthday card. To Sopot. The letter I care the most about, however, is the one I sent last Monday (3.7.50). In it I asked you to take care of something for me of the utmost gravity. Please let me know immediately if you got it or not. If not—I will have to go over it all over again. It must be taken care of in Warsaw at the international department of the Party. Thus I anxiously await your response, at least a note to let me know if the letter arrived and whether you will be able to take care of it, because I myself cannot write there directly. I'm sending today's letter registered mail. Did you get the glasses, the vitamin D3! I know literally nothing at all about you, there were only cards to our friends, and it pained me, Alu. There's nothing else really to say. Just remember how you reproached me when you were in the hospital, and I came late by a few minutes. While here I've been without any word from you for a month. A whole month. I've also come to the conclusion that writing letters, given the uncertainty of receiving them, makes very little sense. This leads to things remaining unspoken and implied, short-circuits, and there come moments of lying awake at night and an

anxiety that eats away at the heart. While a letter ought to be rather a bandage that can be wrapped around the heart. I've given a lot of thought to our concerns. I have tried to evaluate as critically as possible my own behavior and have come to some categorical conclusions, bearing in mind our shared life, which must be strong, dignified, full; in which we could take satisfaction and joy in duty fulfilled. As I have already written you, it is difficult for me here to find an occupation that would enable our material well-being, and even if I were to find such a thing, it would be at the price of demeaning myself morally, not to even mention overstraining the trust that my superiors place in me. That is why the matter that I am asking you to take care of is so important. When you talk to them, try to talk as impersonally as you can. Use strong arguments and emphasize that you are responsible for transmitting my urgent request because given relations here, I am unable to transmit my request myself by correspondence. Let them make up their minds. The consulate can best provide references. When you see Adaś, consult him if you feel he is favorably inclined toward you. Do, however, request total discretion on his part. I am looking forward to seeing you, Alusieńka, so alone, believe me, am I, and I miss you so, my dearest. If you were to come a few days earlier, you would still be able to see four great sculpture exhibitions (Salon de la Jeune Sculpture, Salon d'Automne, "American Women," Maison de la Pensée).

[NOTES:]

Kiss your mother's hand for me and wish her happy birthday *en plus*.
Alusieńka my darling I send you a kiss, but when will I be able to really hold you?

Your R.

62.
SZAPOCZNIKOW TO STANISŁAWSKI
POSTCARD, *VIEW OF A BALTIC BEACH*,
JULY 6, 1950
NOTES →[P 313]

6.VII.

Today I received your first letter to Sopot. Of course, I will try to deal with your request as best I can in Warsaw. From your letter I deduced that you had not received all the letters I sent you or one of the telegrams. (I sent two). This worries me terribly, since there were so many important issues concerning us both, as well as many intimate things, so I would prefer for them to remain between us. That is why I am writing a postcard. And I confess that I had been awaiting your letter with great impatience, love, and longing—unfortunately it was cold and only matter-of-fact. Rysiek, do you no longer love me as you used to? 23.VII I will be with you. What will it be like for us to be together again? Rysieńku, I nestle into you and kiss, kiss you, all of you, with all of me

Alina

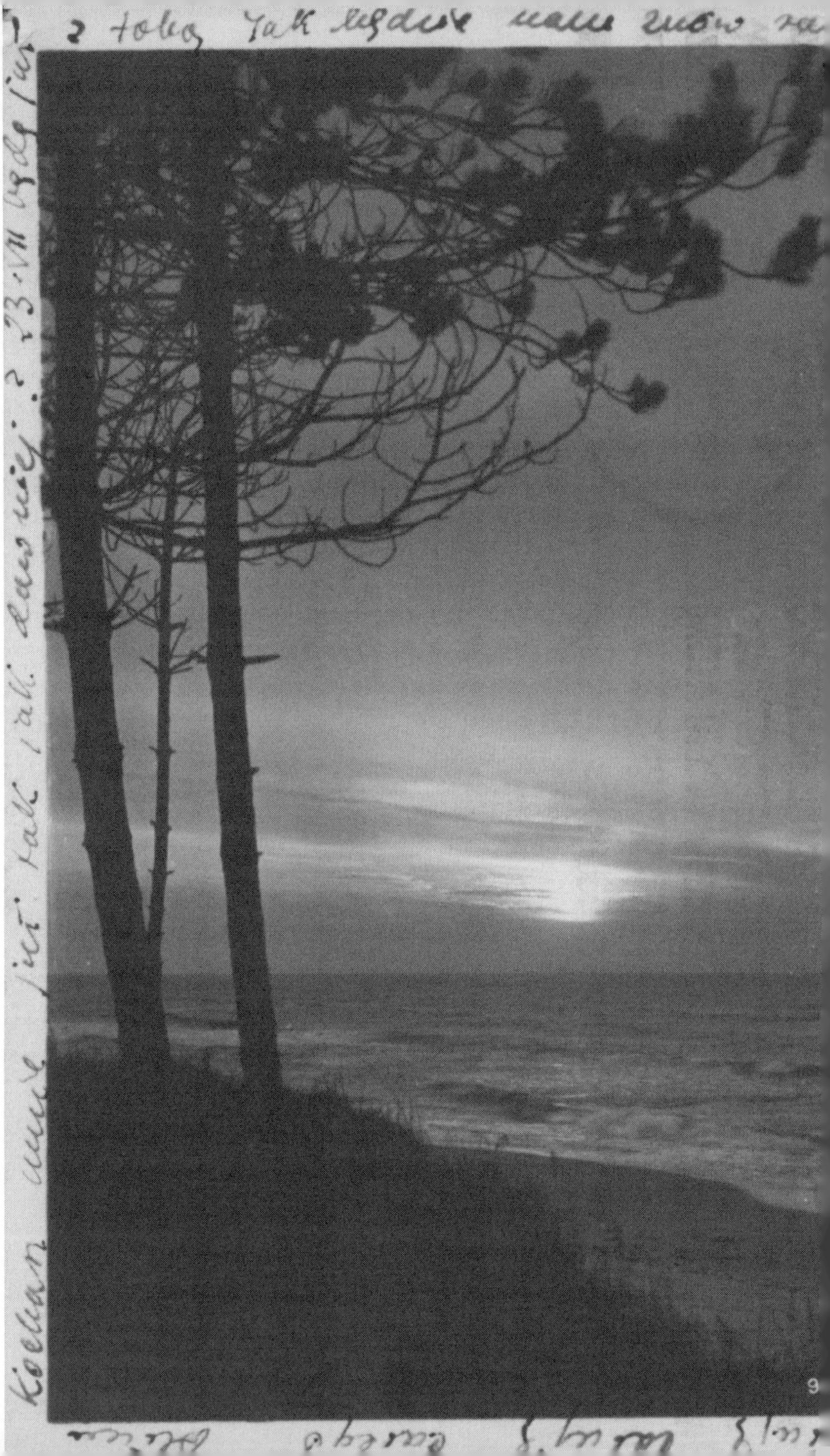

63.

SZAPOCZNIKOW TO STANISŁAWSKI

POSTCARD, *VIEW FROM THE BEACH ONTO THE SEA*, [JULY 9, 1950]

I'll just write postcards from now on, because maybe at least you will get them. Lots and lots of news, I will tell you all Rysieńku dear, darling, my sweet—be strong. Take care of yourself, we'll soon be together. I am going to Warsaw. I ran into Ważyk here, he is on holiday. I am healthy, and the future lies before us. I miss you to madness. And the bushes are in such bloom here. But writing like this makes no sense at all—this is not correspondence—it's a fraying of the nerves. I am receiving your letters. When will we be together at last and alone: I have so much strength! And how I miss my work. Kiss, kiss

Alina

[NOTE ON THE FRONT OF THE POSTCARD:]

write to my Łódź address now

64.

SZAPOCZNIKOW TO STANISŁAWSKI
POSTCARD, *THE POLISH SEA. SUNSET*,
JULY 9, 1950
NOTES →[P 313]

9.VII.50

Rysieńku, I hope you received my last few cards. Please ask G. to get the stone ready for the head of Simone. Are you only studying? What are you living on? Please send the photograph of the shepherd to my Łódź address, 14.VII. we are leaving here. I am going to Warsaw for one day, as well, and then coming to you. Just be brave. Ryś—I still believe in you—because I love you. Did you receive the letter from my mother?
Very soon you will kiss me to death, and we will finally be together again—forever this time—

Your A.

Is there a bookshelf yet? And at the atelier?
My mom sends her warm regards. Thank you for the birthday wishes.

SZAPOCZNIKOW TO STANISŁAWSKI
POSTCARD, *GREETINGS FROM THE BALTIC*,
JULY 13, 1950

13.VII.

My darling!
I received your card, your telegrams, too. We are leaving tomorrow, and on Sunday I am going to Poznań. After that it won't be long. I have realized a lot of things. I bade farewell to Kachu today. We talked a lot. My mom says thank you for your wishes, today is her 60th. Did you get her letter? My mom says hello, and I miss and kiss you.

Your A.

What are you doing?

66.

SZAPOCZNIKOW TO STANISŁAWSKI

POSTCARD, *GREETINGS FROM THE BALTIC*,

JULY 14, 1950

NOTES →[P 314]

This will be our third July 14th. And then we will always be together. Ryś, I am with you this day with all my heart. Please do not forget to take Gaston to the exhibition of works from the *Grand prix de Rome*, it's usually until July 15th in the front gallery of the Beaux-Arts. I got your important letter and will take care of it in Warsaw.
Just be healthy—study.
I kiss you with all my might

Alina

67.

SZAPOCZNIKOW TO STANISŁAWSKI

POSTCARD, ST. ANNE'S CHURCH, WARSAW, EAST-WEST EXPRESSWAY, JULY 15, 1950

15.7.50

I am now in Łódź, after a phone conversation with your father, and tomorrow I am going to Poznań. I will be with you the 24th (Mon. morning). I got all of your cards as well as the telegram. I will do as you wish. I feel healthy and am impatiently looking forward to you and to work. —The two lovers to whom I wish to be faithful. Kisses

Alina

Hello from Łódź, wishing you all the best

Mother

68.
SZAPOCZNIKOW TO STANISŁAWSKI
POSTCARD FROM PRAGUE
[JULY 20, 1950]

Expect me the morning of the 24th.
Kisses

Alina

SZAPOCZNIKOW TO STANISŁAWSKI
POSTCARD FROM WISŁA-GŁĘBCE,
[DECEMBER 22, 1951]
NOTES →[P 314]

It's prettier than expected, quiet, and the hotel is comfortable. Today I was overcome by what has become quite an uncommon joy in life, and laughingly I skipped along the rocks of the stream in the sunshine. It's too bad you are not here to breathe in the freshness and peace. My sweet. x x x x x
There are a few miners here from Kleofas—great people, a breath of fresh mountain air. All told 15 people and with all *ça va*.
I sent greetings to Mr. Stanisławski, but if I got the address wrong, or if they don't make it on time—wish him a happy one for me, and to the kids.
How's the workshop—I'm dying of impatience. How are you?

Your A.

NOTES →[P 315]

Tuesday

Dear Rysiu and Piotrusiu!
I've only been here three days, and already I would very much like to come home.
The conditions are shabby as they can only be for a person who, without an "organized" stay, single-handedly, wants to spend some time in a "nationalized" town.
A clean home (the kind I spend so little time in, unfortunately) and pure, homemade food, those are the things that keep my spirits up.
Meanwhile my work is going well, for I dream only of its being accepted as soon as possible. My working conditions are even worse than my living conditions.
For 10 hours per day I stand on a stone floor, and my legs at the knees are just about bawling. I complain so much because even hard labor in Siberia people bore with serenity when they had their comrades by them and so forth, when some zeal lit up their way for them. Here around me there is such dullness and limitation that I have begun to want them to just be cruel—but let them be something. Hicks and backwater—and "in terrible dwellings dwell terrible dwellers."
I saw such an awful presentation of *Halka* and a film that all I could muster up was a sentimental smile—because it's almost exactly the same as in Pabianice 20 years ago.
I am buoyed by the thought of the money I will have earned, which will allow us to enhance our home and our life, but I ask you as a friend, Rysiu, never let me take on such dull work again.
By comparison I see what a talent and sensitivity I have, and how vigilantly it must be guarded.
The sculpture is even quite pretty, it's over 6 feet, and it was only today that I began coping with the physical work and loading the clay, because there is no one here to help.

I miss Piotruś very much and am anxious about you two not looking out for him enough.
Rysiu, if you come to the Council, please bring a camera to photograph the sculpture for me. It is as sad and full of melancholy as I am. It's a shame you have not written me anything thus far.
I kiss you both sincerely and with all my might.

Alina

Hello to Jadzia

Tuesday

Rysiu darling!
This is kind of out of Godot, I think, those of us in the house can't stand each other, yet alone it's likely to be worse. Yesterday I felt very much amongst strangers. In fact those artist gentlemen only show their "artistic" faces, that is, the "axes" that they have to "grind," in the chitchat amongst themselves. Generally speaking it was quite grim, I'm sleeping in a room with two other gals and Mrs. Stępniowa (whose skis you used last year) snores horribly at night. It was only when Ludwisia brought me breakfast in bed, and I lolled around till noon, and no one wanted anything from me—that I understood that I am, however, resting—but it's so boring and wet that I will probably leave on Saturday (after a week). Fortunately today at lunch Jacek Żuławski showed up, and for a break tomorrow he is taking me to Pięć Stawów for three days (I borrowed boots and skis from the Fajkoszes), apparently at the top there is snow and sunshine, young people from Bim-Bom and some carefree recreation. Here in spite of the bad weather I immediately breathed easily, and I don't feel short of breath and have no heart pain. I saw one artist I know (Wilden) who told me that he has (very) low blood pressure and that his doctor sent him to the mountains here, and that he instantantly began to breathe completely freely.
Today I went to see Brzozowski, he's very kind, our drawings are with Mietek Porębski. I'll tell you about it when I get back. And in general I've really been thinking lately that we really must talk when I get back.
Zosia complained to me over the phone that she is angry with you, please try to be understanding with her—in spite of everything she is very devoted to us.

The whole trip without Piotruś was like that time in Nieborów where we felt so bad about it, but now I am actually happy about it, because there is no room (the Bronisław Czech Memorial), it's muddy, and Marcin has a sore throat again—and I want to go back in a couple of days, actually. Here, at Magnolia, everyone asks after Piotruś, and Franek is very big. The food is considerably worse when Maryta isn't here.
I also want to go to Szaflary and look around, because there are enormous quarries with all kinds of different stone, which I saw today at Kenar's school, very good material, noble, and apparently for free. Besides, that will help me kill some time. Don't forget about Piotruś' ears. I send you a big kiss,

Your Alina

P.S. I found out a bunch of things here that I'll tell you about after I get back.

Piotrusiu darling!
Everyone is asking about you, especially your friend Franek. But there is no snow, and the weather is ugly. Zakopane is covered in mud. I think you are being a good boy and listening to your father and eating lots. I'm looking for a toy here that I will bring you in a couple of days. I send you a big kiss,

Your mom Alina

72.

SZAPOCZNIKOW TO STANISŁAWSKI

POSTCARD, *ZAKOPANE AT NIGHT*,

[FEBRUARY 17, 1955]

NOTES →[P 316]

I'm just coming back from Walter's, who is also really impressed by the mountains and by Zakopane.
The weather today was magnificent, and I felt very sorry that you weren't here with me, Rysiu.
Skiing and sleeping are my two most pressing occupations, and I am finding myself in a completely abstract world. In my subconscious I know that I love you and Piotruś and will probably come back quickly from here all rested up.
Kiss kiss

Alina

73.

STANISŁAWSKI TO SZAPOCZNIKOW
LETTER ON AN INVITATION TO THE OPENING OF THE "EXHIBITION OF MEXICAN ART" FOR FEBRUARY 19, 1955

NOTES →[P 316]

It's a shame I am so tired and cannot even, as I would like, talk over the telephone. In fact that sort of talk makes no sense beyond the fact that I would hear your voice. The past two nights I haven't slept at all, I was writing for Leszek, and for some reason that's been hard for me. Today *Przegląd* finally came out—it's good, and people are buying it *en masse*. No one comes over, and I'm glad, because I find it soothing that way. I am looking forward to seeing you. I would like you to let me know when you're coming. I would really like to go and meet you. It's very good that you are resting, it might actually be good to stay on a bit longer in the mountains, but I miss you so much. Piotruś constantly asks where his mom is. He knows she's in "Kopane." Zosia is taking better care of him than I originally thought she was. She doesn't leave the house. I think she's damned fed up of it and also looking forward to your coming back. Ali my dearest, all [CROSSED-OUT]
—Take care! Accidents are so easy!

[NOTES:]

Today was the opening, all pomp and ceremony, of the Mexican exhibition. I saw lots of friends and went for coffee at the Bristol.
The exhibit was great, crowds of people.
Say hello to Walter!

SZAPOCZNIKOW TO STANISŁAWSKI
[SUMMER 1955 OR 1956]
NOTES →[P 316]

Rysiu dear!
After a tough journey we finally made it in one piece. Nothing has changed in Karwia. There is fish, which we took advantage of already last night at dinner. They sing *Karolinka*. The kiosks are new and bigger. Leszek's mother from the co-op and the man from the post office said to say hello to you, our hosts as well.
No one gets nervous or upset.
Piotrek wakes up at 5 a.m.
Please send 10 lbs of flour right away and cough syrup. There is no flour here, I can't make him noodles or anything.
Call Hanka unless she's already left, she could take some flour with her, too.
Thank you for the kind farewell. Director Wroński is a very kind, peaceful, and far-sighted man.
Kiss,

Your wife

SZAPOCZNIKOW TO STANISŁAWSKI
[SUMMER 1955 OR 1956]

Rysiu dear!
What could be great is in its current configuration nightmarish. My nerves are in a state of total depletion.
—A person that no longer has his own world, or interests, or passions, begins to rot, and meanwhile their fat body hangs like a thick noodle on the lives of their so-called nearest and dearest. Poisoning them with hideous worries with the aim of keeping their own disintegrating cells alive. I am cynical or cruel—call it what you will. I'm referring to my mom. I am not capable of living with her under one roof without some degree of spiritual shrinking. I am being ruthlessly honest with you so that you understand the constant struggle between these cruel sentiments and the deeply ingrained feeling of duty that we all have.
Overall I am coming to the conclusion that artists absorbed in their work ought not to get entangled in family at all.
After all, family is not a goal for me—I do not work for family as others do, but feel rather that with its warmth it ought to invigorate my work.
That is why these things out of obligation scare me, I prefer things icy, but free, and "somehow..."
I'm writing you all this to inform you of how unsettled I am by my pervasive need to work. My head is seething with a few sculptures I have to do—it keeps me from sleeping at night, and during the day I am barely conscious. Yet unfortunately I cannot take my easels and leave everything—but I have to be in the workshop to work.
I am also writing you this so you do not come, because it will be awful, our hostess, my mom, bathing, lunch, sleeping, your nerves, etc., I am really horribly afraid of that at this moment, because my nerves, which are nor-

mally strong now, are rebelling against me.
<u>Send string and paper</u> to pack everything up.
Prepare Piotruś' room.
We are coming back as soon as possible—and then, if I do what is pervading me, then I can, if you want, take a trip with you and Piotruś, wherever you want.
Piotruś is growing and developing in a lovely manner, I love him very much, and he helps me wonderfully with the creative inspiration of life.
So don't come! I can manage—I so want to come back!
Write me back immediately

Alina

Monday morning after phone call

Rysiu Darling!
I am completely stupefied by Paris, which has not changed at all, and which is still our Paris. I immediately recognized everywhere. I took a shower right at the station and bought myself some shoes from here and immediately got *cet air parisien*. Unfortunately, the first day was depressing, because I couldn't reach anyone. The Jaśes aren't even here, and the concierge woman has changed and knows nothing. Ivo went with Kika to St. Tropez just the day before I arrived and will be there a month on vacation. The warehouse on the bld. Poissonnière was shut down, and I can't find Max—maybe he died. De Gallard got married and didn't even invite me in—he had his exhibition recently. Grabowski was seriously ill, apparently he's wandering around somewhere half-paralyzed. The Musée d'Art Moderne is being dismantled because it started to collapse, and there is general resentment on account of this, because no one knows when they're going to be able to re-organize it (the paintings were taken down to the basement). I went to see Ms. Goldscheider at the Musée Rodin. I was received by a middle-aged lady, very *soignée*, in a hat and veil, who did not get out of her car (in which she had just arrived, behind the wheel), with a very pleasant politeness, and I felt, with her whole *allure*, like a girl from the provinces. She said that the sculptures are already here, at the customs office, and that I should send her an address so that—in case she needed something—she could let me know, though essentially there is no hurry, because everything is moving along as it should, fine, no fuss, and the opening won't be until 15.VI. She is arranging everything with the old concierge lady from the museum, but it is so

stunningly simple compared with Warsaw that there's really no comparison, no personnel, no fracas, *commissaires*, etc. The exhibition will be just like the thousands of other exhibitions, no big deal, then it will close, which is fine, no one gets worked up about it.
This all has a strange effect on our over-frayed nerves, and I am increasingly convinced that we are the abnormal ones in this arena of life. Yesterday I was at the Weisses' and spent a very nice afternoon there, they send you their greetings—they have two American cars and are just heading to Italy for 15 *jours de vacances*. Mme Honoré is no longer the concierge there. In general nice, heartfelt people who would feed me if need be, like the Lustres, for example, they are so removed from our interests, *si encombrants*, that to just be with them—it's a waste of time to even be here. In any case I'll tell you all about everyone when I'm back. Please call Styczyński, give him my address, and please have him send me *a. s. a. p.*—or you send it—the pictures of Naya in the wood—before the opening of the exhibition. My sculptures from the photographs are going over well, and I am in the process *tout de même* of making contacts

[PART OF THE LETTER IS MISSING]

if he saw what I see here and what those folks that are leaving see. But to people like our neighbor this offers <u>only</u> a little material advantage and a little poverty complex.
I have to come here with Piotruś, I feel so badly about every banana I eat. I am sending a present for Piotrek through Nieciuński. Write me a lot about him, because I pine very much every time I see children. Does he ask about me and miss me? Write me. That nervous atmosphere at home now seems to me an awful thing, and I can't imagine why it's that way. I intend to live slowly and work completely differently after I get back. I am in

some process of thorough cleansing. From what I've seen thus far amongst the young people in the ateliers, it seems to me we have the great force of creative possibilities, and that we could, with no inferiority complexes, create the art that is truly expected here in that mood of mad intellectual tensions and impotent anarchy. In any case, we'll talk.

Tomorrow I'm going to go and try to get my Italian visa—and maybe we will see each other. You just have to completely reevaluate your ideas, and our possibilities are not really that bad. In spite of everything I am more and more glad that we returned to Poland, it's always cramped here. This trip is helping me a lot with a lot of problems.

I'm tired of this writing. If you can, write to me very often, so that I can be in constant contact with home, because sometimes it seems to me that that life doesn't exist, and that it never did. I'm really in a bit of a stupor these days. Kiss

Alina

Remember to arrange for the Zahorskis to organize something, in Karwia, for example, or somewhere else by the sea, because the grandma with the two kids definitely wants to come, and I think she should do it. If Karwia, it's high time.

Wednesday 23

Rysiu Darling!
Finally your first letter. Write to me more often, because I pine for Warsaw. I am sending a check with Nieciuński. He's going in a week, and a letter takes about as long as that to get there, and this is always safer. I regret writing in an amount, because I don't know how much will be there—I've given checks to so many people!
I saw a lovely exhibition of Calder and a load of other things. Dante and Abrasza happen to be here right now, too.
Rysiu, <u>please go right away</u> and at the nearby Cepelia get those <u>unglazed</u> bowls that I bought for 2 for 3 zlotys. They're those bigger ones, and the big ones are 6–12 zlotys and more, those red ones with the black-and-white design [SKETCH], and go over to Chmielna, I think 124 Chmielna, quite a ways down, near the corner of Żelazna, to the customs office—they pack it up for you there, too. Maybe some little whistles and figures in the 11–15 zlotys range, too, but do it right away—dedicate 2 hours to it, it will help me survive here <u>a lot</u>. No matter what do it right away. If they don't let you send more than one object, then put down different senders. I'm really depending on it.
I can't write anymore, I'll tell you all about everything and assume we'll be meeting in Venice. A big kiss to you both. Don't forget about Piotruś, and say hello to Zosia

Alina

Dear Rysiu
Alina and I have been remembering Polish and Parisian times. Warm regards to you and your son

Dante

to odrazu – poświęć 2 godziny, to mi
ogromnie tu pomoże bardzo. Koniecznie
o zaraz zrób, jeśli nie można prze-
słać więcej jak jeden przedmiot,
o od różnych nadawców napisz!
3. na to czekam.
Już pisać nie mogę wszystko
będę opowiadać i wierzę że się
spotkamy w Wien. Całuję Was
mocno obydwoch. Pamiętaj
o Piotrusiu i pozdrów Zosię

Alina

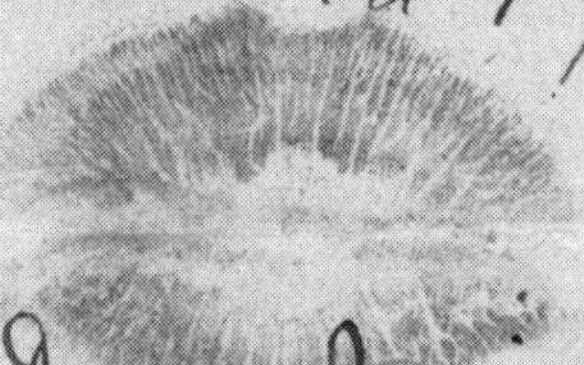

Drogi Ryśku

Przypominamy sobie z Aliną piękne
paryskie dzieje. Pozdrawiam Cię serdecznie
i Twego syna Danuta.

Drogi Ryśku!
Przyjmujemy Halinkę z wszystkiemi
honorami „digne à vous". Byłbym Ci b.
wdzięczny gdybyś poprosił Kostka, aby postarał
się w Ministerstwie Spraw Zagranicznych aby m[illegible]
[illegible] paszport. Serdecznie ściskam

Ryśku dear!
We'll take in Alinka with all the honors *digne à rang.* I would be very grateful to you if you would ask Kostek to try and get the Ministry of Foreign Affairs to arrange for my visa and passport as quickly as possible. Kind regards and respects.

Abrasza

78.
SZAPOCZNIKOW TO STANISŁAWSKI
[MAY 30 OR JUNE 6, 1956]
NOTES →[P 319]

Wednesday

Dear darling!
I think you will receive this letter before our Sunday phone call, because I'm giving it to Mr. Nieciuński tomorrow, and he's going to Poland on Friday morning. The fact that your letters take around 10 days to reach me is terribly annoying, and from what you write it doesn't seem that mine to you get there any faster. Given which any correspondence of a sentimental nature or having to do with our impressions makes no sense, my impressions here change at enormously speed, feelings of delight and disgruntlement follow fast on each other's heels, and your epistolary reactions occur at exactly the opposite point they should. To where I feel embarrassed about my previous letter, and all those things I will tell you with more precision when we are together. The fact is that I see so many wonderful shapes and colors here every day, the eye bursts into music. Only now do I see that I really don't know how to do anything, how immature I was, and I think that this is the first stay that really counts as a study trip, much more so than those years at Beaux-Arts. Because I now independently organize my impressions.
I am very homesick. Particularly for Piotruś, and I worry about him. Why is he not going to see Danielewicz? Write, too, what the situation is with the money, if it made it to the bank etc., how you're managing. Life in Paris is now extremely tiring, especially because I have no space of my own to relax in, or most importantly, to bathe. All of the people I know that I visit greet me enthusiastically, but all of them are terribly overworked, and somehow despite the fact that they all live perfectly comfortable lives, I can only stay with the Lustres, where the conditions are terrible. I am,

however, hoping that I get an apartment next week with a bathroom on the Île St.-Louis from Dr. Monsaingeon's brother, who is going to Morocco for 3 months. Jean Cassou invited me to a reception at his home, Antoine Pevsner, Bernard Dorival and others were there, but I've become very disenchanted with that society. In any case, they're inaccessible, anyway, over the border—I'll tell you when I'm back what that's about (it's the generation, too). I don't think we can count on any level of success with the exhibition at the Rodin Museum, which in any case is but one of many exhibitions. I saw a wonderful film on Picasso by Clouzot. A wonderful completely new exhibition by Braque—unfortunately I can't even buy catalogues or reproductions, because it all costs something in the thousands. I've seen exhibitions by Laurens, Klee, Bores, Lardera, and many others. French poster art is very bad.

The Taminiaux came today, Jacques is staying till the end of the week. We arranged to meet tomorrow to talk over lots of concrete things having to do with the exhibition in Brussels they want to organize. —Here, unfortunately, they are totally insignificant youngsters without a cent, like me. I think it's different in Brussels. You can't imagine how much I'm getting out of being here, and I see clearly how I will work after I return, and that we must completely change our lives.

I've found the Jaśes, Wita, Miecio, and some others. Their situations are all very good now, because the need for workers in Paris now is great. Tomorrow I have a meeting with Anzelm and Auricoste, I don't even really have time for all these visits—I haven't even managed to get to Niclausse's yet. The embassy naturally behaved abominably toward me in every sense of the word, they don't give a shit about me, they have no idea who I am, because they haven't gotten a letter from Warsaw about it—just unnecessary hassle. Unfortunately I have to go back there, because I am supposed to appear on television

etc. I can't do that without them. Kott, Lorentz, and others are here. I'm giving you the Jaśes' number, maybe it's better if in the future you call them, not Mossé. M.E.N. Menilmontant 45-97.
I'm sending a car with Mr. Nieciuński, explain to Piotruś that it's from me from Paris. Check for 2000 zlotys. Write to me about Piotruś and what's going on with Brussels. If they announce anything, telegraph!!!
Mr. Czarnocki from Venice came to see me—you can stop by and see him there, he's very nice, but an awful Londoner.
Please give me the address for Ramponi, because it's very likely I will be able to go to Italy *tout de même*.
I may also have some little gig through the Lerendus (a portrait or something like that for the cemetery, very cheap, around 20 thousand). But it's not sure yet, and as for that seated one, I don't think anything will come of it, and I don't know what to do—it's just an unnecessary nuisance. In any case we'll see after the vernissage. Please call Czyż 900-77 and ask if they have photographs from the competition, if so—have them send them to me as soon as possible before the vernissage.
I am already very tired and sleepy, maybe I'll add a little something tomorrow

kiss kiss Alina

Please call my mom to let her know you have news from me, because I am not writing anyone.

Zosiu dear!
Thank you very much for your letter—it is well written and with no mistakes. I am hustling and bustling around all the time here and have so much to do that I have not a moment to spare. But please do send me letters, Zosia, because that's the only thing that calms me. Are you remembering Piotruś' ears?! That's the most important thing. I am probably going to cut my stay a

little short, because I really miss Piotrek and Warsaw and our home. I look forward to your letters, sincerely,

A. Szapocznikow

<u>Please do not yell at the child</u>

Piotrusiu!

I am sending you a lovely car with Mr. Nieciuński, who has been in Paris. When I come I will bring you another one that's even nicer and a little bunny.

Just be good, listen to your daddy and to Zosia. I am very sad we're not together, but I'll be there soon. Write a letter to me, too. Big hug and kiss

Your mom

NOTES →[P 321]

Venezia, 9.VI.1956

Ali my dearest, you must have received the photographs of the model that I sent you this morning *par avion* from Venice. You can't imagine how happy I am that you are to come here. If you could feel my impatience somehow—you would surely hasten your arrival. I am staying, then, at the Astoria hotel, but write to me at RS. HOTEL PATRIA—TRE ROSE, CALLE DEI FABBRI VENEZIA. It's run by the same people, and TRE ROSE is where we dine. And the one is 80 meters from the other. I have a lovely room, quite expensive, although I have to spend that money on the hotel in any case, and I am really LOOKING FORWARD to you. Ali mine, you can't imagine what Venice is like. Such an unbelievably strange city—not a single car, and no dirt. Fantastically lovely and fantastically dressed women from all over the world. The Italians seem to be even kinder and a lot more polite than the French. There are stores selling things I never even imagined existed.

Ali mine, write absolutely, or send a telegram to the above address: when are you coming and where to await you. I absolutely want to wait for you even if I have to go for you in the middle of the night. Once more—write or telegraph when, by what means, and at what time you are coming.

Tomorrow I'll have a phone call from Warsaw, from the office—so I'll have to make plans with Zosia and Romek for next time, and also with Olek, who turned out to be a really good guy, and in the end he cares for Piotruś and our home more than anyone.

Working like mad here. The pavilion was in a million pieces when we got here—others are already ready to open. From Monday the 11th to the 17th [JUNE] the individual pavilions will be opening at the rate of 2–3 per day, with associated receptions. Opening of ours: the 13th at 12. We were stuck there—dust sticking to us—from 8 in the morning to 7 in the evening. Great hullabaloo at the Biennale. I surveyed the whole terrain. The Greeks have ferrocement and a lovely sculpture (though somewhat superficial), lots of good abstract art. I was talking with Nedoshivin at their pavilion. He doesn't know any language other than Russian—Gerasimov, etc., there's going to be an uproar. The Soviet Pavilion seems to be a real revelation, that is, a total sensation. The Italians have a gigantic exhibit—among others a gargantuan painting by Guttuso: *The Beach.* By the entrance very nice abstract sculptures out of iron and colored stones and pieces of glass that are simultaneously fountains. Yugoslavia—like France. They have their sculptor that alternates between ripping off Brâncuşi and ripping off Pompon (odd combination!). I was talking with him—he doesn't seem to be very intelligent. The USRR—3 sculptures of Mukhina's—weak, it seems to me, and aside from that, in sculpture—naturalistic XIXth-century kitsch along the lines of Tchorek—awful. Beautifully dressed men and women—for now just curators and organizers—roam between the pavilions, which are situated on amazing grounds by the seashore. I think I saw Auricoste, although I wasn't sure whether it was him or not.

When you get here, we'll go and bathe at the Lido. There we have the cabana of our friend—prof. Cini, who *nota bene* speaks Polish.

Aluś mine, my dearest—really, don't fret about anything and come. Piotruś is getting good and proper care. I made sure of everything before my departure. I want to buy him lots of presents. I saw some beguiling little sandals for him here, but I am awaiting your arrival for their purchase. They have pencils made of chocolate and real gold coins made of chocolate—there are many, many pretty things he will be delighted with. And for you?—better not to talk about that—something wondrous. Although none of that is really important—Ali, I love you so much I don't know what to do.

Your Ryszard

80.
STANISŁAWSKI TO SZAPOCZNIKOW
[JUNE 1956]
NOTES →[P 322]

[PARTS OF THE LETTER ARE MISSING]

Forgive me, Ali, for this chaotic letter, but I am sitting at Florian on the Piazza San Marco, and that is the biggest cafe here—the terrace is probably 80 meters—and there are people and pigeons milling about everywhere.
Ali, I was so looking forward to seeing you yesterday. I went to meet every train from Milan. I was at the Lido, at the airport. Nothing. In the evening I was thinking that something would happen to me—I was that distressed. I was thinking of when we would be together—there is so much to see here. I am putting everything off until your arrival. Without you, Ali, it's empty here, and I have no one to share my sensations with—I go around in a stupor, and constantly return to you in my thoughts.
Ali my dearest—

Your Ryszard

(The worst evenings!)
Without you

With my presence here a great deal will go easier for you in Venice and at the Biennale—I will try to facilitate a variety of things.
Among the larger retrospectives at the Biennale there are:

Delacroix
Chirico
J. Gris
Mondrian
Villon
De Pisis
Wouters
and others

I am writing this letter in the thought that it will reach you in France before you leave.
I lift my gaze to St. Mark's Square: it is beautiful here, and that uncommonly blue water and that lacy church

with the golden mosaics, people, smiling, happy people—beautiful. Ali, Ali—I think constantly of you—I must be sick, or hopelessly in love—and this after so many years...

R.

SZAPOCZNIKOW TO STANISŁAWSKI
[JUNE 12, 1956]
NOTES →[P 322]

Tuesday

Rysiu darling!
I am completely knocked out due to events of the last few days. I am summarizing, please write back with some sage advice immediately.
What should I do?
1.) The vernissage has been postponed from the 15th to the 22nd, and it might be all dragged out further (the weather is dreadful—the cement plinths are not drying etc.)
2.) I had arranged to go to Italy on the evening of the 15th, that is, right after when I thought the vernissage would be. It could be that I might be able to stay a week and then come back for the new date of the vernissage on the 22nd.
That was my plan until this morning, since I will not have my Italian visa yet before Friday anyway. And every evening until Friday I am booked (Auricoste, Cassou etc.)
This morning along with your very tempting letter and several things by pneumatic post with invitations from Wogensky, de Gallard, Jan Kott etc. I got a telegram from Warsaw: Definite extra round stop deadline July first stop come back now Jerzy
You know I stand by this work with all my heart, that this is one of the great opportunities in the life that we are facing. Besides that according to the pictures and what I've seen here and learned lately, I can really help them. In the end, this is a truly shared project. And now the dilemma!
I have a *sortir et retour* visa that the embassy issued me for my trip to Italy.
1?) Should I just go ahead and go to Warsaw now, and after the competition ends on 1.VII come back on the *retour* visa (question of the 800 zlotys for the trip)? The

press issues for the exhibition at the Rodin Museum, and the question of the sale of the sculptures, will not really be relevant prior to that time—right now aside from social-studio matters I don't have anything really that I'm doing here.
2?) Should I go and see you for 3–4 days, and then straight to Warsaw to stay and leave the Rodin matters and the sales to friends, because truth be told I can be perfectly dispensed with when it comes to all that?
3?) Should I not pay any attention to Jerzy's telegram and come to you for a week, then (after the vernissage) stay 10 more days in Paris and around July 10 go back to Warsaw like nothing's happened. —You know I am including this third option as a real last resort, because what I really feel is that the most important matter at this moment is the Brussels one, while the rest is more a series of delightful pleasures that it's hard to renounce.
Thus I ask you to advise me really disinterestedly and sagely, what should I do!? Not to go to Italy having an opportunity like this one—unthinkable.
To leave everything in Paris without saying goodbye—unthinkable.
Although both of those matters are questions of an opportunity that could always come up again.
Brussels is now or never, and of course it opens up possibilities for us in the wider world.
I am totally dazed by all of this. To add insult to injury ever since my arrival it has been pouring all the time and cold, and since I don't have anything to wear, I got a cold and have a constant headache, I'm living [ILLEGIBLE]
—But that doesn't matter, because it will pass. Write to me how long you'll be in Italy and generally what am I to do?!!!
I await your immediate response, a letter takes 18 hours. Kiss

Your wife Alina

Respond by telegram, Alina

SZAPOCZNIKOW TO STANISŁAWSKI

[JUNE 14, 1956]

NOTES →[P 322]

Thursday,
11 in the evening.

Rysiu!
I just received your telegram, which rattled me enormously anew. This whole thing could be considered ill fated. "Ill fate has parted us." Today I was supposed to pick up my passport and my visa for Italy at our embassy, and they refused first and foremost to grant me an extension, with which goes my Italian visa. For two days I have been taking part in Paris-Warsaw phone calls, and yesterday the Ministries of Internal and Foreign Affairs said they knew nothing about it. At which the ambassador swore that the matter was under the Ministry of Art and Culture, which I had told him based on your phone call. Today the MAC said they didn't know anything about it, and basically I get the impression that they don't want to give me the extension just so that we don't see each other.

I feel all the more sad and embarrassed that just yesterday I made a date with Germaine Richier to meet in Venice. I've become good friends with her, and we set a place and a time for Sunday. And of course I have so much to talk to you about. But that's going to be tricky...

I can't kill all birds with one stone. Since it turns out that it will be better for me not to be at the vernissage, and they're dragging things out so, I've decided to go over to Warsaw for 12 days, i.e. till July 1st, to use the *aller et retour* visa I have in my passport. This is also based on advice from Gajewski, who turned out to be really nice, and after my return we're going to organize a *soiree* with French sculptors at the embassy. It would be really good if you could manage to return through Paris. I'm telling you, these past two days I was living in such a state of anxiety that I'm just happy that something, anything has been decided on, and that I am going to Poland after all. Everyone here is delighted with the project. Cassou, acting on France's behalf from Brussels, was truly delighted and really praising me. I do think that I'll be a lot of help in Warsaw, even just with my connections. And I'll see the child.

With regard to buying things, do so for yourself and for Piotruś. Sandals for a 5-year-old. But they say that shoes for children are expensive there. ~~The "jupon" is a bit stiff for me in terms of keeping my skirt wide.~~

You might get me some publications with sculpture (here I got the 3rd volume of Malraux on sculpture and one by Marino Marini). Maybe you could get Moore? Buy strong nylon stockings—you can never have enough of those. In any case I got a little money and am stocking up on my feminine "cravings."

But please <u>definitely</u> try to come through Paris. I am furious, I feel like someone's punched me in the face. I can't even begin to understand why you said it had been taken care of, and yet they are refusing to grant me the extension. And I had really been counting on it and was so happy about it for all sorts of reasons. Maybe I'll still go later, when you return—but to miss each other like that!! Preposterous!!

Try definitely to come through Paris, I will be here from 7.VII.

Darling, I send you a kiss

Alina

I'm including the letter from the Taminiaux that I received today.

You can buy me a nice trench coat, black, gray, or yellow. I wear a size <u>44</u>, anything that's ready-made is a 44. Come to Paris!!!! July 1st

[NOTE:]

Un grand bonjour de ton vieux Julien et pour toute la famille.

CALL NOW MORNING ROMA 550298

RYSZARD

NOTES →[P 323]

Rome, 1.VII.1956
2 p.m.

Alenko, my dearest,
Today, after the telegram that you saw, Romek and Olek called me, and I finally found out what is happening to you. They could not explain to me—it might have been uncomfortable over the phone—why you went straight to Paris and didn't get your passport extended. I don't understand, although anything is possible in this big mess of ours.
So please write how all of this happened and if there is any chance of your coming. I would preface this by stating that if you are going to run into any problems, desist from trying to make the Italy trip. After my departure from here you will run into great difficulties not so much in the financial realm as in the political, which might seriously influence your official return here in the future, which sooner or later must occur (would that it were sooner!). I am not going to set out the details of my judgment, but believe me, as I am not mistaken. Teresa Pągowska made a very bad impression here and did a very bad job. Everyone here is biased—perhaps it was precisely this fact that influenced their denying the extension of your passport. The matter is very complicated in any case, and I will recount it in detail when we see each other. Independently of the fact that I am curious about a number of things, the Brussels competition, Warsaw, above all—Piotruś—I will proceed immediately to the most urgent issue, that is, to the possibility of our seeing one another, which, my dearest, I so earnestly desire. Counting on your arrival here, I have bought almost nothing of the clothing or the shoes for you, desiring for us to determine together what to choose from this sea of wonderful things—while many of them I have already seen on you, and you so

beautiful, as always, Ali, my dearest. You must therefore answer the following questions immediately—express to the address: RS... ROMA, via S.CHIARA 5 ALBERGO BOLOGNA. (Tel. 551736):

1.) Do you intend to and can you come here, or not? (If you experience trouble, then give it up, as I already wrote—if there is no trouble, telegraph to the address given above by Thursday morning inclusive, at the very latest. I will be in Rome till Thursday, then I fly to Venice and could wait for you here even 5 days insofar as I could be 100% certain of your coming, we could in that case remain together, without exposing you to any potential costs, for an additional 5–6 days. My official stay here concludes 8.VII, but in the case of your arrival I could extend it somewhat.)

2.) In the case of your not being able to come, of which inform by telegram to the Rome address (Necessary here, Aluś, is your manly decision, and do not fool yourself with empty promises from the embassy!)—I will attempt to return through Paris—the steps in conjunction with the embassy here in order to receive an extension of my passport, however, I will not undertake until I have received word from you—because all such formalities take forever—TELEGRAPH IMMEDIATELY OF YOUR DECISION, so that I might be able, while still in Rome, to apply (before Thursday or potentially in that case I would stay longer) for a French visa.

Telegraphing your decision, send simultaneously an express letter, so that I may become more closely acquainted with the details I note below.

The difficulties with my trip to Paris are these:

a) extension of my passport—I believe that this can be arranged by the consulate here, although I am not 100% certain.

b) French visa—the French may say that they will give me a visa for two weeks—meanwhile the matter simply sits there. That is why it would be good if you could, for

example, ask Mr. Cassou or someone to intervene in order to ensure that no one causes any trouble for me here—in which case you would need to go about that immediately, without waiting for my response, if, of course, you have any such possibilities.
c) financial matters—For the trip to France and a stay in Paris I do not have the money—I could borrow, however, some amount (for the voyage) from Mrs. Marczewska's brother in Venice—I don't see any other option. I have already borrowed 30,000 lira from him—that is a very small sum by local standards—which I will return to his sister in Poland. Independently of whether I come to Paris or not, I will borrow a little more money from him—which he very much wants, in order to buy something for you of the sort that people in Poland can't even dream of. On this subject I would need to write more extensively, but I will not undertake to do so, so I ask you in this respect for total trust. I will proceed with the utmost prudence I can manage. In your express letter, then, write what you would like to have especially, give me your mesure (44?) and shoe size. For Piotruś I will buy things for a 5-year-old. Give me, also, your size in pantyhose, and if need be the colors of the materials (taffeta, poplin, linen, etc. etc.). Do this regardless, and do not take finances into account. Of course we are not talking about a massive purchase, but there are a few things that I want to buy you no matter what.
3.) —Particularly important is what I wrote above, if things turn out in such a way that we couldn't see each other by any means. In that case, Alenko, do not stay too long in Paris, and return as soon as you can—we could go on holiday together—I miss you so much, my dearest Ali—you can't imagine it.
My plan for my stay is as follows:
Today is Sunday, 1.VII. Tomorrow I am flying to Naples for two days. I am coming back to this same hotel in Rome on Wednesday, the 3rd. I think I will find, at that

point, a telegram from you—in that case I will immediately go to the embassy to apply for the extension of my passport and for my visa. If that is successful, around the 7th or 8th I will be in Paris, stopping of course in Venice along the way—in any case, however, let me know immediately how things stand.

If my departure turns out to be impossible (for Paris), on Friday or Saturday of this week I will go to Venice, where I will be for approx. two days, and then straight to Warsaw. This is the plan. Depending on your decision and the options available to me, this plan can be modified appropriately, in which case I will immediately communicate to you said modifications.

On which I conclude this *express* letter—later on today I will write you a few details about my stay here, because my friends have been calling for me for ¼ of an hour already from downstairs, and I would not like to keep them waiting any longer.

Ali my darling—I beg you to send a quick, manly, and telegraphic response!

I love you, Aluś, more than ever—I think about you always.

Your Ryszard

In your *express*, write about your encounters with Mrs. Marczewska from Łódź—in detail, everything you know. Did you bring something for our friend in Venice? Respond in this regard to my express letter (the old one) that you found, I'm sure, at the Lustres'. Say hello to them. Once more, Aliś ++++++++

Ryszard

If you were to come here, write, telegraph, when and where—I will come pick you up.

R.

(If by chance you wanted to call—I am in the hotel between 11 at night and 8 in the morning)

SZAPOCZNIKOW TO STANISŁAWSKI

[JULY 2, 1956]

NOTES →[P 323]

Rysiu darling!
You can't imagine what all that was, the work and the travel. I can't wait for us to talk about everything, or to talk at all. I shuffled around every day after Lucek, and that completely ruined everything for me. Yesterday at 6 in the evening at the passport office on Szucha I got my passport, and only for two border crossings. I had a ticket to go out this morning. You can imagine my nervous tension. Although maybe it's good that I'm not going to Italy this time, because of Piotruś. I am very worried about his condition and want to return as soon as possible, in order to take care of him myself. And that is why: Rysiu! The one thing is you have to go one more time to Danielewicz, and have him make a final decision on where and what, if Zosia still has not, with the aid of those guardians, arranged anything.
Keep writing me at the Lustres'.
And phone! I am returning as soon as possible, because I pine.
Big kiss

Alina

Rome, $11^{\underline{00}}$ (4.VII.56)

Alenko mine,
today is Wednesday—11 o'clock, and I have no news from you—I do not know, then, if my letter (express) got to you or not (I sent it from Rome last Sunday). I am essentially writing this letter blindly, then—not knowing if you are coming here, or if I am going to you, which is beginning to take on an aspect of likelihood.
The embassy extended my passport to include France. Today I was at the French embassy, and without waiting for your response, I applied for a French visa. It normally takes two weeks to receive this visa. In this case, however, because I would like to visit the museums and talk over the matter of the Polish exhibition with Cassou—they promised to arrange it telegraphically by next Monday (without giving, however, a precise date). Tomorrow, then, in the afternoon, I am going to Venice, where at that French consulate I will find out the results of my application. If everything were to go well, then I would be in Paris next week—insofar as the visa is clear and it makes sense to invest money in this trip (around 13,000 French francs). So you see how necessary it is to have news from you—I am counting on the fact that it might yet come today—give me some sign of life, and I will be able to somehow narrow down my plans. That's it, as regards our potentially seeing one another, which you know how much I desire—so much that I don't have the words to write to you.
Italy is a wonderful country—thanks to the tickets that were reserved back in Poland I have been able to visit, besides Venice—Padua, Florence, Rome, Naples, and even Capri, Sorrento, etc. Venice, Rome, and Florence are not cities to me, but genuine events. Museums with tremendous painters, churches where Titians, Tintorettos,

Bellinis, Veroneses, etc., are just hanging there like the most ordinary thing in the world—alongside frescoes in other places—Giotto, Masaccio, Ghirlandaio, Fra Angelico, etc. etc.—these are EXPERIENCES whose character is difficult for me to specify, but which remain, however, in my consciousness as something great, unforgettable. Such ones as, for example, the Bargello Museum in Florence—the place of Donatello and Verrocchio—an old palace of monumental, Renaissance architecture, and more than a dozen of the most beautiful Donatellos—St. George, David, St. John the Baptist, the polychrome bust of Niccolò da Uzzano, the lion with the shield, a second David (marble), bas-reliefs etc.—and besides that, Verrocchio, Luca della Robbia, his brother Mattia, and Andrea, Brunelleschi, Ghiberti, Pollaiuolo, Riccio, and a gargantuan room of Cellinis. It's a whole museum of the most beautiful sculpture of the Italian Renaissance. I was so happy, Ali, that we were going to see it all together. And the Italian landscape is full of charm—the landscape made famous by the *Quattrocento*—still the same, nothing in it has changed, and the electrical lines running here and there only bring its beauty into sharper, more powerful, relief.

Despite all this, this visit of the mind holds only half its value, since I cannot exchange views with the person that is dearest to me in the world, cannot tell of my joy. I think, Ali, that the time will come for us to find ourselves here together—I am somehow almost certain "deep down."

Of the Brussels competition Romek told me, so I am more or less "up to speed." I know nothing, however, from you or about you, which puts me in a state of sort of psychic helplessness, as we have, after all, always talked about everything, and that, Ali, is what I miss the most here. I am also curious how Piotruś seemed to you and where he will be in Zakopane. I wrote him a series of postcards. Did they arrive? Thinking he would go to the sea I bought him an oversized fish made of plastic, pretty, colorful, capable of keeping him above water. I'm sure it will be of use next year. I think a lot about our child, and only here have I fully realized how attached to him I am. I am curious, too, Ali, how your participation in the Rodin has gone. In the latest issue of *Arts* there was just a laconic note about "Polish classicism (!) and primitivism (?)". Next Sunday an article is supposed to appear in *Lettres françaises*, were there any mentions in other magazines?

I'll give you my plan once more, with regard to my time abroad, if of course you are not coming to Italy, which Romek and Olek told me.

Tomorrow evening (the 5th) I will be in Venice, where I will stay probably until Monday (possibly leaving Rome not tomorrow but the day after, but that does not alter the situation). In Venice write to me at this address: R.S. —ALEBERGO PATRIA TRE ROSE, CALLE DEI FABRI, SAN MARCO, VENEZIA. So, if no drastic changes occur, I will be in Venice until July 8th.

Then there are two alternatives:

1) I go to Paris, with a one-day stopover in Milan (if they give me the French visa, of course)

2) A trip of 2–4 days to Milan and from there return to Poland around July 12–14.

Regarding whether I am coming to Paris or not I will obviously let you know immediately by telegraph, but obviously not earlier than Saturday-Tuesday, as it is within that time I expect to receive my visa. If I don't get it before Tuesday (maybe Wednesday)—I probably am not coming to Paris.

I would like to know, Ali, what your plans are—what you are doing, how much longer you intend to stay in Paris. Please write. I cannot tell you how much I would like to see you.

Ali my darling, mine—I send you a kiss

Your Ryszard

NOT COMING ALINA

SZAPOCZNIKOW TO STANISŁAWSKI

[JULY 4, 1956]

NOTES →[P 324]

mercredi le 4

Rysiu dear!

Finally we managed to communicate, because we were so lost in the world that I didn't even know where to write to you. On Monday I sent a letter to *poste restante, bureau de poste principale*, Roma. Try and pick it up. I didn't write anything there, really, it was just to find you. But now I have your letter, and I will try to respond to you in a straightforward manner. A moment ago I sent you a telegram informing you that I am not coming to Italy. The matter is as follows: In Warsaw I asked Lucek why I was denied the extension; here he began telling me that they had gotten hauled over the coals by the Ministry of Foreign Affairs, which receives radio dispatches from the Polish embassy in Italy and France, for sending people out on official passports without funding, and that they should be ashamed of themselves, etc. He led me to believe that he was talking about Teresa and me—but that in view of the fact that I am not without resources (friends, a cousin, and you)—they are going to extend my passport. The matter appeared so delicate, though, which of course—I see from your letter—you yourself understand, that when in the end they did not grant me the extension, I did not insist, just to be sure they didn't think that I had some secret business, resources, or that I was trying to deceive them. Besides, why torture myself over it when in fact there isn't much time, nor do I have the money, the trip itself was really tiring, and right now I am getting a lot out of being here. Besides, I believe I will still make it to Italy—and officially, at that.

As regards your coming, there, too, I think there's no reason to push hard, although you must know how much I would like for you to come, see how good I look in the exhibition, and many other things, and of course how much all of our friends would like to see you here. But 1° there's no reason to beg (if it doesn't go smoothly) at the embassy in the hopes of an extension, because they will just send a telegram to Warsaw, and again people will start talking about trying to take advantage, and the like, "it's not enough that they..." 2° Here the Lustres' apartment is terribly inconvenient, and I don't see any other options. 3° time and money—I don't know where they're to come from.

When I left to deal with Brussels I spent everything I had, down to the last franc, because I didn't know (you know the times we're living in) for 100% certain that I would be coming back. I have now received 10,000 francs in aid for the exhibition—which is nothing (one meal 1,000 fr.). Jean Cassou expressed a desire to buy a sculpture for the Musée d'Art Moderne, which he's paying pennies for, around 30 thou fr., because it's an honor to have a sculpture at the M. d'Art Mod. Besides at the vernissage (fortunately I wasn't at the vernissage, because they really wreaked havoc) he talked to the ambassador about me, they wrote about it in *Trybuna*, a big success for Poland, they said, although in any case it is not as though I have other options. Aside from all that, I don't know when he's going to follow through on that promise (yesterday I went to see him, he was charming and said that he would let me know me soon—but when—I don't know). For the time being I am working miracles to try and stretch out that 10,000 fr. as much as possible.

I went to see Danielewicz with Piotruś, his ears are not in the best shape, and he really doesn't hear well—we definitely have to send him to Zakopane, not to the seaside, if only because of the medical care they have there. Fortunately Maryta was moved by his mother being in Paris and his father in Italy and made room for him at the Magnolia—which I think is actually in the end the cheapest and the safest. I wrote to Gaffka that for now we are not coming—maybe in August, but since the deposit is set, and if we make the reservation, we'll have to pay 600 zl. per month, it'd be good to give that room in Karwia to someone, because it's just a waste to throw away 1200 zl. I think you'll easily find a taker in Warsaw, but if not, then write to Gaffka and have her cancel our reservation and apologize, I'm sure everything in Karwia is booked, so it will be easy and even appreciated for us to give up our room. Take care of this as soon as you get back.

From Zakopane I would like to go and see the professor in Krakow with Piotruś.

They'll tell you about Brussels there—I think it was very good that I was there those 10 days, although I got terribly sick on the plane because of the change in pressure and the lack of oxygen (I didn't throw up), to the point that I am actually scared of returning.

In Warsaw I collected the rest of the money for the monument, I used the entire raise of around 18 thousand to pay all debts: plasterer, Wojtek, Mr. Kordiasz. and 1000 zl to Mrs. Mrozowska for the 20 dol. her brother gave me here. The rest (very little) I left with Romek, who will pass it on to you, but I beg you not to spend it, because it's still not enough for Piotruś' stay, and I would like for us to go to him too, and I would really like to rest after my return at least just a little and be with Piotruś, so please put that money aside for that now. As regards shopping, buy only (as others do) insofar as you will have something left from your *per diem*. I don't need anything, I already bought myself a few of the most pressing things (I bought myself 4 pairs of shoes) when I was going to Warsaw the first time. For you there are ties in the wardrobe, cigarettes on the shelf, and pencils in the desk drawer. Please don't take anything else from Mrs. M.'s brother, 30,000 is already more than 1000 zl, and the only thing that I really want is to just

work in peace for two years, and not to earn, I mean, not for the sales, but only when something is really mature, not churn out sculpture by the yard. I now have a few ideas that I <u>must</u> work through as soon as I get back. They are smaller sculptures, expensive to make, and cheap to sell according to our price list. I will really and truly <u>do everything</u> in order to not earn my living by sculpting for two years while not having to worry about Piotruś' expenses or domestic ones. So I ask you once more, do not buy anything for me that doesn't come out of your travel allowance, do not take out <u>any</u> loans. And I really don't need anything.
Write, too, if you bought glasses for your father? I bought him *anchois*, they're on the shelf next to the cigarettes. Tell Mr. Czarnocki that I'll write in the next few days—my mom came to see me in Warsaw on Sunday, and she took those sweaters to Łódź and the money, and she phoned that Mrs. Mrozowska was delighted.
<u>Remember to buy Zosia a present</u>.
I did not bring any silk for Mr. Czarnocki, because actually there wasn't any, the season for it is before carnival, and it can always be sent to them when the time comes.
When I get back, I'll tell you about all the ups and downs and successes and failures here in detail—and a lot of it's good.
Tomorrow Mr. Lustre and Michelle are going off to Champagnole, and maybe I will be able to live a little more easily here. For the time being I am taking advantage of Paris and experiencing the sculptures I will do when I get back.
Please make note of all this, write to me what you've bought so that I don't buy the same thing... Write as soon as possible, and where I am to write you, and what day I am supposed to be at the Jaśes' for you to phone from Warsaw (figure that out), I send you a big kiss, and we'll talk about everything when I get back

Your Alina

NOTES →[P 325]

Thursday eve.

Rysiu dear!
I just got your letter from Rome written at eleven in the morning—and I get the impression that our letters simply sailed past each other, and you know now what my situation is.
Nonetheless I will briefly write you now about my likely plans so that we can go s'according our actions.
You know how much I would like for you to come—but it seems to me that for just a couple of days it's simply a waste of money—and where would it come from, for that matter?! (I myself at this moment am in a similar situation, down to my last 500 fr., I can't go to anyone's place to eat anymore, because one ought not get carried away, I want to telegraph Mr. Czarnocki to borrow something, which is also why I don't want you to take anything from him, because that would simply be too much). I want to stay here, though, until the reception the embassy is organizing on my initiative next week for sculptors here. Besides that I still believe that I'll hear from Jean Cassou like he promised (that he would let me know) any day now with regard to that purchase [SKETCH OF A SCULPTURE].
Now I am walking around and looking at things. Unfortunately, however, either the cuisine or the climate is bringing on terrible allergies (remember the eczema I had here before?). Presently they're attacks of a runny nose, respiratory trouble, and headaches and so forth. I have repeatedly had to get off the metro amidst already, and once I even felt sick, and I was taken to the little café. It is terribly stuffy, and my heart breaks down. Life at the Lustres' is unbearable. Fortunately she went off today to Jura Champagnole.

So I want to come to Warsaw somewhere around July 22nd—I will be, I think, unveiling the monument to friendship at that time. I would go to Piotruś to rest for a week or so. Then—I hope, he will be recovered for now. I would take him on the way to the ear doctor in Krakow—which even Danielewicz advised, and we could all spend the last 2–3 weeks or so of August at the seaside, for example. But we do have to think if it's worth paying so much for a trip hither and thither, or if it might just be better to stay together till the end in Zakopane. Although that doesn't seem to me to be a real rest for us like a village or the sea, where the climate has the best effect on us.

Write what you think about that plan? I came up with it, among other things, because I wouldn't want to take such a long break from work again, and we have to give Zosia 14 days off. And as for you, I am almost certain that you won't be able to go on holiday before August, because when I was in Warsaw Cesia was complaining that she can't handle everything all by herself, what with Brussels, and her being sick, Nieciuński on vacation, you flitting around—she has to rest etc. Unless of course you were actually to quit, but right after the trip it doesn't seem like it would be appropriate to do that. And besides that it would be good if you earned a little money when you get back, for this vacation and for the debts we've incurred now on our travels. Maybe you could write something about Italy and the problems there, and about the Biennale. Olo will probably also take financial advantage of the trip. Maybe you could pull something off together—since you have so many ideas and impressions. Tell me who you are traveling with. Are Stanisław Zamecznik, Juliusz Starzyński and Olo Wojciechowski still with you?

I guess that right after you get back you'll probably set the dates of your vacation with the C. B. A. V. A. and will telephone me with the what and the how. It won't be long before we'll be talking about everything. Are people all worked up about the incidents in Poznań there, too? That is also making it difficult to get around or get letters out of Poland. Last Monday Zosia was calling with regard to her departure for Zakopane and it was only at 12 that they were able to connect her, and only for 3 minutes. But do write when exactly you will call from Warsaw, so that I can arrange with the Jaśes to wait there. I would really like for the last couple of days to have a little money and not have to see the idiots who are supporting me, just freely and by myself go around and pay for all my own entrance fees and see lots of things. I don't need to purchase anything. Maybe that way I would get some rest. Please, Rysiu, don't let slip to anyone in Warsaw about my difficulties here, because after the article in the *Trybuna* everyone was advising me what brand of car I should buy here and other ridiculous things.

Write me more and about everything
big kiss

Alina

Saturday 7.VII.56

Aluś mine, I have been in Venice since morning. Today is Saturday 7.VII. I received your telegram and your letter while I was still in Rome. As I (told) wrote you, I was granted an extension of my passport for France and Switzerland, I will most likely also receive the visa, on Monday, here in Venice—however of the trip to see you nothing will come. I have to be in Warsaw as soon as possible, I spoke with Motyka on the phone, regardless I will be abroad a couple more days because I am awaiting the return plane ticket they've sent. A trip to Paris for 2–3 days simply exceeds our means (the cost is over 35,000 lira)—I don't know if you can imagine what it means to me to decide not to see you and not to spend July 14th with you, Ali.

In Venice I will stay only until I receive my ticket—I think until Monday, Tuesday—and then right to Warsaw. When will you be back?—Respond to that question in a letter to Warsaw, but if you can, immediately, and then I may find a letter already there when I arrive home.

I bought you among other things 5 pairs of the best nylons. For Piotruś sandals, socks (3 pairs), short pants with suspenders and ¾-length pants also with suspenders. For you also a few little things, and I intend to buy something on Monday that is in Italy the most fashionable and most elegant thing for everyday—a kind of dress suit, a little skirt and little jacket. You'll look good in it. I just don't know if I will get it in Venice—and I ran out of time to buy it in Rome. I really lament that despite my request you did not supply me with your shoe size—they have incredible shoes here, and they are the cheapest of everything, but I can't even buy something based on what I think, because shoes that are too big or too small completely lose their value.

Aside from that I bought quite a few different trinkets (even for the kitchen). For Zosia I bought a nylon pinafore, and I have to buy her something else, as well. I am not going to buy glasses for my father. The most mediocre (like what you can get in Poland) cost as much as two pairs of shoes. I'll most likely buy Olek a watch, obviously a cheap one, but Swiss. In fact I don't really know what to give to whom, and I will probably wait in Poland until your arrival and not unpack anything. I bought myself a suit (light), two shirts, two pairs of shoes, and some little trinkets. I also bought a very nice suitcase, and a traveling bag. I economized, as you can see, a great deal, and yet despite that in Italy I did not pass up anything I could afford. I am writing you about those purchases, which are of course of merely secondary importance, so that you don't happen to repeat the same purchases. Besides that you can see from this that had you been here with me from the beginning—my savings would have been enough for us both to lead <u>an affluent life and to travel</u>. I have also spent a great deal of money on books and other pleasures—coffee, juices, soft drinks, etc.—of which one <u>must</u> drink lots, because the climate is unbearable. In Rome the heat waves reached up to <u>40ºC</u>, from 12 to 5 all of Rome lay one after another at home behind closed shutters.

I returned to Venice with real pleasure (I greeted the hotelier and all of the staff as though we were old friends). This city has an extraordinary charm. I am alone, and I am quite happy about that. You know how I value solitude. Obviously, if you were here, Ali, our life would be fullest.

I won't see Mr. Czarnocki until tomorrow, as he is not in Venice now. Don't write to me here anymore, because I doubt the letters will arrive in time. I will write to you again before I leave. In the meantime, Ali, a hug and a kiss

Your Ryszard

I'm ending here because some friends have arrived, and I can't keep them waiting, and I want to send the letter right away.
Darling!

Venice,
Wednesday, 11.VII.56

Ali my dearest,
Thanks to the kindness of a friend, Mr. Czarnocki, I am sending with him ~~5,000~~ 10,000—francs for you, which, I hope, will make your stay in Paris somewhat easier. I borrowed just a little more money from Mr. Czarnocki, thinking of you, among other things, so don't ask him for a loan at this time. I received your letter and am very worried about your ailments. Take care of yourself, my dearest, and if you are not flourishing in your present climate—return home. Your health is the most important thing. Here there are terrifying heat waves, too—the famous sirocco, which might drive the uninitiated absolutely mad. I am somehow bearing the climate, however, resting for 2–3 hours in my room during the time of the greatest heat, though it is very stuffy in my room. I saw the photograph of your sculpture in the *Lettres françaises* and read the flattering note. The exhibit must in fact be fantastically interesting, judging from the names—Moore alone is enough. Don't forget, Ali, bring me and Mietek a catalog, have the embassy buy it. Aside from that don't ask for anything at the embassy, after everything you wrote and what I know here about Teresa—it's not worth it. It's obviously nonsense and a waste of our time and [CROSSED-OUT]. Just think, I could have been in Poland three days ago already, and yet I am still waiting for that return ticket they promised, which from Warsaw could be sent by telegraph within a ½ hour. Lucek, with whom I spoke on the telephone, promised to take care of it for me, but nothing has come of it. Tomorrow I am going to Milan and will keep awaiting the aforementioned ticket there—if it doesn't arrive, I will just go back by regular train, although it's tiring, but I'm sick of their bullshit. Only from here are

you able to really realize how all of this works. As for the long-term plan and our holiday, I agree with you. I will simply wait until you return. Aliś, I didn't buy you that little suit that I wrote to you about—however I am sending you money, and I would really like it if you bought yourself a bit of the lingerie and the things you need so much. Do not buy anything for me. If you had some extra money by some miracle, think about Piotruś and about winter for yourself—do not let yourself be influenced by the heat, which is passing, but think instead of our Polish weather.

I got interrupted by a phone call from Mr. Czarnocki a moment ago. He had just received a letter from you. Since you clearly mention 10,000—I am sending you a further 5,000—a total of 10,000 fr. I think that that ought to more or less ensure your stay until the end, at least in terms of the bare minima. Maybe you would be able to sell your sculpture? I am curious as to how expensive life is there. I saved money where I could here, even on food. I bought various little things for our home from just those savings.

You ask who I am traveling with. I have been completely alone for a week now. Before that I was hanging out with Olo and with Starzyński—Staszek was a bit on the periphery, staying in a different hotel, though still we saw each other on a daily basis. After my return to Warsaw I will try to write something about the exhibitions here. I have quite a few observations and a lot of material. I have one excellent idea floating around in my head, but it would be fairly difficult to pull off, and I need to talk to you about it.

Olek and Staszek are in the same position, also awaiting their return tickets, but they are in Rome. And so, tomorrow, I am going to Milan. From there meanwhile, depending on that ticket (it could take another 2–3 days)—straight to Warsaw. I miss you very much, Ali. Over a month of not seeing one another is horrifyingly

long—I would so like for us to finally be together. Definitely try to get back before Piotruś' birthday! I will call you in Paris from Warsaw, but at the moment I still don't know when. Before that I will simply send you a telegram with the day and hour of the phone call—the hour we can in fact establish right now—it will be 9 in the evening, so in the telegram I will just give the day. I will phone to the Jaśes'.
I don't know anything about the article you mention. I will try to find the *Trybuna* in Milan.
Obviously the Poznań incidents are being talked about here a lot, and opinions are varied. In any case we are going to find a Poland that is very different from the one we left a month ago.
I send you a hug and a kiss my dearest.

Your Ryszard

[THREE SKETCHES IN PROFILE—A MAN AND TWO WOMEN]

92.

SZAPOCZNIKOW TO STANISŁAWSKI
[JULY 17, 1956]

Rysiu Darling!
I was awaiting that phone call with such impatience, to finally hear you from home. Meanwhile with phones it is always the case that a person hurries and in the end doesn't know what to say, all the more so because all those Jaśes were standing around. Although they are all very solicitous, and I bathe at their house and eat breakfast. That tone of yours, once again upset, worried me terribly. I don't want to live like that anymore, always worked up over something, and nerves frayed. I have decided to completely change my lifestyle after my return and make completely different sculptures—beautiful ones. I also pine terribly, but it is precisely now that it is most important for me to be here, and instead of soothing me, you get hysterical as you did when I was in Zakopane, which you regretted once I had returned. I do think I can be back by the 28th. If you want to go away for 14 days with me, however, then take your vacation during the last 14 days of August, and we'll give Zosia a holiday and be together with Piotruś. I have so much work that I won't be able to holiday for more than 14 days, anyway, so I want our trip to coincide with Zosia's vacation, because when she's not there, I can't work anyway.
I have seen a plethora of wonderful things and have heard some brilliant jazz that completely "swept me away." When I come, we'll listen to it, and I'll tell you about it. I await our phone call on Thursday.
Big kiss

Alina

NOTES →[P 325]

Rysiu darling!
I am terribly upset after each phone call—but I don't want to write any more about that, because it won't help anything. Two days after you receive this letter I will already be in Warsaw, and we can talk about everything. Piotruś especially worries me terribly, while on the other hand I have the horrible feeling that I haven't been doing anything for two months now. Besides that I've grown accustomed to freedom and the free determination of my time, which is why I am not at all amused by submitting to plans that are in fact Cesia's plans. I will obviously need to go and see my mom at least for one day after I get back, meet with the plasterer so that he can cast that standing figure for me so that it's ready when I get back from holiday. Besides which I want to enter a competition I will tell you about when I'm there. And actually lately—because I have a little money here, and an empty apartment—I feel like I'm on holiday, and I have no need of a new holiday in a *pension*, and I am dreadfully afraid of being bored. I would like for you to be able to understand me—truly and as a friend. Meanwhile it seems to me that your stance is despotic and selfish. Besides I get the impression that you also need the kind of psychic decompression often provided only by work, and not a *pension*. I'm sure it will all work out somehow.
Yesterday I saw *The Good Person of Szechwan* in a festival performance of Israeli theater in Hebrew. The production was much better and simpler than ours, but it turns out that when you compare, Mikołajska is irreplaceable.
At the embassy from the 20th to the 24th they're having receptions and cocktails in honor of July 22nd, I'm invited to all of them, and in general my time is filled

out in a lovely way, unlike in the first weeks, when I was feeling impatient and very lonely. I think we'll spend our first night telling each other things.
For now a kiss from afar

Alina

94.

SZAPOCZNIKOW TO STANISŁAWSKI

POSTCARD *TATRAS IN THE SNOW*

[WINTER 1957]

I now pine terribly for home and cannot get through by phone. I'm going tomorrow, with supplies of strength, I think.
Zosiu, please be good to Piotruś.
Rysiu, a big kiss to you and Piotrek.

Alina

NOTES →[P 326]

Dear Rysiu,
For now everything is fine, I saw the exhibition and lots of people. I'll tell you all about it.
Now this morning we are going to Kuźnica. I spent two nights in Sopot because my period was really killing me. Kuźnica is apparently awful, as I learned here, and I am still planning to try and snag something in Karwia. A director friend of Zula's with a Wartburg, has a wife in Karwia. He rented one of the last rooms there last week and wants to take me with him from Kuźnica to Karwia on Saturday to look for something. In that case maybe Zosia?!? I would send a telegram in that case, but meanwhile start hinting a little, that perhaps... I know she would really like to. But we'll see.
Piotruś is a wonderful child, darling, but spoiled, and he has a cold. P I O [CHILD'S WRITING]
Mr. Honig cares for us just like a father.
The sea! The sea renews as always, there's something unusual and infinitely, magnificently wonderful about it that conveys both restfulness and joy. The weather took a turn for the worse today, and it's pouring now.
My heart is not at all sore. The air is refreshing, with the wind off the sea.
This pen is awful for writing.
I don't want to go to Moscow, but I'm afraid to phone the committee without talking it over with you first. I think I'll be able to tell them in a week that the child is sick, heaven forbid, knock on wood, or something like that. I've heard terrible things about scheduling coming back. How are things with Poleszczuk? Don't forget to make the preschool arrangements with Cesia, call her and remind her. Big kiss because I pine a little.

Alina

Friday

Rysiu darling!
I'm writing you now after being in Kuźnica for 1½ days. We arrived to fabulous weather and immediately went to the water, first the bay, then the sea, and of course you know how the sea is able to be beautiful, and in the bay a wealth of fishing boats, yellow-black, yellow, white-brown, or Indian red, and this incredible peace and happiness that can't be described. This is a real port and fishing town. There was a commotion by the sea at the appearance of these unheard of schools of sprats, brought in by little boats practically submerged under a silver that filled them to the brim. Piotrek was just as happy as a clam, by the time we had covered about 100 meters of the shore he had already gathered a whole panful of those sprats. I really wish you had been there. In any case, I'll tell you about it when I head back [to] those lovely parts. But... our room is disgusting, between the kitchen and the shitter, sounds and stench coming in from both sides. Two narrow beds, although you couldn't fit any more in anyway, because it's 10 feet × 12. Right by the street, where there are a lot of cars, and right by the tracks, where there are a lot of trains. The inner and outer ugliness of the little house is total and unbearable. To the point that I don't dare bring that Mrs. J. from Katowice here. But the landscape and the sea here are such wonderful things, only now do I realize how worthwhile it is to make the effort and live here for a bit, in the conditions available to us. Everyone is free to go anywhere, even take boat rides with the fishermen, and I hanker after Karwia ever so much, I think about the dunes near Dębki, where we would be able to sunbathe in the nude. So the one remaining hope is in that gentleman with the Wartburg

that we are supposed to go to Karwia with tomorrow. I'll write you right after that and let you know what I've decided. Beyond that it's a question of cash. Mrs. Ostaszewska, Kasia's mom, who I go around with all the time because I don't have anybody else, spent 2 thou. zlotys in two weeks, and I believe it, because fruit is over 30 zlotys a kilogram, and the kids want something to eat every second of the day. Kasia looks terrific, and this really is a way of storing up health for the winter. And Piotruś is so happy and just asks "that we stay here till winter comes." Mr. Ostaszewski is supposed to come by car, maybe you could give him a bowl, two large sheets, and two sets of silverware (knife, spoon, fork), toilet paper, because we really need it. If you could just come for a couple of days even, but try to bring a little money, too—maybe you could get an advance on some work or on the articles you're doing now. Because although Honig gave me another 500 zlotys, I no longer have anything at all, and I'm waiting on 1000 zlotys from my mom. But wait for news of where I am, because in this room there's no point in either coming or staying. I'm very lonely, Piotruś is sleeping now, and I'm just thinking now why even someone so stupid as Mrs. Ostaszewska is faring better, and I think the only thing really worth striving for is to just be with the child in a carefree and peaceful way among these miracles of nature. And what is the point in constant struggles, better to have peace and quiet and a bit of a comfortable life than empty fame, and over nothing, and for nothing.

Rysiu! now for the most important thing!
Call the Festivals Committee room 16 Smolna 40 and tell them that your wife has written to request that they find a substitute for that Moscow thing, because I don't think I am going, tell them because the housekeeper has left, the child is sick, etc. Just say what you want and whatever you think, because I do not want to go.

I prefer to spend a week with Piotruś by the sea than there. I discovered that people never come back from there as planned, and I really just don't want to with all these political eventualities, I just don't feel like going there. So please make sure it's appropriately resolved, and I'll go by there, too, when I get back.
Also, don't forget about the preschool, it's a very important thing now. Big kiss, and I really really feel like speaking with you.

Alina

[NOTE:]
I'm terribly curious about how your things are going, but don't write, because I don't know where yet

A.

NOTES →[P 326]

Monday

Rysiu dear!
Finally my first news from you today, and it made me so sad that you're not here. You know how it is at the seaside, how delightful the weather is. Schools of fish go out, and they just can't keep up with them. The post office continues to be besieged, and telegrams: you all should send in vehicles, ice, and boxes, because they're not bringing in anything anymore from the sea because they don't know what to do with it. Piotruś looks great and is totally happy.
I arranged a very nice room in Karwia with a view of the fields in that little house where Brzechwa lived, 600 zlotys for August.
Karwia is incomparable. I think in August, or maybe around the beginning of September, after the opening of the exhibition, we'll be able to go for at least 1 week together. Just don't forget to get me out of that Moscow thing.
Today (right after I got back from Karwia) I wrote to that Mrs Jadwiga from Katowice by registered express mail and told her to come, and as soon as she's here and gets to know Piotruś (one day), I'll go back to Warsaw immediately. When I saw here and in Karwia these little groups of soldiers, I realized we can't have Zosia do it.
I think you should get ready to sell that diamond ring so that we don't need to sell it in haste later.
I'll tell you everything, and we'll talk, by now I am really pining.
I want to go to Łódź on the 13th (my mom's birthday), and then get started on that ceramics thing.
Welcome Hela Lustre warmly and invite her over, and when I get back, I'll do the rest.
Kiss, see you soon

Your Alina

SZAPOCZNIKOW TO STANISŁAWSKI
[LETTER LEFT IN THE APARTMENT, 1957]
NOTES →[P 327]

Friday

Rysiu dear!
I'm so sorry to do this (all the more so because the apartment is all clean and my joints hurt in this weather), but I've gone to Nowolipki to sleep because I just can't stand it with them. Maybe you'll be able to talk Ewa and her husband into not staying another night, because they want to until Sunday—after all she's closer to you.
During the day I'll be in the workshop as usual, I'll be back for dinner at 4 a. m.
So you don't worry, know that Mr. C. gave me a response by phone regarding the Ministry of Foreign Affairs—he found out more or less the same information that you had. Meanwhile he pledges there will be some housing options before then. At the moment he is very busy, but in the next few days he'll summon me by telephone to come in with the reference number of the response from the Council of State (that green paper).
See you

Alina

99.
SZAPOCZNIKOW TO STANISŁAWSKI
POSTCARD, *VIEW OF THE TATRAS*,
MARCH 26, 1958

Dear Rysiu
There is nothing lovelier than Cyrhla in the winter. The weather is great, sunshine and snow. We are skiing and breathing deeply. Piotrek is very pleased.
Big kiss → Alina → Roman

SZAPOCZNIKOW TO STANISŁAWSKI
POSTCARD FROM PARIS,
[1958]

No nostalgia now, Rysiu dear, because it's changed radically here since our time—it's a different Paris, and we are different. Although of course that "monstrosity" is wonderful and charming.

Tomorrow I'm going to Rome for two days, and then your Venice

kiss Alina

101.
SZAPOCZNIKOW TO STANISŁAWSKI
POSTCARD FROM ROTTERDAM,
COLOR REPRODUCTION OF BOSCH,
JUNE 21, 1958
NOTES →[P 327]

Before I leave for Brussels I send my greetings from this town, where everything modern is being carried out now and everything ancient being exhibited in the most modern way.
Hugs for you and Urszula

Alina

NOTES →[P 327]

Paris Wednesday

Rysiu dear!
There was a whole pile of letters awaiting me at Mrs. Lustre's, and I was finally able to put my mind at ease with regard to Piotruś and to also learn your latest (though Marysia had already passed along your regards). Only from here can I write you a real letter. I came from Brussels (I'll tell you about the masterworks, I'm bringing heaps of catalogues and documents) on Monday night on Sabena, and immediately felt, after being in Holland, right at home and 100% happy. In sum: my stay is coming together happily, because in the very beginning I was received by (completely fortuitously, in fact) César. He's got a huge car, a bunch of contacts, etc. He arranged with his contacts (the owner of the metallurgical factory where he does sculpture) a great apartment on rue Soufflot. Telephone in my room, bathrooms, etc. In addition tremendously kind people, in love with him, with art, etc. He did the appropriate introducing me around, too, and they are terribly proud that I am staying with them. He wants to do an exhibit at the Cordegardie?! (put the sculptures into the *bagnole* etc.). I automatically entered *tout Paris*. Vernissage at the Stadler Gallery etc. And I also met Mr. San Lazzaro that way, and then once they found out *que je suis l'amie de Marie la polonaise sa femme! Ça alors*. San Lazzaro does put me somewhere in the *XXe siècle*!! I have a bunch à propos to tell you. The *comble* was that yesterday at Odeon I met Jean Cassou, who kissed me up (they're going on holiday in Normandy today), basically just a delightful conversation in a café for two hours. All roads are open to me! He was very taken by the latest sculptures. There are offers and more offers! And also everyone's expression changes *quand je dis que je suis logée par César*.

Thanks so much regarding Venice, it's a shame that that Auschwitz competition is galvanizing me to return (people are talking about it quite a lot here) so I will no doubt not take advantage of everything, *mais pour la prochaine fois.*
The one disaster is that the Lustres want to come for August—what can be done with them?!
Regarding Holland, when you were in Italy, I wrote quite a bit to Romek, so he can tell you about it. I saw Walter in Brussels, I asked him to call you, I also have the Sonsbeek catalogue for you. Walter took one for Romek—you'll see, there's an enormous amount of rubbish in it, and just a few good things.
Essentially Holland is extremely interesting and extremely boring. I spent two evenings with Leszek Kołakowski, who is bored to death there. People basically darling everywhere. Jaffé also wanted to top the hospitality of the Poles and made things nice for me where he could.
I have so much to tell you! But I have to run already.
Darling, please, especially for all the reasons and Piotruś etc. be friends with Romek, that's the way, the truly lovely, European way, this was confirmed for me yet again here now. It's also the only way to maintain the milieu that is the basis of our life and activities, and to which after all you both belong. These are things above and beyond sleeping—and even so you cannot sleep always with the same partner, it becomes disgusting. So no hang-ups, let's be human!! kiss

Alina

best to all

Paris le 1 juillet

Rysiu dear!
I am tremendously saddened to be leaving Paris today and going to Rome, although I'll only be there for two days because the ticket's been bought already (sleeper car). And then just Venice. I had a great hairdresser at Odeon and a kind of Paris *genre* has come out in me. I feel so good here, everyone's all being so kind to me, I am living on Soufflot. I haven't seen Roland at all. I've been very choosy in who I go with and the things I go to see—I only have one week, after all!
I have a little money (not much), write if there's something you especially want me to buy you that you forgot in Venice. Write me in Venice now, to Cini's address or whatever one you think. I told Romek *poste-restante*. I really, really miss Piotruś. In comparison with Parisian children, he is turning out to be a completely delightful real boy's boy. Go for a walk together somewhere maybe on Sunday, with Romek, too. Please calm him down a little, because he is really pining and hysterical (Romek).
I'll bring a bunch of catalogues etc. We'll talk about everything when I get back.
I asked Walter especially to call you etc.
I really have to get on with it now, I send you a heartfelt kiss.
Your ex-wife, as always sincerely etc. loving

Alina

Best to Urszula. I really need Romek, too, call him and cheer him up.

best from the lands of yore
was calling all evening and morning, too bad you didn't pick up

Alina

NOTES →[P 328]

9–XII–1962

Dear Dad,
Sorry I haven't written in so long. On Friday have no school because there's a strike. For Saint Nicholas Day I got: six chocolate bottles with liqueur, a ballpoint pen with four colors, four bars of chocolate—milk, rice, hazelnut, and the regular coffee one; a white American airplane, very modern and I really like it. Thank you very much for that airplane. The watch does not run slow or fast. Meanwhile the calendar runs slow. One day, I think it was the 16th, the calendar showed just the 14th. How are you feeling, Aunt Urszula and Ewa? I'm doing fine.
A kiss to Ewa from me.
Kisses to you both

Piotrek

Rysiu dear!
Finally after the flu etc. I got down to work, so time is passing extremely quickly. It seems like just yesterday that we saw one another, we have fond memories of your visit, it's just a shame you didn't have time to come to my studio.
The stereo works wonderfully, and we are expanding our record collection. Aside from that nothing to report. Piotrek is doing his best in school—his collection of writing instruments is fit for the head of a bank now.
Write to us, goodbye for now

Alina

Happy holidays to you both

Rysiu, your business cards could be quite quick, but only in Półtawski (you know that typeface)—although on

very good cardstock. Write if you agree to that, and you'll have them this year yet. That other typeface isn't possible.
Best to you and Urszula.
A kiss on the hand for your daughter.

Romek

SZAPOCZNIKOW AND PIOTR
STANISŁAWSKI TO STANISŁAWSKI
POSTCARD FROM TRIESTE, JULY 14, 1963
NOTES →[P 329]

14–VII–1963

Dear Dad,
I'm in Italy. I am really enjoying this trip.
Love, Piotr Stanisławski

Everything is going as *ça va* as you can imagine. A wealth of impressions—we crossed the Furka Pass in a Fiat—2500 m., eternal snow. Romek has already gone from Zurich to Germany. Everyone was very kind to us in Zurich, Lausanne, Geneva, etc. 1000 wonderful proposals and plenty of hospitality, but we're just about to cross the border today at Trieste. See you later from Yugoslavia, Alina

107.

SZAPOCZNIKOW AND CIEŚLEWICZ
TO STANISŁAWSKI
DECEMBER 20, 1963
NOTES →[P 329]

Paris le 20.XII.63

Rysiu dear!
Thank you for the greetings and the very lovely book.
Piotrek left yesterday, excited and proud in his new skiing gear.
We're working a lot and have been met with a lot of problems and a lot of satisfaction, drinking up the vital juices and obsolete values of Paris, down to the very last drop.
We wish you and Urszula all the best this holiday and in the New Year of 1964

Alina + Roman

Paris 9–I–1964

Dear Dad,
Thank you for the steam engine, the book, the coin purse with money in it and the postage stamps. How are you feeling, Dad? And how is Aunt Urszula? I really like the engine, the book too. On Sunday I went to the Grand Palais de la Découverte. I saw the design for a tunnel to go underneath the English Channel. It is a moveable design.
Pleaze [SIC], Dad, write to me right away because I haven't gotten a single letter from you since the holidays were over, and I wrote you a whole month ago. I got a *Bien*—A + at school. Mom decided to buy me the book *The Chase of the Golden Meteor*. Today I had lunch at a Chinese restaurant. I ate with chopsticks there. Lunch was sharkfin soup, rice, duck, seaweed salad, and sweet pork. For dessert I had pineapple and Mom and Dad coffee.
Kiss to you Dad and Aunt Urszula

Piotr

Rysiu dear!
Piotrek came back from holiday in fine form, very pleased, in love with his instructor Michel, plus he made a lot of progress in French. But alas, the holidays are over—for us, too, now that we have to get up early to wake him up for school.
I'm in fact already working, full steam ahead, and I already have a couple of bronze pieces—the Susse foundry offered me castings with payment *conditionnelle*, i.e., if the sculptures sell, which is a great sign of their faith in me, because the costs get into the millions in old francs.

I've also got a couple of interesting offers, but I won't write about that just yet, because I don't actually know how to pull it all off, if I should withdraw from the exhibit in Rome, because where am I supposed to come up with so many sculptures in such a short time. If I sign something concrete, I'll write you.
Romek has more work every day, but he also has a fair number of issues to deal with. Both of them miss Warsaw, as well.
Hugs to you and Urszula, from Romek, too.

Alina

NOTES →[P 330]

Paris 10.IV.64

Rysiu dear!
I waited quite a while to write you this letter because I wanted to enclose the photographs that were taken at my workshop, as well as give you a report on several serious proposals that are being finalized. —Unfortunately Piotrek broke his leg skiing, and we find ourselves helpless in every possible way: 1° financially (no insurance policy), 2° yesterday he was brought back in an ambulance from Evian and will be immobilized for another 6 weeks (cast up to the hip and groin), and we have to cook for him, serve him, sit him down, etc. and are bound to the apartment, 3° before his trip to the mountains he had brought back his first *classement* from school and actually had really good grades, like 9 and 10 in *récitation*, and he was to accelerate by the end of the year and move on with honors to the next grade, according to the principal. But nothing of that now—rotten luck.
He wrote this letter in French completely on his own, with no corrections from me. What of that—after 6 wks at home he'll likelier move backward than forward. For now, then, we are making no plans, we'll wait 6 weeks.
Best to your father and write to me about everything in Warsaw.
best to you and Urszula,
from Romek, too

Alina

Dad!
I am writing this letter after the "Easter" holidays, I broke my leg skiing on them! I put the site of the accident in blue on the postcard. Pion and Michel were

right by me. I got off the trail and fell down into some soft snow. I hollered out till Mr. Pion came. Michel went to find a toboggan. Then they took me to the shelter. At two they took me to the hospital. They did an X-ray. The big bone is broken, I am eating a lot at the hospital. Thank you for the books, the chocolate, the magnetic animal, and the ball.

Thousands of kisses.

Pierre S

SZAPOCZNIKOW AND PIOTR STANISŁAWSKI TO STANISŁAWSKI
MAY 3, 1964
NOTES →[P 330]

Dear Dad,
The book *Robinson's Island* by Arkady Fiedler is really great, I like adventure stories. Especially about Indians. Thank you for the postcard with the view of Krakowskie Przedmieście. Today I am going to a boarding school where the priests are Poles. I will be with French kids. I will be able to see how they learn printing and how they print books
Please write me a letter.
Bye, kiss

Piotr

Sunday
3.V.64

Rysiu dear!
Finally, after overwhelming difficulties, we managed, through the intercession of the publisher Julliard where Romek was working, to place Piotrek at a printing boarding school on beautiful grounds in a small chateau just outside of Paris. I went there yesterday and think it will be the perfect place for him until his cast comes off (28.V.). There are 20 boys there aged 15–18 all studying printing. Piotrek will share a room with two of them who will be giving him private lessons in French, he has a window with a view of the grounds, there is a television, good food, and he can even go fishing in the pond. Can you believe that we found out when we got there that the boys are watched over by two young Pallottine priests from Poland? We're taking advantage of the holiday today to take him there ourselves.
Yesterday evening we went to the Théâtre des Nations to see a Polish play, and we saw everyone we know from

Warsaw and from here. Among others Janek Lebenstein and Olga Wirska etc. Janek had an exhibition in Brussels and is now getting ready for a Paris one and not really going out at all. There is a really interesting surrealist exhibition here, which André Breton spits upon, but that's probably because he wasn't invited to be on the committee.

I did a demonstration at my workshop, and it was attended by the *crème de la crème* of critics and gallerists (it was just for them). I have a couple of very tempting offers, but I'd have to actually commit, so I have to make sure I'm really ready. Why are you not writing to tell me who was chosen to go to Venice from Poland?

I am sending you a few photo proofs. That large sculpture with the tubes I am sending to the Jeune Sculpture salon that they invited me to participate in in June.

Piotrek is upset, too, that you only sent him a postcard for his leg. It's the height of spring in Paris now, all of the chestnut trees are in bloom, it's very nice.

Hugs to you and Urszula,
from Romek, too, and from
our mutual acquaintances in Paris

Alina

111.

PIOTR STANISŁAWSKI TO STANISŁAWSKI

JUNE 25, 1964

NOTES →[P 331]

PARIS 25–VI–64

Dear Dad,
Thank you for the dream gun with 10 packs of cartridges. Today (June 25) was "my day," because I went to the hospital, and they took off my cast. I went to see Dad at *Elle* and then went with Mom to pick up the package you sent. And now I am writing this here letter. I had been dreaming of just that kind of gun. The plastic cartridges work well. I came in 20th in the end-of-the-year classification and am going to get a prize, which is a book.
Kisses PIOTR

PIERRE

Paris le 17 juillet 64

Rysiu dear!
I got your letter from July 10th at my new address now, tel. 842-02-87, where we are currently living in very lovely fashion in an enormous white workshop with a loggia and a little garden. The heat is really killing us, though. Fortunately Piotrek is in the country (I sent him your letter there so that he would write to you), in a week we are going to pick him up and will be spending some time together at the ocean near Les Sables-d'Olonne. We've decided to live in Paris for another year, and Piotrek is supposed to take a math exam on September 14th (which he is doing fine with) as well as a French exam— very difficult, to get into the Lycée Michelet (a boarding school with Russian, state-run, very select).
With regards to the exhibition, just take what you need from my studio. Mr. Lau from Zachęta has the keys: 1.) bronze hand, which was at the Biennale in 1955, just make sure to mount it properly on the pole, i.e. like this, not like this [SKETCH→]. 2.) the bronze sculpture called *Unmarried*, 170 cm, is currently in Opole for the plein-air exhibition (196[2–1963]), Zachęta will also provide the information (make two pictures for them). 3.) —*Biological*, which I am enclosing a photo of, bronze, 1964, approx. 80 cm, along with the rock it's on, which is approx. 130 cm. It needs to be picked up from me in Paris. I don't have any more in bronze, because a few of them are in galleries. After the Biennale I participated in: Bronzetto 63, Carrara 63, Portorož Symposium 63, Salon Jeune Sculpture Paris 1964. I think that's it, you'll figure it out.
Where is Bochum? I doubt we'll go, because I lost a lot of time when my studio by Père Lachaise was destroyed, and I won't have a new one until August 1st, thanks to

Co do wystawy to weź z mojej pracowni
klucze są u p. Łana z Zachęty 1 rzeźbę
w brązie co była na biennale rok 19
tylko uważaj żeby ją dobrze zmontow
na tyczce t.j. tak 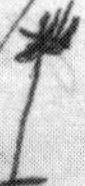 a nie tak 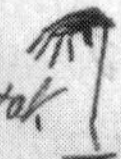. 2. rzeźba
w brązie p.t. „panna" 170 cm. jest w t
chwili w Opolu na wystawie plenerowej ro
Zachęta też Cię poinformuje. zrobi im też 2 zdjęcia 3 - „biologi
której foto załączam brąz 1964 ok. 80 cm wra
z kamieniem na którym jest ok 130 cm. To
do zabrania u mnie w Paryżu. Więcej b
mi nie dyspozycję, bo mam w kilku ga
Po biennale brałam udział w: Bronzetto 63, Carrara
Sympozjon Portorož 63. Salon jeune sculpture Paris 196
To chyba wszystko i dasz sobie radę.
Gdzie jest to Bochum? Chyba nie przyjedzie
bo dużo czasu stracę tam w zw. ze zburzeniem
mojej pracowni przy Père-Lachaise i dopiero od
1.8. dzięki Galerie de France będę miała wspa
tą pracownię blisko domu. Poradzimy pojechać
chyba do Wiednia, gdzie Romek ma mieć wys
plakatu. Narazie więc pozdrawiamy
Ciebie i Urszulę Alina + Roman
Jak przyjedziecie z Mietkiem
to pogadamy

the Galerie de France, which will be wonderful and close to home. Aside from that, I think we are going to Vienna, where Romek is supposed to have a poster exhibition. So for now all best to you and Urszula

Alina + Roman

We'll talk when you and Mietek get here

Sables d'Olonne
2.8.64

Rysiu dear!
I didn't get a chance to write you before I left because Herta (Wescher) was staying with us and was telling me all about the museum in Bochum (she was supposed to do an École de Paris exhibit there, too). Apparently the center is very beautiful, it's just that the director is eternally drunk. So I thought it over, and if your grouping is going to be more from recent years, then what about taking two sculptures from here (that is, from Paris), that is, one bronze, which I sent you a picture of, and another one about 120 cm, which you had on that tiny little picture, which is called *Machine en chaire* and which the critics really liked. That would be instead of the hand, which admittedly is bronze, but which is fairly old now. Beyond that, decide if *Unmarried* is going, or maybe that *Armored,* which was in the Desa gallery window. Write me please immediately to let me know what you've decided—in Paris. We will be here another 7–8 days, and then Piotrek will stay until the 20th with Mrs. Mossé, Michelle Zahorska's mother. Then he will go to a Nadeau *cours* in order to prepare for his exam. We are doing very well here, taking full advantage of our natural surroundings and of the wonderful summer. Heartfelt greetings from us all

Alina + R. + P.

Dear Dad,
I have been on the Atlantic for 3 days at a campsite. Mrs. Michelle Zahorska is at the same campsite, and in a few days she is going with Dorian to Bulgaria, where Mr. Leszek Zahorski is to meet with Dorian.
I go swimming three times almost every day.

How are you feeling? Is the market square the same as it was a year ago? How is your dad feeling? I'm supposed to take an exam on September 15.
Kiss

Piotrek

SZAPOCZNIKOW, PIOTR STANISŁAWSKI AND CIEŚLEWICZ TO STANISŁAWSKI
AUGUST 21, 1964
NOTES →[P 333]

21–August–1964

Dad!
Thanks for your letter. The water in the Atlantic was really good this summer. I saw a movie called *The Hole* during our vacations, it tells the story of French prisoners that dig two holes to get free but when they start to escape, the prison guards discover the holes. My vacation this year was really very nice. The movies were for free; I also played pinball with my friend. I have a good time with Dorian's cousin who is named Jean-Luc, and he is nice and cool and changes clothes all the time. My leg is okay, it doesn't hurt, just once a week my knee hurts. Everything is fine. Mommy feels fine, Daddy too, and me, too. Big hug to you and Aunt Ursula,
Your son

Piotrek

Rysiu dear!
Piotrek has decided to write in French, because he writes even worse in Polish. He came by himself by train from Sables, and I was simply mortified that Mme Mossé had simply placed him in the care of his fellow travelers, he came out of the train such a grown man, with people calling him *jeune homme*.
As for the letters that you've supposedly been writing, it strikes me as something of a fantasy, because everything was registered under all three last names, and the mail is forwarded regularly from Sextius Michel. And did you not get that decorative announcement from Romek?
In any case the point is that it's very lovely here, and we're living really well—when you and Mietek come you'll see.
I'm sending you a photo of the sculpture that I want to exhibit in your show, among others—I think it will be

something like *Embodied Machine* or *The Embodiment of the Machine* in translation, although that sounds awfully figurative for just a machine that has grown a body (flesh). Please put a picture in the catalogue, Jean-Louis Bloch-Lainé does my pictures for me here, and please credit him. I am doing lovely sculptures now, and everything *ça va*. The only thing worrying us is Piotrek's exam. Yesterday he went by coach just outside of Paris for his *cours Nadeau cours révision et préparatoire pour lycée*—we shall see.

Best to you and Urszula

Alina+Roman

[NOTE:]

The big sculpture with the revolving ring from the salon was bought by the museum [CUT OFF]

Paris le 26 sept. 64

Rysiu dear!
I got a letter from Dr. Leo a few days ago—very correct and in consultation with Mr. Lebenstein we are dealing with the transportation issue. I also wrote Mr. Leo back, giving him precise details (*Machine en chaire* is iron + cement, not bronze) dimensions, prices, etc. of the sculptures. I think it could be a very fine event. I am therefore writing you this very quick note to tell you to choose as the third one *Unmarried* and not *Armored*. It will be a newer and more fitting combination. Besides *Biological Sculpture* is a mixture of bronze with stone, so I prefer (absolutely) that that third be just bronze and newer than what was already at the Biennale and that I don't like at all anymore. Besides, if you are going to be there as it is being installed, please take care that the sculptures have an empty backdrop without any paintings and that they stand fairly concentrated as a whole (as being by a single artist), and not scattered around the rooms as amuse-bouches between paintings. If you're not going to be there, then write that director that—because lately at all the major events all the sculptures are always getting split up. I'll send you new photographs in the next few days, because Jean-Louis is going to be coming. It's really wonderful to work in this new studio, and I'm very happy that you and Mietek are coming.
We've been having a horrible time with Piotrek of late (among other things he has to wear glasses now because he's short-sighted!?!). Although the experts say that getting into middle school after a year in France was next to impossible. He speaks and even writes fluently (they fail you for three mistakes in dictation), but the literature and grammar program was immense, and

he doesn't even like to read (even in Polish), and he doesn't enrich his vocabulary with the dictionary, which they care about a lot here, and they have very competitive examinations, because they push the young into the crafts. I don't know what is going to happen because he exceeds the *limite d'âge* and any further process of elimination would mean technical trade school. But we'll see, for now he's doing his best, and this new school seems good—it's just burdensome and costly for us. Anyway you'll see everything for yourself when you're here.
Best to you both

Alina

[NOTE IN THE MARGIN:]
Buy him (Piotrek) a good Russian watch

116.

SZAPOCZNIKOW, PIOTR STANISŁAWSKI AND CIEŚLEWICZ TO STANISŁAWSKI

OCTOBER 2 [1964]

NOTES →[P 334]

Paris le 2 oct.

Dear Rysiu,
I received your letter of the 28th, it must have crossed paths with my last one. We'll probably talk soon, so for now just the specifics.
1. I would prefer if you didn't send *Duo*—I don't want to try and sell it because the cast is awful, and the model has been destroyed.
2. If you want me to have four sculptures, send *Unmarried* and *Armored.*
3. The prices for the sculptures sent from here I will send straight to Mr. Leo in francs, because that has nothing to do with Desa.
4. The price of *Unmarried* in bronze—1400 dol. = 700 dol. + 700 × 24 zl or 1400 × approx. 70 zl.
The price of *Armored* (*unique cire perdue*) 1200 dol. = 600 dol. + 600 × 24 zl or 1200 × approx. 70 zl.

Be so kind as to pass those prices along to Desa, because with the two possible exchange rates it's hard for me to give them in zlotys. I'm giving prices based on the estimate for the *Sculpture with a Turning Wheel* made from cement that's been bought by the Musée d'Art Moderne.
Piotrek is starting to really apply himself, his last little incident really upset him. Aside from that nothing new, for now hugs to you and Urszula

Alina + R. + P.

Paris 20.XII.64.

Beloveds, we wish you nothing but the best in the New Year of 1965.

Alina, Romek, Piotr

P.S. The stereo record player works perfectly, by now we've spent all we have on records, although even so they keep coming out with newer ones. Piotr brought home a distinction again for December. Your letters crossed paths. He (Piotr) will write himself in 3 days, he'll be on vacation.
Aside from that *ça va*! Business cards being printed.

SZAPOCZNIKOW AND PIOTR STANISŁAWSKI TO STANISŁAWSKI
[JANUARY 1965]
NOTES →[P 334]

Dear Dad,
Thank you for your letter from 3–I–1965. On the 1st of 1965 we drank champagne at midnight. We had turkey for three days. Our tree was big and pretty. We ate by candlelight on Christmas Eve. I got: roulette, shoes, a shirt, and a Soviet tank for Saint Nicholas Day. On Saturday the 16th our teacher was sick. Our teacher gave me a book by Curwood called *Les cœurs les plus farouches*. I have an A- in shop. I am doing good in school, I am the best at math. Kisses to you, my Aunt, and Ewa!

Piotrek

Rysiu dear!
Piotrek is enormously enamored of his teacher and has gone totally crazy about studying. I don't even recognize him anymore, I don't check up on him at all and he still studies all the time, and with results, in fact, because he managed to take a dictation with just one error (up until now he's been making 30–35) as well as to conjugate his verbs with no mistakes. It must be a question of motivation, because he's fallen in love with the teacher's daughter (10 years old).
Thank you very much for the Infeld, I read it, I found it very "timely," though it's full of truisms like "scholarship serves humankind," past that it reminds me of that old man that writes about death that posed for me at my studio very recently, not always comporting himself as would suit a scholar so distinguished.
I have heard nothing from Leo, nor anything about Kassel, nor about the return—so I await news.
Today's news of Churchill's death throes also means time has been passing.

I am working a lot and waiting for spring in order to begin glistening in the sunshine.
Best to all of you, i.e.
Urszula, you, Ewa, as well as
your friends and relatives

Alina

119.
SZAPOCZNIKOW TO STANISŁAWSKI
[FEBRUARY 22, 1965]
NOTES →[P 335]

Monday 22 [CUT OFF]

Rysiu dear!
This morning your postcard came from Amsterdam, which reminded me of my stay in that city and of its splendors. We went to La Coupole for dinner on Friday with Mrożek (who came here for a week), and Karpuszko showed up (straight from the plane), he'd just missed you in Holland, Restany came, too, Gamza and a couple of other friends of ours, international art brokers—the only person that wasn't there was you, and once more I had this sense of all the little pathways of contemporary art production intersecting.
Apropos—I've already spoken about this to Mrs. Olkiewicz, who says that the matter can be handled on the basis of a conditional clearance—it would be really important, then, that in addition to the two sculptures sent from here, *Unmarried* and *Armored*, the things from Kassel would come here for a bit. I have a string of very serious meetings and visits that I am putting off until my sculptures get back from Germany, this should bring "fateful" consequences, and it's important to me that the studio be full. Then I am supposed to exhibit at *Réalités Nouvelles* and at the Salon de Mai, and then on my own. Those sculptures would return to Poland with me and with my work from here if Desa asks for it sooner. And please write me when Kassel finishes, when I can expect my sculptures here, and who there is responsible for sending them, i.e. give me a name and an address in Germany in case anything comes up.
We're trying to help Mrs. Olkiewicz in terms of the exhibition insofar as we can—today we're supposed to hear back about a place that would be perfect for it. She'll tell you all about it.
Mr. Lebenstein invited us over (to reciprocate) and was

very nice up to the third bottle of Beaujolais, while over the 4th he told us that he knows about these little Warsaw games, that he doesn't give a shit about them, and that we played them all masterfully, in relationship to him, of course?!?! I think you'll "play" this with him again in Warsaw, although I wonder what he is talking about, maybe I am just too simple, and this is over my head?! Best to you and your ladies U + E. My men R + P— *ça va*— both progressing splendidly.

Alina

Paris 27.II.65

Rysiu dear!
I just wrote you a full letter that probably Mrs. Olkiewicz has given to you. Now I will just repeat the questions about the Kassel issue, because I already have invitations and precise dates for the exhibitions I'm taking part in.
So for *Réalités Nouvelles* I need to give them the sculpture by March 30th, and for the Salon de Mai March 25th. Please write to me immediately to let me know if I can count on the sculptures arriving by March 25th so that I can show them to someone prior to that date and choose.
And please try and make sure that all four make it here, because Very Important Sculpture People have scheduled visits. I await your answer
best,

Alina

Paris 1.IV.65
prima aprilis

Rysiu dear!
I'm writing only now (seriously despite the date) because I was waiting for Lebenstein to return, and thought he might tell me about some things I would need to respond to. We saw each other yesterday and went to a concert together. I got Piotrek's package, thank you, he'll add something in a moment, too. He didn't really say anything new. There's nothing new here, either, you'll probably see Stefan G., who can tell you about us, we've seen each other several times.
The sculptures from Kassel have not arrived yet. I got a letter from Desa. Mrs. Radziejowska adds that I should do something about that Perry woman, but I can't do anything, I don't even have her address. Could you please convey that to Mrs. Radziejowska if the opportunity arises?
Meanwhile I am informing you as the commissioner of "Sopot Similitudes" that I was happy to receive the invitation, and that I wrote to Stanisław Teisseyre, who had signed it, to ask for assistance with transport, because I would like to exhibit something new from here. He wrote to me after three weeks to say that he had the flu and that he was illiterate (in financial matters), and that Szymczak was on vacation, and that I should write to Giza and to Wilski, which I did a couple of days ago, and I am informing you of it. Maybe you could say something to them, too.
It's already spring here, and that is really "breaking" me, and we are dreaming of going off on vacation. We saw the movie *King Kong* recently. *Réalités nouvelles* opens Monday, so I have stage fright. Aside from that I'm just working, although slowly, or so it seems to me.
Best to you and the ladies,

Alina

Dear Dad,
The watch works good, the chocolate is really good, I haven't read the books yet. I saw *GOLDFINGER*, it is really neat. I am eighth in my grade.
The weather is wonderful, 68 degrees of warmth. How are you feeling, how are my Aunt and Ewa?
A kiss for you, for my Aunt, and for Ewa

Piotrek

NOTES →[P 336]

Paris 8.IV.65

Rysiu dear!
Piotrek set off today with Mme Mossé (Michelle's mother) and three other boys for a two-week vacation. I hope he'll write to you from there, because I told him to do so. I'm writing to you on business, or rather with a request that is very important for us. —Dobrochna probably told you that we will be here in the fall still (in connection with the Desa exhibition), assuming we receive the passports we asked for. —So we applied for them, Romek, me, and one for Piotrek, four months ago, with the support of Breza, and they were supposed to be issued by the beginning of March. We were supposed to come, then, for Easter, as a kind of surprise. But they screwed that up, and they said at the consulate that someone in Warsaw should intervene, because they have so much work there (in Warsaw). I wrote to Lucek about this, I even went so far as to say that you would explain to him the issue of my difficulties with the French visa, because you know what my files have been bogged down by starting back in canteen times—namely by you and your visits to the miners. So please find out at the passport bureau what the situation is now, and meanwhile I will describe our plans to you briefly, which in any case are set forth in the application: So—you know that I received a sculpture studio in Sopot—it was Horno-Popławski's, but he's retiring in two years. So the perfect period for Piotrek to be in school, because it's only now that he has really started studying, because he's supposed to be accepted to <u>boarding school</u> next year (I breathe a sigh of relief, and he's really getting his grammar and spelling down, and he will have Russian as his foreign language, so he should not have any problems making the transition to

school in Polish after that.) I have the kind of studio I won't get again, and lastly the sculptures and contacts are very promising. Romek is supposed to become the art director (he promised to let them know if he accepts as soon as he gets his passport), he is supposed to do a book on Eisensztajn for Julliard in the fall. But we can't be here for so long without a stay in Warsaw (apartment, studio), besides, if we could go, I could sculpt for 2–3 months in Warsaw and take part in exhibitions, Romek could come and oversee the credits he's doing for Wajda for *Ashes* and other things, he could also (if he had that passport) do fall fashion in Kazimierz, for example, as art dir. But nothing will come of these things, because it's not even trying again for the Polish passport that scares us, but the fact that we can't give up our *carte de séjour*, because it was given to us as a favor (in connection with my past). Meanwhile on the consular passport we can be in Warsaw even up to 6 months on an *aller-retour* visa. Please keep that information to yourself, I hope that this description has clarified the situation for you, and that you will know where to go for information and what to do. I would really like them not to disappoint us now and for us to be able to come for the summer. Please write—very best to you and to the Ladies,

Alina

[NOTE:]

The sculptures from Bochum still haven't come yet. ?

123.
SZAPOCZNIKOW AND CIEŚLEWICZ
TO STANISŁAWSKI
MAY 23, 1965
NOTES →[P 337]

Paris 23.V.65

Rysiu dear!
Thank you for your last long letter, which worked me up into a real travel fever. I saw Boudaille recently, he's also setting out for Warsaw, our voyage may even coincide with his. Our plans have crystallized a bit, in terms of the upcoming months. Everything was in enormous chaos in connection with the exhibits, invitations, etc. I was even supposed to participate this year in a symposium in California, but I didn't get in in time. In any case I will take part in the "Sopot Similitudes" thing. Our Commercial Councillorship is helping me with the transport of the sculptures, which I am sending some of straight to Sopot by sea, and then I'll do a bit more, because in June I'll already be in Warsaw. It would come in really handy if you could take Piotrek on some trip or other between 20–25 of June and July 20th. Romek unfortunately committed to working here until the end of July and won't be in Warsaw until the beginning of August.
Other than that there is an avalanche of exhibits and vernissages here right now, as well as friends passing through from Poland and the world. The May salon brought me new social and business contacts and the need for new work leads to an ever-increasing lack of time. I feel, though, that in Warsaw I will be able to work more peacefully.
I'm sure we'll run into each other somewhere in passing, and I'll tell you about everything in more detail. Please let me know if that exhibition Dobrochna was talking about here is going to happen?
Say hello to Marchiori for me and tell him I am going to be exhibiting something this year in Carrara, maybe he can be on the lookout for me there.
Best to you and Urszula and Ewa

Alina + Roman

SZAPOCZNIKOW AND CIEŚLEWICZ
TO CZARTORYSKA AND STANISŁAWSKI
DECEMBER 22, 1965
NOTES →[P 337]

Paris le 22.XII.65

Dear Rysiu and Urszulo

Meilleurs souhaits pour les fêtes de Noël et la nouvelle année!
Serdeczne życzenia Świąteczno Noworoczne!
With best wishes for Christmas and the New Year!
1966

I hope that between Warsaw and Łódź these wishes somehow reach you. Actually from within the walls of Paris I really envy you those 130 km that you traverse over snowy fields. I would really like to come back again for a bit but—impediments of a technical-financial nature restrain me from those unwise voyages at a heart's leap.
Piotrek is coming today for a 2-week vacation that we'll spend together, and then he is switching boarding-houses. I hope he'll manage to eke out a letter to you today about his scholastic progress.
Specifically we're all going to be working on things over the summer, and especially Romek, because of the Biennale. Apropos—Rysiu, I have a favor to ask of you—you probably remember Robert Wogensky, he's a tapisserie teacher in Paris and very connected with Aubusson textiles etc. Apart from that he's now doing very lovely things etc., etc. He would like to go to Warsaw for the Biennale (he's a friend of Picart Le Doux) and see all the people on the jury. I also told him about Abakanowicz, and he could do a lot around Paris in terms of spreading the word. So he needs some kind of invitation, to give a talk or something like that, if only just for our authorities and his. For official reasons, he wants to pay his own way. He is our very kind neighbor and friend, we could all travel together by car. In any case ask whoever

you can (Płaza?) (Władzio? UNESCO) to have some kind of invitation sent for him, to thank him if nothing else, R[OBERT] W[OGENSKY], 9 rue Bargue, Paris XI.
Let me know what you think but no matter what do something for him.
Otherwise Paris is defending itself as best it can against op. pop. stop, super op. and is getting more and more boring in its exhibitions in neglected rooms and galleries.

Dear Ones,
All I ask of you is that you accept my very best wishes to you all.
Did you see the new SECOND REALISM and SUPER POP —that the Americans did? I write and publish reproductions in the *Times* from December, 65.
My MINI-OP—is coming along richly, beyond expression. I've already applied for the '67 exhibition—I'm sure by then someone will be doing it better and more interestingly, but such is life. If Urszula's paper on my *photocherches* happens to come out, send it to me here. And what should we send you? Again my heartfelt good wishes and hoping that you are all in good health

—Romek

SZAPOCZNIKOW, PIOTR STANISŁAWSKI AND CIEŚLEWICZ TO STANISŁAWSKI
JANUARY 25, 1966
NOTES →[P 338]

Paris 25 janv. 65
[OBVIOUS MISTAKE IN THE YEAR: IT SHOULD BE 1966]

Dear Rysiu
Our letters crossed, because I was writing to you about various things while you were in Głuchów. In the meantime Piotrek has probably managed to squeeze out the letter he promised from the Golovanoffs' house, where he is currently staying.
It's a much more normal atmosphere there, because all 15 children are in the same situation, that is they have their parents in Paris, where they all come together for Saturday and Sunday. He also immediately improved in academic terms, as he is not being dumbed down by obscurantism with its pseudo-Makarenko methods, and he may skip a grade.
For now Romek is the one that has skipped ahead, and he is currently working at *Vogue*—which I think is enough said.
Aside from that can you believe I finally got the Copley Prize ($2,000 = 1,000,000 [CUT OFF]) for achievement in art. Among others on the committee were Marcel Duchamp, Darius Milhaud, Jean Arp, Man Ray, Sir Herbert Read, and the other winners were: Soulages, Matta, etc. We are finally relaxing now and can calmly think about returning to Warsaw.
Please call Stajuda about that prize, because I swore to him that I would inform him so that he could fit it in. Meanwhile the letter from Copley went to Warsaw, and it was a month before I actually got it when it came back.
Aside from that I am still working and beginning to destroy what I do over and over again, because I can't quite get at what I want. Almost like with Giacometti, in a way, whose death was a real ordeal for us personally. We recently went to a cocktail hour at Cérès' in honor of Penrosa and also some Brazilian critic, "an admirer

of Ewa Garszt." All of societ*ay* was there, and Cérès said that you were also coming to Paris soon, is that true?? She (C.) has now split up with Jean—the Brazilian-Romanian-Slav and is now I think romancing with Corneille, the Dutch painter. At Restany's I saw your friends the Morales, but they made almost as much fun of happenings as Sandauer, who is here now.
I'll stop there, and just ask you not to neglect to use the above information as appropriate.
Greetings to you and Urszula

Alina + Roman + Piotr

SZAPOCZNIKOW AND CIEŚLEWICZ
TO CZARTORYSKA AND STANISŁAWSKI
FEBRUARY 9–10, 1966
NOTES →[P 339]

Dear Rysiu,
We got your letter and the catalogue from Sweden. There were quite a few things left to take care of in accordance with your letter. Since a number of the matters you write about involve me—allow me to go ahead and "check them off" one by one.
1. We thank you for the <u>lovely</u> Pałka catalogue, exceptional plates—for that kind of paper and just generally interesting layout. You should all "use" Pałka more—he is one of very few authentic Polish graphic artists—living in oblivion, because he does things that are not that "snazzy," but very wise.
2. Thank you for the compliments on my posters. Did you see all three posters 1) *The Trial*—Kafka, 2) *The Circus*, 3) *May 1*? I sent that last one from Paris and still don't know if it made it on time, I don't want to ask either Mroszczak or Eryk—I would be very much obliged if you would let me know next time you write.
I sent Bojko the names of several people that ought to be invited to the Poster Biennale as journalists. These people are Georges Boudaille, Michel Ragon, Mr. René Salanon—a restorer at the Museum of Decorative Arts at the Louvre, etc. (I talked to them in person at Cérès' and they expressed a great desire to come!)—I have enclosed names, addresses, and telephone numbers with this letter on the assumption that neither Mroszczak's talk for *Trybuna Ludu* nor the interview with Ćwierciakiewicz in *Kultura* will give anyone in the world an idea of what the 1st Poster Biennale means. Strangle Bojko for a good cause! (If you find the time for it.)
3. With regard to the reproductions of your postcards, there is no question of contacting blasé Braun, or the others—that would just be a waste of time.

I can arrange for all of those things to be printed at the publishing house that the Polish priests run. They are very leftist, and there is no question of mistakes or distortions. Piotrek stayed with them when his leg was broken. They are anti-Wyszyński and anti-Piasecki—they have their own political agenda—making Poland into the center of the universe—and they carry it out with some success. They would probably agree to the postcards immediately, but I won't say anything to them until you agree. The technical conditions—Swiss—are top-notch (Skira!), and it is mutually beneficial, because it brings them great joy to be able to do something for Poland.
They were the ones that printed your business cards, because they're the only printing house in Western Europe that has a modern typeface with the Polish letters "Ł", "Ż", "RZ", "Ó", "Ę", "Ś" (and they are now printing you a second set, but not before late March—it's already ordered, though).
4. It's better at *Vogue* than at *Elle*—an incomparably better technical base. I don't know if it's available in Poland, but here they have four versions of *Vogue* that come out—the American one, the British, the Australian, and the French. The March issue is being done entirely by me, but I already have authorization for pages in the January and February issues, which I will send you (the French version).
5. I reiterate my request for Wogensky.
6. Copley—it's called the William and Noma Copley Foundation.

Officers and Directors:
William N. Copley
Noma Copley
Marcel Duchamp
Barnet Hodes
Eleanor Hodes
Darius Milhaud

Advisors:
Jean Arp
Alfred Barr, Jr.
Matta Echaurren
Max Ernst
Walter Hopps
William S. Lieberman
Man Ray
Roland Penrose
Sir Herbert Read
A. James Speyer
The grant is $2,000 (no reason to spread that around), and you'll have Chablis and steak or truffles (your choice)—to celebrate.
Our son has grown bigger even than expected. He is already wearing my shirts, ties, shoes.
Alina will give you the address and write you about what all has happened besides the Copley thing. Best to Urszula from me, I hope she writes us sometime, too.
Best

—Romek

[NOTE FROM SZAPOCZNIKOW:]

It's not a grant, as Romek mistakenly put it, but a prix for "young" artists for their activities and contributions in the field of the fine arts. I have the feeling that Speyer put me up for it, if you remember he really liked my work at the Biennale, and his sister has a salon here and sometimes invites me. I was complaining quite a bit about financial hardships in her presence a year and a half ago, and then I got a little note from Duchamp that on behalf of the Copley Fund he would like to visit the studio, and he also liked it, hence our friendship with M.D., which continues. In May of 1965 he told me that he had put me up for the prize for 1965, and that I would find out in November. I confess we were kind of counting on it, in coming, but we stopped believing it was going to happen, and in December I was very depressed that I had lost. Meanwhile the letter had gone on December 15th to Warsaw, and then returned to Paris on January 25th, and it was only then that I found out and collected almost 1 million AFS = 9,760 NF. Alina

[CIEŚLEWICZ'S NOTE TO SZAPOCZNIKOW'S NOTE:]

Its official name is FOUNDATION, so like funding or a grant, not a prize!

Paris le 9.II.66

Rysiu and Urszulo, dears!

Please convey our sincere congratulations to Ewa on her wedding. (I'll bring her gift)

Piotrek's address: chez Mme Golovanoff, Homme "La chanson," Janvry S-et-O.

Today I sent the pictures to Dr. W. Zanini.

Romek has written you about the Copley Fund, so disseminate it as you see fit in the fatherland, because for the first time just a humble old Pole etc., but make sure, though, that all the different officials and envious people don't kill it.

Pierre Restany just told me about Sweden, he made the same rounds just before Rysiek. He (P.R.) is a correspondent at *Vytvarna Prace* in Prague, and if it would be possible to invite him to the poster biennale in Poland, then he could write both here and there.

I've been invited to the symposium in Hořice—Č.S., I think I'll go, the conditions are good, and there are grand *rendez-vous* because of AICA.

Cérès asked me to tell Ryś that Candida was at her house to *dejeuner*. Cérès and Jean—the Brazilian—separated, and now she is "seeing" the painter Corneille, the Dutchman.

Past that much loveliness afoot for me, but I won't write about that yet so that I don't trip myself up. I'll let you

know next week the what and how, but write in the meantime.
I've done a lovely sculpture!
Romek was working till four in the morning all last week with different Avedons, Penns and others, because there was a collection photographed, and they hung up the models on real advertisements dug up on the street and brought into the studio.
We are probably going to the south for Easter, to reclaim our enfeebled health.
That cousin from Israel that Rysiek gave my address to came to visit and was horribly boring. That stranger poisoned our whole Sunday.
Find out from Stajuda the particulars, did he get my writing, does he want more, and will he put it in, and what will he put in?—because I haven't heard a peep from him.
A kiss, best wishes,

Alina

127.

SZAPOCZNIKOW TO CZARTORYSKA AND STANISŁAWSKI, POSTCARD FROM CARRARA, [MARCH 15, 1966]

NOTES →[P 341]

Rysiu and Urszulo dears!
Can you believe that a fan of my "fine arts" has funded this wonderful trip and rest cure following my chronic bronchitis? Thus I chip away at marble all day beneath the sunny skies of Italy and *sono tanto felice*! It is absolutely brilliant here. The mountains, the sea, and this sort of Italian Nowy Targ, the nicest people in the world, and all around nothing but renaissances. There are a couple of sculptors you know, Rysiu, Moore bought a little house from a peasant, and I think I shall do the same. Viva Carrara!
write something, Rysiu, best

Alina

128.
SZAPOCZNIKOW AND PIOTR STANISŁAWSKI TO STANISŁAWSKI
JULY 23, 1966
NOTES →[P 342]

23–VII–1966

Dear Dad,
Today I am writing you from VRNJAČKA BANJA (Yugoslavia). It's a town like Vichy in France.
Mom already finished one marble sculpture here.
Elle est trés belle, et maintenant elle a commencé une seconde sculpture.
I have to go back to Paris by August 22nd because I'm taking some classes so that I can go over 7th grade, because I'm skipping it.
How are you feeling, and Aunt Urszula?
Mom and I are very well.
My dad stayed in Paris. In about ten days Mom and I are going to Paris along the seacoast.
Where are you going on vacation?
Kisses, best to Aunt Urszula:

Piotrek

Rysiu dear!
We are in the heart of Serbia, somewhere in between Sarajevo and Belgrade, and we're doing very well here and are very well taken care of.
It's a lovely event, because it's not a symposium, it's just that every year the most distinguished sculptor that is a friend of the Republic does a sculpture for them in the beautiful park with hot springs. I'm the second. Last year Ernst Neizvestny broke out a 20-foot Centaur, so you can see that the order of the countries is being preserved.
I have the quarry they have taken marble from for the American Embassy in Warsaw available to me, so you must know it, a lovely blue-gray. I have two workers and a student from Belgrade on an apprenticeship, so the

work is moving along quickly in spite of me, my sculpture is just 8 tons, so by USSR standards directly proportional. Write to us here how you're doing, we're here till the 8 or 10th of August, and then we'll go to the sea for a bit. In September I'll be in Warsaw.
Lea Lublin left a very large file for you at my place in Paris, which I will bring in September.
Best to you and Urszula

Alina

Best to your friends and relatives

Paris le 19. sept. 66

Rysiu dear!
Today I received your letter from Poznań bearing the news of the death of your father.
All three of us send our sincerest condolences (what an idiotic word), but we are sincerely very saddened, and we feel for you.

Alina + Roman + Piotr

I'll be in Warsaw on the 25th, so the rest in person.

A.

Paris 4 12 66

Dear Dad!
Thank you very much for the three books and those two records. Everything is going good at school, except for English my best subject is math. I am going to Val d'Iser for the holidays. I'll be there at a camp of the Montaigne school in Paris. My parents are looking for an apartment right now because the one we are living in is too small for us. The weather is not that good. It rains a lot, and most of the time the sun doesn't shine.
How are you guys?
Everything is fine here. I have a runny nose, but nothing to complain of, really.
I'm ending there, it's seven o'clock. Big hug to you all.
Piotr

5.XII.66

Rysiu and Urszulo dears!
Already three weeks have passed since I made it safely back to Paris. I fell immediately into the mill of jobs and problems—i.e., looking for an apartment, because we have truly gotten sick of life in this room. We finally decided to do it and chose, based on different pros and cons, a modern apartment near Invalides and on the 10th floor with a so-called panorama. I think that within a month we'll be fully installed, and we hope to receive Ryś there when he "stops by" Paris.
The vernissage of my exhibition with Houston Brown has been nailed down to between April 3 and 12, 1967.
Rysiu, now down to business: Pierre Restany is going to be writing the introduction and also the introduction to the catalogue of the exhibition at the Zachęta that I am supposed to have in July. He's gotten very enthused

about that "presentation" and wants to come to Warsaw with us for the occasion, and to take the opportunity to give a lecture, something titled—and on the topic of: "Is Today's Rome New York or Paris?" with slides etc. You know he (Restany) is very clever and will do a great job, and for free, I think. But he did say it would be good if he were to receive a plane ticket *aller et retour*. I wrote to Giza about this. I haven't had a response, and he is already making some summer plans and so forth. Could you please take care of this or push them a bit and maybe you could take advantage and be able to do something in Łódź. I've been telling people here about the museum, which I really think is going to be very high-class. Write soon! What and how. Thank you for the kind reception in Poland. All best wishes Alina + Romek
p.s. write for now to Croix

—A.

131.

SZAPOCZNIKOW, PIOTR STANISŁAWSKI AND CIEŚLEWICZ TO CZARTORYSKA AND STANISŁAWSKI, DECEMBER 16, 1966

NOTES →[P 343]

Paris 16.XII.66

Urszulo and Rysiu dears!
I'm writing a second letter, because we're moving tomorrow already, and I have the new address: —14 passage Du Guesclin XVe. The apartment is lovely, on the 10th floor, and from the balconies you can see all of Paris. Unfortunately there is no telephone as of yet, but we should be getting one soon.
Rysiu! I got a letter today from Giza saying that she had gone to the BICC about that Restany thing, for them to invite him to come for a couple of days in conjunction with that lecture I wrote to you about. It's really important to me, because he is supposed to also be the one spearheading my exhibition, besides that the lecture and the problem are of great interest. But according to her letter she asked for a stay of just a couple of days— which is actually not that important, because he could even stay with us.
The main thing is the LOT ticket *aller et retour*, and of course the necessary invitation for him to get a Polish visa. Please push this with Markowski or wherever it is that it needs to be done, they really might as well send it to him, at least instead of the one Boudaille didn't use, and how much more interesting this guy is!
Besides that I have made a couple of interesting things out of plastic with light, Romek got a new journal to work on, *Opus International*, formerly *La Revue de poche*, J. C. Lambert, Lévêque, Fall etc. Piotrek bought himself a navy surplus coat (the latest in fashion) and now looks like a cadet from the movie of *Doctor Zhivago*. The holidays promise in these empty rooms to be nice and peaceful. How are things with you all?
We wish you happiness health and sweets in 1967.

Alina + Roman + Piotr

Paris 12.I.67

Rysiu dear!
Thank you for the letter. We are very pleased that you shall be gracing us soon. Here is our address: 14 passage Du Guesclin, Paris XV. There is no telephone yet, because the place is new. The métro stop is "La Motte Piquet" or "Dupleix." 10th floor. On Saturday or Sunday you can just come. Any other day in the morning before 10 and in the evening around 7. You can also call Romek (at *Elle*) any day but Saturday or Sunday from 11 to 1 and from 4 to 6: GUT88.00, extension 537, or call Mr. Santelli 253.45.74 and ask for me in the studio from 11 to 6.
Best to you and Urszula from all of us

Alina + Roman + Piotr

Vyšné Ružbachy
18 August 67

Rysiu dear!
Thank you for your letter, which soothed me somewhat. Maryta plagued me in person all the way up to the border at Łysa Polana. I deduce from your letter that you did not get the card I sent you immediately upon arrival. I'll do the photographs of the sculpture once I'm done with it, and you'll see it once you get to Paris, or else I'll send it to you from there. The conditions here are quite "Czech." I am enormously curious to know how you displayed my works at the Museum, did they have the right lighting? I.e. normal top-side + backlighting the transparency of the mouth.
If you are taking pictures, please send them, along with a picture of *Corrida*, which I don't have any photographs of at all.
I will be in Paris around September 1st, Piotrek is coming back on August 28th, Roman is complaining of loneliness. Restany wrote fondly recalling his trip to Łódź and saying he "prefers" Poles to Americans, from whom he has just returned to "cheer up" Roman with some nighttime excursions to Falstaff.
My very best to Urszula
Write immediately to let me know if Piotrek has a sister or a brother
Best

Alina

Paris 29 August 67

Rysiu dear!
I hope you received my letter from Vyšné Ružbachy.
Yesterday I returned to Paris after an arduous trip.
Piotrek is coming back from London in a week.
I found quite a few letters when I got home and many things to be taken care of.
Among other things, a letter from Maryta that made me very sad, in which in a sweet tone she assures me that I should not worry, but...: The two checks (each for 10 thou.) that I made out to her on August 15th could not be cashed and have now expired. Just in case I also gave her an authorization for Desa, for them to give her my advance for *Coffee Table,* and apparently they also received her quite badly there. Her check for 10 thou. remained but was dated August 30th and expired on September 9th. From Maryta's letter it turns out that she wasted her vacation because of me, and she can't fix her roof this season, and I put her at risk of getting into trouble with the bank and subjected her to Desa and to needless running around. Furthermore I am not supposed to worry because Maryta, if she doesn't get the money by September 9th, thinks she'll just collect it in the amount of 1000 N.Fr. and will finally be able to come to France. Rysiu! 100 kg of Maryta in Paris is a blow not to be borne! Besides which I am tremendously depressed that I have disposed of the most interesting works and have so many problems and even so can't even pay for our short vacation in Poland.
I am sending you a check for 20,000 zl, which is the amount I owe Maryta. Rysiu, I beg you to take care of this. I believe that you are the only one that can take care of it in the European manner. The check needs to be taken to the so-called "Roundagon" P.K.O. It's made

out to cash, and you receive the money without any formalities or issues. I'm dating it September 1st. If that money happens not to be there yet, add a zero, and it will be September 10th, and it is valid for 10 days, meaning it can be cashed in that case up to September 20th. By then the money will definitely be there, because what the Toruń Museum sent was transferred to me two days later by PAVA. —Take that money to Maryta. She lives on Kanonia 16a, you can find her phone number in the book, anyway. If she has already picked up the 10 thou. from her check, then just give her 10 thou., and with the remaining money open up a savings book for a car in my name. If she hasn't picked it up, give her all of it, and have her destroy her check. I don't think it will cause you any major inconvenience, and you would really be doing me a huge service, in any case I don't see anyone else that could take care of this matter for me in an equitable way.

I came back from Slovakia through Prague, Nuremburg, Zurich, Ronchamp (Giacometti, Le Corbusier). I stopped for a couple of hours in Zurich and looked in the windows at Globus. I saw Mr. Kaufmann, who has already received the sculpture and expressed great satisfaction with it. So I don't understand why Desa received Maryta so poorly, and why they don't send my money. Please ask about that, and write and tell me what I should do and what seems to be going on.

I would really like to get down to some quiet work, but this constant nonsense keeps tearing me away from it. I withdrew from the Borrolatto exhibit, I don't want to get distracted.

I've already spoken on the phone with Restany, he is back from America, tomorrow we are supposed to meet, he said to say hello to you and that he recollects his Polish experiences with great pleasure.

Romek is at work on all fronts, I think you'll be seeing him soon as well as on Polish walls.

I look forward to hearing back from you as soon as possible.
Best to you both
kiss

Alina

135.

SZAPOCZNIKOW, PIOTR STANISŁAWSKI AND CIEŚLEWICZ TO CZARTORYSKA

OCTOBER 9, 1967

NOTES →[P 345]

Paris 9.10.67

Urszulo dear!
I am returning the card that came after Rysiek left.
I am writing to you because Rysiek told me how kind you were about dealing with the 10,000 zl. that were left after paying my debt to Maryta.
Thank you and apologies for the inconvenience. Please send me the number of the car savings book that I heard you've opened in my name. This will allow me to follow the results of the drawing in the papers, which we buy here on a regular basis.
As long as nothing has changed with those books, you should still have 1000 zl. Mr. Józef Borzym, our administrator from Old Town, is going to contact you, be so kind as to give him that money, because this is another of my "pressing" debts.
I hope you still feel as well as you were feeling when I last saw you in Poland.
We eagerly anticipate the announcement of Piotrek's brother's or sister's name.
All most favorable etc. wishes
Best to you
and to Rysiek

Alina + Roman + Piotr

Paris. 13.V.68.

Dear Rysiu,
Thank you for the letter. The fulfillment of your request for copies of *Domus* is under way. Thanks to Alina—Restany will prompt the sending of more than two issues straight from Milan to your address in Łódź. I understand your concern about this well, I've been asking Mroszczak, Bojko, Wróblewska, etc. for a year—for 1 (one) issue of the latest *Projekt*, and I can't wait. I know Restany's article, but I felt it to be more of a glorification of your institution.
The biennale in São Paulo is no longer an option, and there's no point in talking any more about the ensuing disputes. They were local issues and just among yourselves. It seems to me that it was César who opened his big Mediterranean mouth—not Restany—they say Restany is a reactionary critic—but he's done more for Poland than all the leftists put together (in Paris, obviously.)
Our holiday plans are very limited despite many invitations. Alina: Italy, Yugoslavia, me: Switzerland, Germany—all of that is professional travel—though our passports have still not come in from Warsaw yet. I really want to be at the II Biennale in Warsaw and Krakow at any cost. Time flies. Everything depends on our passports. We have a letter from Boguś P. from November '67 saying "Things are underway." While we call the consulate about every 10 days. —Nothing.
Thank you for thinking of me and putting me in the exhibition. Please send the catalogue. I am sending you Lebenstein's catalogue, which I had the honor of doing. I'll send you the 6th issue of *Opus* if I get a big print run. Student riots still going on in Paris—cars and shops burning, strikes, some streets with no one in them.

Polish May: exhibiting Kwaśniewska, Buczkowski, Pągowska, Lebenstein. Alina at Objet III, Salon Jeune Peinture, Jeune Sculpture, Viètnam [CUT OFF]
I've printed a few posters, and I'm now putting together the biggest collage in the world. —Alina will write you the rest, about Piotrek and about life.
Sincere good wishes to the three of you

—Romek

Dear Stanislawskis,
One can't endure any more here, every day someone opens something very important, and sometimes there are 3–4 events a day. Even Ms. Darthea Speyer has started up a huge new gallery, probably to spite Mr. Sonnabend next door, and enormously American, even her brother James came from Chicago.
I don't go anywhere anymore, because we spend our days at a factory for these totally sensational plastics, where we're conducting experiments, photos of which I'll send you soon. You'll see the first in *Opus*, repeated for now, a model in plaster. There will be up to 50 of them made out of soft plastic, while two like in the model will be made in Querceta in white marble, 240 cm tall. I'll go there, then swing over to the biennale, where we will probably see each other?! Pierre wrote to *Domus* to have the whole so-called press print run, i.e., 6 issues sent to your address, and here you are already "heading out," which will probably be even faster than our possibly sending out things. Too bad you didn't give *Modus* the pictures of my sculpture at the museum. What is the deal with São Paulo, and how should I get going with it?!
Piotrek is taking his end-of-the-year exam in a month and is cramming as much as his inborn laziness allows
Ciao! Kisses

Alina

Rysiu, I hope that in Rijeka you award me a prize for my very beautiful drawing, and let it [CUT OFF]

A.

SZAPOCZNIKOW, PIOTR STANISŁAWSKI AND CIEŚLEWICZ TO STANISŁAWSKI
OCTOBER 16, 1968
NOTES →[P 347]

16.X.68 Wednesday

Dear Rysiu
Your letter arrived right as I am leaving for Brussels. But I'll be back by Friday.
You can stay with us and sleep in Piotrek's room, he has a second bed now. It's low season anyway, so if you aren't comfortable here, you'll be able to find something else whenever you wish. You have the number, although we're not at home during the day. Call as soon as you get to the airport.

best A + R + P

we're very happy that
we'll get to talk with you

NOTES →[P 347]

Paris. 20.XII.68.

Dear Rysiu, we wish you, Urszula, and Olga a good year for 1969. Strumiłło was here. We hope you are informed as to the difficulties and to the advantages.
I can start on the poster and the catalogue now, I'm just waiting on the formatting, text, dates, etc.—from you. Olo W. called us yesterday and will be here the 26th. When he returns, we will send you Pluchart's book *Du cubisme à l'abstraction réaliste* with him, which contains a few pages dedicated to the main figures gracing your museum. That's all for now, we await your news
Kisses to the family —Romek

P.S. Piotr is skiing in the mountains.

1969
Heartfelt wishes for the holidays and the new year for all three

Alina

Rysiu, I told Andrzej in great detail about (and showed him) the book that just came out today in which François Pluchard describes, with <u>all</u> the names and titles, the history of Polish Unism as one of the most important movements in the daily realities of art today, Andrzej showed no interest, so we'll send the book with Olo, with whom Janek Lebenstein put us in touch

A.

139.
SZAPOCZNIKOW AND PIOTR STANISŁAWSKI TO STANISŁAWSKI
LETTER LEFT IN STANISŁAWSKI'S APARTMENT IN WARSAW, [JULY 1969]
NOTES →[P 348]

Saturday

Rysiu!
In the end we're leaving only now, Saturday, 7 a. m. I'll be here on the 30th for Romek, and we'll go August 3rd. Then at the end of August we'll be here again for three days before we leave. I hope that's no problem. I've already used up 1449 zlotys and 99 groszys on phone calls, but I suppose we can settle accounts at the end. A couple of morsels were left over in the refrigerator, so please eat them and then maybe unplug it. It doesn't quite shut (the fridge), you have to slam it. I got three ordinary letters from Romek yesterday, but I still no sign of the large envelope with the materials in it (?!?)
best

A + P

NOTES →[P 348]

Chałupy 18.VII.69

Rysiu dear!
Thank you for the letter you sent.
I really don't understand how that happened with your poor refrigerator. Piotrek and I were so happy to be leaving you a couple of tasty morsels (including an excellent duck pate), evidently in my morning haze (it was 5 a.m. when we were leaving) I simply unplugged it.
Aside from that I forgot to include in the note that we took the liberty of borrowing Simenon's "Maigret" series, very useful here. The weather is lovely, and one is really able to rest up wonderfully here. We saw Urszula and Olga, and both look terrific. It would be great if you came.
I hope we see you again before our final departure.
Best

Alina

Dad!
Thank you for your very kind words that you sent to me by letter.
I hope to see you here at least one day. I have already gotten my first birthday present from my mother, it is a Zorka-4 that I think is very good.
I am having a great time here and have a ton of girlfriends and friends. Yesterday Mom and I went to see Urszula. Olga is great tanned with golden hair.
I'm waiting for you and send you a big hug.

Piotrek

SZAPOCZNIKOW AND CIEŚLEWICZ
TO STANISŁAWSKI
JANUARY 24, 1970
NOTES →[P 348]

Paris 24.I.70

Rysiu dear!
Yesterday I applied for a Dutch visa and am slowly starting to get ready for my long stay in Amsterdam. I'm also starting to pull together my documentation, so as to have it with me. Please send me that transparency from *Domus* that ended up with you and that you promised to return. Obviously if aside from that you could make me slides or at least black-and-white photographs of *Corrida*, *Leg*, and *Portrait*, I would be very grateful and would reimburse you immediately.
Nothing new here. Fortunately Piotrek's surgery went wonderfully well, and yesterday Dr. Gotlieb used a special microscope to show me the new eardrum that has already "taken" inside his ear. The surgery (anesthesia) took 2½ hours, was not dangerous but was extraordinarily delicate. July 5th they'll do the right ear. Because this is all taking place at one of the most elegant clinics in the XVIth (Clinique Spontini), as Dr. Gotlieb is a collector and will be receiving a sculpture, Piotrek laments he doesn't have a third ear, he so likes all the little buttons and devices around his bed, the little tables on wheels and the food they give him when he wakes up. We are hoping the next surgery is as successful as the first, and that Piotrek will be fully recovered in time for summer vacation.
Best to you and a kiss to Olga, Urszula and you.

Alina

My dears,
I will write you shortly
a full letter, for now a big kiss
to all three

—Romek

NOTES →[P 348]

Tuesday 28.9.71

Dear Rysiu
It appears from your letter that you will be in Lausanne when I am in Geneva. I am coming to Geneva on Monday the 4th.
Romek is coming on the 7th for the vernissage. It would be nice if you would come, too—after all it's an hour away, and it would give us the opportunity to drink to all the vernissages.
Besides that on the 7th there is the general opening of the Geneva gallery season, and the collective vernissage of the old town
best

Alina

NOTES

AGATA JAKUBOWSKA

1

LETTER →[P 13]

[AUGUST 2, 1948]

The village is utterly tiny, 110 inhabitants, beautifully ensconced in a valley. [...] *My hosts' home is a half-destroyed little cottage*—In early August, 1948, Alina Szapocznikow took a vacation in the village of Champagne-sur-Loue in the French Jura. She stayed in an old house belonging to Helena and Julien Lustre. Helena was Jewish and had known Szapocznikow's parents in Poland. She helped the artist at the beginning of her stay in Paris, providing a studio in the form of a closed textiles workshop. Szapocznikow would remain in touch with the Lustres for many years and would stay with them during her trips to Paris in 1956 and 1958.

They played musettes—musette means "bagpipes" in French and is also the name of an eighteenth-century dance, which in time grew to be the name of folk celebrations set to accordion music.

they kept playing "Pigalle"—"Pigalle" is the name of a waltz played by such village accordion bands.

Mosquitos = moustique (moo-steek)—Szapocznikow sometimes supplies Stanisławski with French words in her letters. It is not known when she learned French; she may have known it already before the war. We know from the statements of her Czech friends describing the beginnings of her stay in Prague in 1945 *that she quickly learned Czech and spoke without any accent*, which may point to unusual linguistic capabilities [Věra Janoušková, for: Tomáš Pospiszyl, *Alena Szapocznikova w Pradze*, http://www.obieg.pl/teksty/13571, date of access: September 20, 2011].

tell Ivo—Probably Ivo Rublič (born 1917), Czech graphic artist and painter.

2.

LETTER →[P 15]

[AUGUST 4, 1948]

The form of your ideas completely reminds me of Camus' Etranger, *and actually the whole thing is a little bit like Dygat's* Lake Constance—Szapocznikow references the titles she is reading both in French and in Polish. She most likely read Albert Camus' novel *L'Étranger* in French (the Polish edition of *The Stranger* did not appear until 1958, while the French came out in 1942), while we do not know what language she read Stanisław Dygat's *Lake Constance* in. It appeared in Poland in 1946, but in France just one year later in a translation by Stanisław Dygat's father, Antoni Dygat.

I never thought that money would get in my way like this—Mention is made often of financial woes in these letters; this is the first time it comes up. Ryszard Stanisławski was not making a great living working nights at Paris' Les Halles (the market, the old Les Halles that was torn down in 1971). In the preceding summer months he took preparatory courses in French language and civilization. From the academic year of 1948–1949 on, he enrolled in the museum studies program at the École du Louvre. After his first round of exams he was awarded a scholarship from the "Entraide Universitaire Française" (International Federation of Students), but it was very modest.

Please, before you do go, send me Mietek's address—Mieczysław Szabliński was a friend of Stanisławski's from the First Polish Armored Division. They came to Paris together, whereupon Szabliński took up his studies at the École Nationale Supérieure des Beaux-Arts. There he met Alina Szapocznikow; he later introduced her to Stanisławski. He was one of the couple's closest friends at the beginning of their relationship. After Szabliński left Paris (probably in 1949), they gradually fell out of touch with him.

pour Alena S.—for Alena S. (French)—Szapocznikow, arriving in Prague right after the war, gave Český Těšín as her place of birth (in fact she was born in Kalisz, Poland). In documents extant from that period she appears by the Czechified name of Alena Šapočniková.

my mom wrote to me that she was sending money—Alina Szapocznikow received financial assistance from her mother, who repeatedly sent her money, always through a third person (the logistical details come up often in the letters).

Szapocznikow's mother Ryfka (after the war she used the name Regina), *née* Auerbach (1890–1961), was a pediatrician. Mother and daughter spent the greater part of the war together in ghettoes and camps, though they were separated a few months before the end of the war. After the war, Szapocznikow was sure that no one from her family had survived. While it is true that her brother Mirosław died in January, 1945, in the concentration camp at Litoměřice, her mother, whose wartime circumstances are also not fully known, went back to Poland and settled in Łódź. She found her daughter through the Red Cross. Věra Janoušková, a friend of Szapocznikow's from Prague, recalls that after returning from her first visit to her mother Alina extracted from her brassiere a wad of bills and said, *"Girls, we're going to the beach!"* [...] *Alina's mother—the mother of a child of the camps, who was humble, simple, defenseless—wanted to return to life before the war. She would give her lovely dresses, dress her. We saw a different Alina, different from the one we had been used to. Suddenly she became the daughter of a wealthy bourgeois family* [Janoušková, *op. cit.*].

3.

LETTER →[P 18]
[AUGUST 8, 1948]

d'abord—first (French).

L'Humanité—French daily newspaper founded in 1904, main publication of the French Communist Party from 1920–1994.

I am more concerned about the fate of my correspondent on the Boulevard Raspail—Ryszard Stanisławski was living at 5 Boulevard Raspail at the time.

It really wouldn't be the worst thing in the world to go to those Polish country folk—The reference is to seasonal work in the country. Andrzej Vincenz (born 1922, Polish literary critic, writer, later a professor of Slavic literatures at the University of Göttingen), a friend of Stanisławski's from Maisons-Alfort, a suburb of Paris where they lived for a time, had taken a job in the country in the summer and was trying to convince him to do the same.

My friend from Prague wrote that he wants to claim his emigration pass [passport] *and come here and live with me*—She is referring to the Czech sculptor Bedřich Stefan (1896–1982), with whom she had had a relationship during her time in Czechoslovakia. From October 1946 he was a professor at the Academy of Arts, Architecture and Design, where she was studying. Neither hid their romance, although Stefan was married, and Szapocznikow was also with someone else, a fellow student named Zdeněk Palcr. After she left Prague, they didn't see each other again until the fall of 1948, when Stefan came for a few weeks to France. In Szapocznikow's letters she speaks of him as "my friend," "uncle," and later as "Bedo."

Mr. S. Dygat wrote about that in his book Lake Constance. *He writes that "love is a negative feeling, we feel its lack when it is far away from us"*—The actual words of one of *Lake Constance's* main characters, Mac Kinley, are: "Love is not happiness, it's simply that not having love is torture. The workings of love are negative."

Les Lettres françaises—A literary journal that came out on the first Thursday of every month as a supplement to *L'Humanité*, publication of the French Communist Party. Szapocznikow mentions it often, sometimes erroneously as *Lettre*.

It might seem a bit paradoxical to you that I am sending you a Madonna—Szapocznikow was Jewish, but she came from an assimilated family and had gone to Polish schools before the war. From her son's account as well as from her letters, we can see that—like the majority of assimilated Polish Jews (or Poles of Jewish ancestry)—she celebrated Christmas: *We always spent it in Warsaw. We would get ready for the holidays for two weeks so that we could spend from December 24 to January 6 resting and receiving guests. —Was it a traditional holiday? —It was a Polish Christmas, with the traditional dishes for Christmas Eve and a Christmas tree* [Excerpts from conversations with Piotr Stanisławski and Joanna Pużyńska in *Pokaz*, no. 23 (1998), p.26]. From Ryszard Stanisławski's accounts we know that living in France after the war, she also maintained contact with religious Jews and sometimes took part in religious ceremonies [Ryszard Stanisławski in conversation with Jola Gola, winter 1997–8, Jola Gola Archive]. During her second period in Paris (beginning in 1963) Szapocznikow also worked with the Society of the Catholic Apostolate (the Pallottine fathers), on which more below. Sarah Wilson discusses the Christian elements in Szapocznikow's work in her article "Alina Szapocznikow in Paris: Worlds in Action and in Retrospect," in *Alina Szapocznikow: Awkward O*bjects, edited by Agata Jakubowska, Warsaw, 2011.

4.

LETTER →[P 21]

[AUGUST 12, 1948]

Kuźnica—"Forge" in Polish, a weekly social and literary publication that came out between 1945 and 1950, run by a group of intellectuals and writers with a Marxist orientation. The editor-in-chief was first Stefan Żółkiewski, then Paweł Hoffman.

Odrodzenie—"Renaissance" in Polish, a weekly publication founded in 1944, a socio-cultural magazine that politically backed the post-war communist regime. The magazine was first directed by Karol Kuryluk, then by Jerzy Borejsza. From the union of *Odrodzenie* and *Kuźnica* there arose in 1950 *Nowa Kultura* ("New Culture"), which continued until 1963.

Les Cafards, the French translation of Maxim Gorky's short story *Lower Depths*, appeared in Paris in 1928.

Je passai près d'un an en prison...—"I spent almost a year in prison. There I made the acquaintance of a band of thieves: that got me out of jail, bringing a swarm of police down on me. I killed people, it's very simple. Now I am a bandit myself. I would also be an executioner. It makes no difference to me." (French)

Jean-Paul Sartre (1905–1980), French philosopher, writer, and literary critic.

Don't go around with that awful spleenful Johnny—Most likely John Carson Parker. According to information from the letters of Andrzej Vincenz [in the Ryszard Stanisławski Archive], Stanisławski *arranged an apartment for him* in Paris.

Maybe Jasio didn't want to go with you—Most likely she is speaking of Jan Jasiński, who is mentioned often in the letters later on.

5.

LETTER →[P 24]

[AUGUST 1948]

My comrade—This is in reference to Bedřich Stefan, mentioned above, who was in France from September 29 to November 7, 1948, sent by Prague's Academy of Arts, Architecture and Design where he worked. The real reason for his trip to Paris was his desire to establish a life together with Szapocznikow, but she rejected his proposal. For many years they remained in touch, as evidenced by the dozen or so letters from Stefan preserved in the Alina Szapocznikow Archive, the last from 1968. She also mentions him on numerous occasions in her letters to Stanisławski.

to Vallauris, Picasso's little town—Pablo Picasso (1881–1973) was living in Vallauris (in the region of Provence-Alpes-Côte d'Azur) in 1948.

6.

LETTER →[P 27]

[OCTOBER 9, 1948]

Amour nouvelle chasse l'ancienne—New love chases out the old (French), a quote from André Le Chapelain's seventeenth-century treatise *De Amore*.

strikes in France—The post-war crisis was intensifying in France during this period, and in 1948, long-term strikes occurred in the coal mines that had been nationalized two years earlier.

11.

LETTER →[P 33]

[NOVEMBER 4, 1948]

come tomorrow (Friday) evening to Crillon to Dr. Russak's house—7, rue Crillon housed the outpatient clinic of the Polish Red Cross (Dispensaire de la Croix-Rouge Polonaise). She is no doubt referring to Dr. H. Russak, the general practitioner and dermatologist whose card is preserved in the Ryszard Stanisławski Archive (Docteur H. Russak—Ancien externe des Hôpitaux de Paris—Médecine Générale—Maladies de la Peau).

12.

LETTER →[P 34]
[DECEMBER 23, 1948]

At the end of 1948 and beginning of 1949, Szapocznikow spent a few weeks in Poland, staying with her mother in Łódź (4 Wólczańska St. apt. 5), spending New Year's Eve in Zakopane, a popular skiing destination at the foot of the Tatra Mountains.

Then Prague, and I am cold, sad, hungry, and then the Polish consulate and now leaving on a Polish train—This stop in Prague may have had to do with the fact that Szapocznikow was carrying documents showing Czech citizenship for some time (cf. note to letter 2). In France in 1948, when she was trying to get a Polish passport, it was realized that her documents contained conflicting information as to her place of birth (the true information about Kalisz as well as the false Český Těšín intended to facilitate her 1945 stay in Czechoslovakia). Szapocznikow was accused of illegally coming to France under an assumed name and nearly deported, though the courts ultimately ruled in her favor. It was a period of worsening Polish-French relations, which manifested itself in numerous deportations as well as in clamping down in visa policy.

13.

LETTER →[P 36]
[DECEMBER 25, 1948]

Because in fact they have everything here [...] *all the good books are getting published here, whether they're by Albert Camus or Vera Panova*—Alina Szapocznikow emphasizes the openness of the Polish authorities' cultural policy, but her examples are a good illustration of the fact that although the process of Sovietization of culture had at that time not yet reached its apogee, the writers that were promoted were above all those sympathetic to Communism. The writings of the existentialists were published, including those of Albert Camus (Szapocznikow is no doubt thinking of a piece in some journal, because no book by Camus had yet appeared in Polish at the time), as well as those of Soviet writers like Vera Panova (1905–1973), whom she mentions here, whose popularity was ensured by the novel *Sputniki* ("Fellow Travelers," published in English as *The Train*, 1946, Polish edition 1947) about the fates of hospital-train personnel members during the Second World War.

While Adam sits with Krysia "at theirs" under the Christmas tree—Adam and Krystyna Leśniewski. Adam Leśniewski went to school with Szapocznikow's brother before the war. He studied law in the late 1940s, while his wife, Krystyna, studied sociology.

They opened up a film school here—The film school in Łódź was established in 1948 (now known as: The Leon Schiller National Higher School of Film, Television and Theatre).

I'm sending you Wiech because on the other side you have little notes on the visual arts in Poland—She's talking about one of the feuilletons of Stefan "Wiech" Wiechecki, commentaries on life in the Polish capital written in contemporary Warsaw slang, published at that point in *Przekrój*, among other venues. In issue 193/194 from 1948, Wiech's feuilleton is located on p. 27, and on p. 28 there is a brief note on exhibitions at the National Museum in Warsaw, in the Palace of Art in Krakow, and an advertisement: *Don't be dummies! Try and get the problematics of modern art. Read* Przegląd Artystyczny *(monthly) and* Głos Plastyka *(a lovely periodical)*.

There's also an exhibit of Dunikowski in Warsaw, and I'm thinking of going in a week—From late 1948 to early 1949 at the National Museum in Warsaw there was a "Xawery Dunikowski (1908–1948) Jubilee Exhibition." The Polish sculptor Xawery (Ksawery) Dunikowski (1875–1964) was considered at the time to be—as the catalogue from that exhibition somewhat exaggeratedly states—"the greatest artist of our time." Although, as Szapocznikow makes clear in her letters, she did not in fact rate him very highly, it is, however, clear that he was a very significant point of reference for sculptors. He enjoyed the recognition of the authorities—at the "Great Exhibition of the Works of Xawery Dunikowski" organized a bit earlier at the Palace of Art in Krakow in the fall of 1948 he was awarded one of the highest state decorations, the Polonia Restituta Order of the Renaissance of Poland.

9 pelotes of black wool—9 balls of wool (French).

14.

LETTER →[P 39]
[JANUARY 7, 1949]

our "Italian" money—Szapocznikow and Stanisławski were planning a trip to Italy that ended up not happening.

In the next few days you should receive a package from some former patient of my mother's, her last name is apparently Kantor. Eat to my health—Sending packages (like sending money) through trusted intermediaries was widespread at that time: *Sending letters and packages to and from Poland was predominantly accomplished as opportunities arose. Sending even little packages by mail almost didn't figure into it at all. They took forever to get from one country to another. And no one wanted to pay the taxes levied by the Polish authorities on even small items of no commercial value. No one wanted to deal with the formalities or have to make small purchases from the customs office.* [Marcin Kula, *Mimo wszystko bliżej Paryża niż Moskwy. Książka o Francji, PRL i o nas, historykach* ("Nonetheless Closer to Paris than to Moscow: A Book about France, the People's Republic of Poland, and about Us Historians"), Warsaw, 2010, p. 472.] The person conveying this package in one of the subsequent letters is not Kantor, but Kantorowicz.

I don't know why I haven't gotten a response from your father—Ryszard Stanisławski's father was Romuald Stanisławski (1890 or 1891–1966), who lived at that time in Sompolno near Koło. Ryszard Stanisławski's mother Maria died in 1931 at the age of 41.

Alina Wnuk—Stanisławski met her in Wrocław in 1946. In a few somewhat later letters she writes to Stanisławski about "our Wrocław spring of '46" [Ryszard Stanisławski Archive]. In 1948 she moved to Warsaw, where she completed her studies in medicine and lived and worked for the remainder of her life.

15 janvier—January 15 (French).

Morskie Oko—A hotel in Zakopane built in the nineteenth century, a cultural meeting place with a theater and exhibition space designed by Stanisław Witkiewicz.

the feast of the Three Kings—The common name for Epiphany, a Christian holiday commemorating the manifestation of the newborn Jesus to the Magi from the East. In the Catholic Church, Epiphany is celebrated on January 6.

Tytus Chałubiński (1820–1889), Polish doctor and naturalist, advocate of the healing properties of Zakopane. Stanisław Witkiewicz (1851–1915), Polish painter, architect, writer, advocate of the Zakopane style. Both were buried at the Pęksowy Brzyzek Cementary in Zakopane.

Crusaders is the four-volume novel by Zofia Kossak (married names Szczucka and Szatkowska, 1889–1968), describing the history of the first Crusades, first published in 1935.

Ewa Olszewska (born 1927), sculptor, the only Polish woman Szapocznikow mentions meeting in Prague in her letters. She most likely did not graduate from Prague's Academy of Arts, Architecture and Design. Her teacher Karel Pokorný (1891–1961) is recognized as one of the most important Czech sculptors of the first half of 20th century.

"Uncle"—a reference to Stefan Bedřich, mentioned above.

Henri Matisse (1869–1954), French painter and graphic artist, co-founder of Fauvism.

Giewont—A massif in the Polish Tatras, important in Polish mythology: the outline of its ridges is reminiscent of a sleeping knight. Atop the Giewont is a tall iron cross.

Please try to get both [crossed-out], *it's the only effective means*—In this and subsequent letters, the details pertaining to health problems were effaced.

15.

LETTER →[P 48]
[JANUARY 1949]

Ballad of Siberia—A film by Ivan Pyryev released in the USSR in 1947.

16.

LETTER →[P 49]
[JANUARY 10, 1949]

I immediately called up 25 Sompolno Kolskie—Stanisławski's father Romuald lived at the time in Sompolno near Koło, where he had settled after the First World War. After the Second World War, he worked in state-owned dairy plants (before the war he was the owner of a dairy), first (until 1951) as director in Sompolno, and then in Poznań, where he was transferred.

Yesterday I went by taxi to Pabianice [...] *My visit also stunned the town, and people would come up to me and say, are you, by any chance, "that one"?*—Alina Szapocznikow's birth certificate indicates Kalisz as her place of birth, though her family lived in Pabianice at that time, and that was where the artist spent her childhood. Before the war (she was 13 when it broke out) she went to Polish elementary school in Pabianice, then to the Saint Hedwig State School, where the number of girls of Jewish ancestry was strictly limited; there were only two in Szapocznikow's class, herself and Rita, later Hilton, from whom we have this information. After the outbreak of the Second World War, she and her mother and brother (her father had died in 1938 of tuberculosis) wound up in the ghetto that had been opened in Pabianice, and when that was liquidated, they were sent to the Łódź ghetto. Pabianice is located about ten kilometers outside Łódź.

he visited his old burg on a consular passport—Passports of this type were issued in the era of the People's Republic of Poland to Polish citizens with permanent residence abroad.

mignonne—cute (French).

Alphonse Daudet (1840–1897), French novelist and writer of short stories.

17.

LETTER →[P 51]

[JANUARY 11, 1949]

Maybe you would go to the Cité and lie down?—Paris' Île de la Cité houses part of the Assistance Publique—Hôpitaux de Paris complex, including the oldest hospital in Paris, the Hôtel-Dieu.

Arts—A weekly magazine appearing from 1945–52 (previously known as *Beaux-Arts*), published by the gallerist Georges Wildenstein. His family had also published the monthly magainze *Gazette des beaux-arts* since 1928.

Polish Folk Art—*Polska Sztuka Ludowa*, a magazine founded in 1947 (the editor-in-chief was Józef Grabowski), is still published today under the name *Konteksty. Polska Sztuka Ludowa. Antropologia kultury-etnografia-sztuka* ("Contexts: Polish Folk Art—Cultural Anthropology—Ethnography—Art.")

18.

LETTER →[P 52]

[JANUARY 13, 1949]

The critics write that he's the Polish Rodin—Helena Blum, for example, writes not only of the similarities between Dunikowski's early *Pregnant Women* and Rodin's *Burghers of Calais*, but also of the artistic vision that predominates in both, which *matures in the psyche of the artist*, and when it comes to the execution of the work, *it is whole, encompasses form as well as the so-called inner contents* [Helena Blum, "Xawery Dunikowski na tle rzeźby europejskiej," *Przegląd Artystyczny*, no.12 (1948), p. 2].

Aristide Maillol (1861–1944), French painter, sculptor, and graphic artist.

Georges Braque (1882–1963), French sculptor, co-founder with Picasso of Cubism.

19.

LETTER →[P 54]

[JANUARY 17, 1949]

140,000 functionaries from the Department of Security and the police were killed at the hands of that enthused (onward, upward) group of youth (as reported by Warsaw radio)—In fact, around 12,000 members of the armed services subject to communist authorities were killed in battles with the armed underground that took place in Poland between 1944 and 1956, (data from *Atlas Polskiego Podziemia Niepodległościowego 1944–1956*, Instytut Pamięci Narodowej, Warsaw and Lublin, 2007; http://ipn.gov.pl/portal/pl/866/15641/?poz=6&update=1; date of access March 30, 2012).

Tadeusz Boy-Żeleński, *Marysieńka Sobieska* (1937), first post-war edition 1946.

Tricots—A journal or supplement devoted to handicrafts.

Teresa Stanisławska-Adamczewska (1924–2003), Ryszard Stanisławski's sister. Worked on Polish literature, later the editor-in-chief of the *Echo Krakowa* daily. Teresa and Ryszard had two other siblings: Aleksander Stanisławski, called Olek (1923–1993), and Barbara Łubieńska (1924–2005).

Przekrój—A social and cultural weekly founded in 1945, a "window onto the West" for Polish readers. Marian Eile was its founder as well as its editor-in-chief for nearly a quarter of a century.

Tygodnik Powszechny—A Catholic periodical founded in March, 1945 on the initiative of the Archbishop of Krakow, Adam Stefan Sapieha. It earned a reputation for being independent of communist authorities. Jerzy Turowicz was the editor-in-chief for many years.

Przegląd Artystyczny—A monthly publication founded in 1946 dedicated to contemporary art, published by the Polish Association of Visual Artists (first by the Krakow branch, then the Warsaw central committee), co-published from 1952 by the State Institute of Art. Ryszard Stanisławski would later work for *Przegląd*.

In Przekrój *there was quite a <u>good</u> article by Margul*—Most likely she is referring to Mariusz Margal's article *"Operacja Paryż" skończona (Reportaż z zamknięcia III Sesji O.N.Z.)* ["Operation Paris" concluded (A Report from the Closing of the Third

Session of the United Nations)], *Przekrój*, no. 1 (1949), p. 5–6. It was at the Third Session of the United Nations, which took place in Paris on December 10, 1948, that the Universal Declaration of Human Rights was adopted.

at the "ball" (at Legendre's)—At Paris' Hotel Legendre.

In the first days of February there will be the grand elegant ball of the Association of Polish Students for the 25th anniversary of the organization's existence—The Polish Students' Association of Paris was founded in 1922. The occupation of France by Germany in 1940 put a temporary stop to its activities, which were, however, taken back up again after the war. The years immediately following the war were a period in which many young Poles came to study in France. The Association was one of the institutions (alongside the Polish Red Cross and the Polish Catholic Mission) that provided significant assistance to students, organizing free meals and offering the chance to receive nominal scholarships.

20.

LETTER →[P 59]

[JANUARY 18, 1949]

We will take our holiday in Italy—cf. note to letter 14.

a collection of Ildefons' poetry—Polish poet Konstanty Ildefons Gałczyński (1905–1953), most likely his volume *The Enchanted Droshky*, published in 1948.

21.

LETTER →[P 61]

[JANUARY 1949]

Ryszard Stanisławski was born on January 20, 1921. He celebrated his name day on February 7. A name day is a tradition in many countries in Europe and Latin America that consists of celebrating the day associated with the saint after whom an individual has been named. [Translator's note.]

22.

LETTER →[P 62]

[JANUARY 1949]

your article—She is probably referring to Stanisławski's collaboration with the official *Gazette Polonaise* published in Paris for a few years after the Second World War (until 1952), known as the mouthpiece for the National Council of Poles in France.

He was terribly afraid that that transformation of yours (a new subject of study, new views, etc.) might be just superficial, might be the result of being under my "spell"—Ryszard Stanisławski, who studied at the University of Technology in Poland, intended to continue his technical studies in Paris, but he ultimately decided on museum studies. His father's suspicion that this decision was made under Szapocznikow's influence was probably correct, since Stanisławski himself recalled years later: *In large part it was thanks to her that that transformation in me took place. [...] She exercised an enormous influence on me* [Piotr Rypson, *Dwie rozmowy z Ryszardem Stanisławskim* (Two Conversations with Ryszard Stanisławski), http://www.obieg.pl/rozmowy/1391; date of access March 2012]. His father was also troubled by the change in his son's views, and by his activism on behalf of the communist cause, for Ryszard had until that point always stayed out of politics. In a letter to his son from January 9, 1949 Romuald Stanisławski writes: *I confess that I have serious concerns, knowing your impulsive character, so easily influenced by others, that your new tastes have been influenced by someone else, and perhaps in large part on the impetus of your friend Ms. A. I have not yet met this lady personally, and it may well be that meeting her may prove me wrong, but I do have impression this is the star that has illuminated your path...* [...] *Nothing would have prevented you, had you completed the studies you had already undertaken, following your attainment of a position, being at least partly independent, from taking up these studies that have so become of your liking now... But the way you have done things... once more you are a student just starting out, in such uncertain times, when every year may be considered wrested from the lion's mouth...* (Olga Stanisławska Archive).

O. + T. + B. these are Ryszard Stanisławski's siblings: Olek, Teresa, and Barbara, living at the time in Poznań (cf. note to letter 19).

Dyková 15—the Prague address of Bedřich Stefan, given earlier by Szapocznikow on passport forms.

Šapočniková—cf. note to letter 2.

23.

LETTER →[P 66]
[JANUARY 25, 1949]

Invincible City (1946)—A novel by the Polish writer Kazimierz Brandys (1916–2000) about life in occupied Warsaw.

over the last ten years, you did not go through that baptism of despair...—One of only two mentions of her wartime experiences in the entire correspondence. In February, 1940, Alina Szapocznikow was confined in the Pabianice Ghetto, and after its liquidation in May, 1942, to the Łódź Ghetto. In August, 1944, she was sent with others from Łódź through Auschwitz to Bergen-Belsen. She probably did not stay there long. The further fate of Szapocznikow during the war is unknown. There is unverifiable information about her having been in camps in Theresienstadt and Buchenwald (the latter occurs in a document she herself signed in Prague after the end of the war). Ryszard Stanisławski was, when the war broke out, a student at the National School of Chemistry in Warsaw. He returned to Sompolno, where he spent the whole occupation, working at the local power plant.

you got married, you wanted (or didn't) to start a family—Ryszard Stanisławski married Barbara Nowowiejska on March 10, 1945, and they had a daughter, Ewa Stanisławska, on November 11, 1945. They were divorced in October 1951.

Climats (1928) by the French writer André Maurois (1885–1967, given name Emile Herzog) is a novel about the two marriages of the protagonist, Philippe, to women with completely different characters, Odile and Isabelle.

24.

LETTER →[P 69]

[JANUARY 31, 1949]

maladie—illness (French).

I am moving out and into a hotel, and we will live there together until we find something—Upon returning to Paris, Szapocznikow lived with Stanisławski, first for a short time in a hotel at 2, rue Damrémont, in the district of Montmartre, and then they moved to an apartment they had rented at 4, rue Etienne-Marey, near the Porte de Bagnolet, where they lived until they left France.

à la longue—in the long run (French).

My regards to your uncle—The reference is to Bedřich Stefan (cf. note to letter 3).

25.

LETTER →[P 71]

[FEBRUARY 4, 1949]

consigne—left luggage (French).

26.

LETTER →[P 72]

[JULY–SEPTEMBER 1949]

In July 1949, Alina Szapocznikow came down with tuberculosis of the ovaries, then a very serious illness. She was admitted to the Hôpital Tenon, near where she lived, on July 19, and then to the Hôpital Paul-Brousse in Villejuif just outside of Paris, where, on August 16, she underwent surgery. In September, she went with Stanisławski to the village of Sirod in the Jura mountains in order for the change of climate to bring her back to health. But she suffered a relapse, reaching a private hospital in Champagnole in a very bad state, and was subsequently transferred back to the Hôpital Paul-Brousse. Szapocznikow and Stanisławski then had trouble paying for her treatment, which was eventually subsidized by the French government. The following section of letters was written by Szapocznikow during her two stays at the Hôpital Paul-Brousse.

28.

LETTER →[P 74]

[OCTOBER 2, 1949]

When I was 17 I wrote in a little yellow book. [...] *Oh! I am so lovely*—Szapocznikow was 17 in 1943; at that time she was in the Łódź Ghetto. Her friend Rita Hilton would recall years later: *Alina, as usual, had a few boys, as did I. One time my boyfriend and I met up with her together. It was a cold winter day, I had a cold and felt terrible. Alina started flirting with my boyfriend, but he resisted her charms. Despite the loyalty my friend felt for me, seduction was her calling.* [Quotation from a four-page fax from Rita Hilton from February 16, 1998, Jola Gola Archive.]

I don't like Your journalistic exploits—cf. note to letter 22.

let there be a "socialist realism"—In the letters from the period of her illness, Szapocznikow writes for the first time about her relationship to socialist realism. Characteristically, she employs precisely this French term, and not "socrealism," as it was being called in the USSR. She invokes here several fundamental elements that socialist realism ought to be characterized by, including a focus on working people and, on the formal side, a classically-styled composition. It is worth recalling that in this period work of this type was developing in France as one of several options on equal footing, while in Poland it was already by this time (from 1949 until around 1954) the only possible way of creating art. Positioning Joseph Stalin as a sort of custodial figure has to do, no doubt, with his position in the so-called Eastern bloc, but perhaps also with the doctrine of socrealism itself. It was Stalin's text *On Party Politics in the Field of Literary Fiction* that formed the basis of the premises of socrealism in literature, ushered into the USSR in 1934, then expanded to incorporate the other arts, as well as into the other countries subsequently left to Soviet domination. Szapocznikow's evident sympathy for the idea of socialist realism is expressed in her early works, for example in the figure of the peasant boy, given the title in the emigré press of *The Road to Socialism*, or *Woman with Child*, also appearing as *Peace*.

The family, that is, the state cell that the state really likes in its entirety, composed of various pieces—Szapocznikow says "composed of various *sztuk*," *sztuka* being the word in Polish for "art," as it is used throughout the letters, but also the word for "unit." She follows this sentence with the parenthetical remark: "Nie od sztuka—art, ale od sztuka—pièce.)" ["(Not sztuka—art, but sztuka—pièce.)" Translator's note.]

hors d'œuvre—appetizers (French).

œuvres—main courses (French).

légumes—vegetable sides (French).

desserts—desserts (French).

32.

LETTER →[P 87]

[OCTOBER 25, 1949]

l'hôpital—hospital (French).

34.

LETTER →[P 91]

[DECEMBER 1949]

On December 13, 1949 Szapocznikow went to a preventorium named after a Doctor Calmette in Jouy-en-Josas near Paris. A preventorium was an institution for the treatment of patients with tuberculosis.

borrow something from Hanka or from someone at the canteen—As is clear from the memoirs of Poles living in Paris at this time, one of the main meeting places of those permanently residing there and those that had come on a scholarship was the canteen in its various guises, always partly subsidized by the Polish government. It was in one such place that Szapocznikow and Stanisławski met. In this letter, Szapocznikow writes about the best-known of those canteens, the so-called "Polish Hall" on the second floor of a restaurant at 3, rue Racine. It is worth noting that in spite of the aforementioned deterioration of Polish-French relations, the scholarship program that allowed many Polish students at least a few months in Paris did continue. The role of "Polish canteens" is described thus by one such funded student, the architect Oskar Hansen (1922–2005), then a student at the Warsaw University of Technology: *Just about all of the Poles on scholarship would meet here, and all the Poles living in Paris: musicians—Skrowaczewski and Żmudziński (students of Nadia Boulanger), the architect Olek Kujawski, working at that time for Le Corbusier, the graphic artist Leszek Zahorski, working freelance, painters—Lutka Pink, Kaziel (Kazimierz Zielenkiewicz), Jerzy Kujawski, Kazik Ostrowski, coiffed like a soldier, the beautiful sculptor Alina Szapocznikow, her "fellow" Ryszard Stanisławski, the physicist Rydel and his colleague, who lamented having come and who would return immediately, but above all the co-inhabitants of my hotel—Warszawska, the violinist, painters—Tadzik Romanowski and, as it soon turned out, my closest friend—Leszek Kunka. I sometimes saw in that canteen, for example, Eryk Lipiński, the quite eccentric-looking set designer Teresa Roszkowska, and the art critic Mieczysław Porębski* [Oskar Hansen, *Paryż, Bergamo, Londyn (1948–1950)*, 1999, excerpt from his memoirs, Oskar Hansen Archive]. Hanka whom Szapocznikow mentions—Hanna Kulągowska, later Kulągowska-Słonimska (1923–1994)—also went there on occasion. She was the Polish literary critic and journalist, wife of the geneticist Piotr Słonimski.

couleur d'argent—silver color (French).

There are moments here when one must tricoter—Tricoter, knit (French). The sweater that Szapocznikow made during her stay at the preventorium became her favorite thing to work in. In 1961, in *Ty i Ja* [*You and I*] monthly, Andrzej Kossakowski wrote: *Modeling a shapeless mass of susceptible material, working it into a shape that then hardens when cast in bronze or terrazzo, in lead or plaster of Paris, is a kind of great mystery. The role of liturgical vestments is played by a thick gray sweater—armor that when placed on the floor maintains the three-dimensional form of a human figure. Szapocznikow is very attached to it—she knitted it herself a decade or so ago, killing time while she was in the hospital.* [Andrzej Kossakowski, "Alina Szapocznikow," *Ty i Ja*, no. 6 (1961), p. 4.].

facteur—mail carrier (French).

35.

LETTER →[P 93]

[DECEMBER 1949]

mamelle—breast (French).

"stud. de Beaux-Arts"—student at the Academy of Fine Arts (French); Szapocznikow was then studying at the Paris École Nationale Supérieure des Beaux-Arts.

I don't think the thing with Mencel is any good—Wiktor Mencel, then first secretary at the Polish Embassy in Paris.

We can see from the letters that in this period Stanisławski was active in organizations existing in France that were financed by the Polish government. This was probably tied to the Polish authorities officially sanctioning his stay in Paris. In 1949, he joined the Grunwald Polish Youth Union (an underground organization founded in France in 1943 on the initiative of Polish communists to sabotage and subvert the Germans; like many other Polish emigré organizations, it was banned by the French authorities in 1950, during the period of worsening Polish-French relations). He also worked for the Bureau of Polish Information in Paris (Bureau d'Informations Polonaises, B.I.P.); there he gave lectures on Frédéric Chopin, organized (on the occasion of the centenary of his death) for Polish miners living in northern France, as well as for students at the Polish high school in Paris, among others.

"BIB"—Szapocznikow makes an error here, she means B.I.P.—Bureau d'Informations Polonaises.

Out of the money from Pac. please give some immediately to the Weisses and Pappé—She may have been talking about Felicja Pacanowska (1907–2002), a painter and Polish Jew born in Łódź who graduated from the Warsaw School of Fine Arts and then went to Paris in 1932.

Jacques Weiss—His business card comes up in the Ryszard Stanisławski Archive: Ets UNITAS exportation, importation, commission.

Julian Pappé (1920–2000), maker of animated films, born in Rzeszów, Poland, moved permanently to Paris in 1948.

36.

LETTER →[P 96]

[DECEMBER 1949]

[Bedo]*'s to turn in a plan for a relief near the "springs of love" in "Francbad"*—Bedo is Bedřich Stefan. In this artist's only monograph (written by Jiří Šetlík, published in Prague in 1961) there is no mention of such a sculpture. "Francbad" is Františkovy Lázně (German Franzensbad), a health resort in the western part of the Czech Republic.

Is it sentimental weakness that I think aboud Oldo and swimming in the spring in the overflowing Vltava, about Zdeněk and the little winding streets of Mala Strana, the green light of gas lanterns and his room packed with sculptures, where we put on that record from Cyrano de Bergerac 100×...—Zdeněk Palcr (1927–1996), a colleague of Szapocznikow's from the studio at the Academy of Arts, Architecture and Design (he studied under Josef Wagner from 1945–1950), and her lover. According to the Czech scholar Tomáš Pospiszyl, cited above, *Stefan and Palcr knew about each other, many years later Palcr still wouldn't speak to Stefan* [Pospiszyl, *op. cit.*]. With Palcr, as with Stefan, Szapocznikow maintained contact for many years—the last extant letter from him to her was written in 1970.

where Ježerský would recite us poetry—František Ježerský (1908–1964), Czech photographer.

trésor—repository, reserves (French).

37.

LETTER →[P 99]

[DECEMBER 1949]

Eryk Lipiński (1908–1991), Polish graphic artist and journalist, creator of posters and illustrations for books and magazines, co-founder of the satirical weekly publication *Szpilki* (1935, together with Zbigniew Mitzner), a collaborator at many other magazines.

œil à la biche—passing glance (French).

38.

LETTER →[P 102]

[DECEMBER 19–21, 1949]

I'll affix them at home over the holidays—Szapocznikow spent Christmas with Ryszard Stanisławski; she was there from December 24–27.

fil pour couper la forme—a thin cord to cut out a form (French); she is talking about a thin line to cut through clay.

libám tě milý jak jen dovedu—I'll kiss you, sweetie, just as soon as I get there (Czech).

Paříž 19 prosince pondělí—Paris, December 19, Monday (Czech).

tvojě čeština je špatna—your Czech is horrible (Czech).

39.

LETTER →[P 105]

[DECEMBER 30, 1949]

while into the telephone through the receiver tears—The exact quotation from Julian Tuwim's *An Unremarkable Story* is: "And along her face, into the receiver, tears."

40.

LETTER →[P 107]

[JANUARY 9, 1950]

freedom, home! Thou art like good health!...—Szapocznikow paraphrases the opening lines of *Pan Tadeusz*, the Polish national epic by Adam Mickiewicz (1832–34) written in thirteen-syllable verse:

O Lithuania, my country, thou
Art like good health; I never knew till now
How precious, till I lost thee. Now I see

The beauty whole, because I yearn for thee.
(English translation by Kenneth R. Mackenzie)

I wrote a letter to Artur—Perhaps to Artur Sandauer (1913–1989), Polish literary critic, essayist and translator, who lived in Paris from 1946–1948. After returning to Warsaw he worked for a year on the editorial board of *Odrodzenie*; an opponent of socrealism, he was banned from publication for some time.

Jan Kott (1914–2001), Polish historian of literature and theater, critic, essayist and translator, in this period linked to the Polish communist authorities, co-founder and editor of the weekly magazine *Kuźnica*, one of the co-founders of the Institute for Literary Research at the Polish Academy of Sciences.

41.

LETTER →[P 109]
[JANUARY 1950]

In the letters from her mother Szapocznikow mentions, sent on to Stanisławski (on the blank sides of which Szapocznikow added her letters to him), the artist underlines, among others, the sentence: *It was for the best that Ryszard lost that night job, working at night and studying is unthinkable, he has to put his health first, after all.* And she wrote: *So you see what my mom is talking about.* Stanisławski was at the time doing manual labor at Les Halles (cf. note to letter 2).

And it also has information about the pardessus, I don't think there's much to get worked up over in it!—Regina Szapocznikow had written to her daughter about those "pardesses" (*pardes* means "orchard" in Hebrew): *You see, daughter, with these pardesses, I can't know, after all, where and when that transaction was entered into, it's on your father's mother's side, why even today I saw one of the Folman's relatives that says that if there was something to be done, then the two Michelson's granddaughters would have taken care of it, as they have been there since before the war.* [Letter from Regina Szapocznikow from January 7, 1950, Alina Szapocznikow Archive]. They are no doubt referring to transactions connected with plots of land in Palestine, where a part of the Szapocznikow family emigrated before the war.

43.

LETTER →[P 113]
[JANUARY–FEBRUARY 1950]

cure de silence—silence cure (French).

First regarding the more burning questions, i.e. transferring out of here—Szapocznikow was never able to transfer to another institution.

service médical—department of health (French), very likely under the auspices of the Assistance Publique–Hôpitaux de Paris; cf. note to letter 17.

Il y a quelques semaines était...—A few weeks ago a young woman sculptor came to see you (here show that paper from

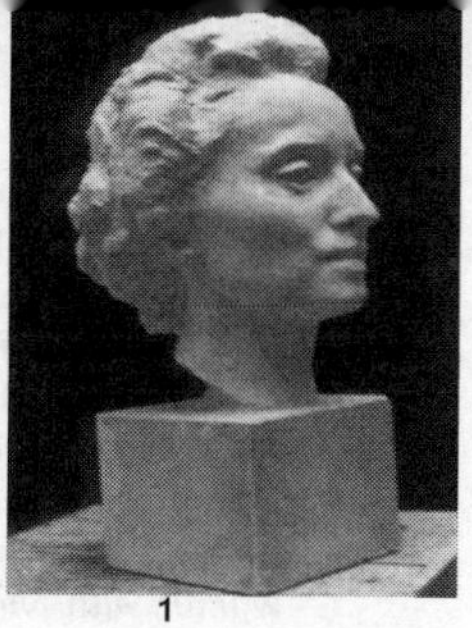
1

from Niclausse), sent by Miss Desjobert. She is now in Jouy-en-Josas. You told her that if she needed a different sanatorium, she had only to take the proper steps. That girl was summoned to the prefecture and is to go to a sanatorium near La Rochelle. She went to the doctor, who suggested that the climate by the sea is very good in her case (tuberculosis of the ovaries). (I talked to her for a long time about my illness, and back then she expressed great feminine sympathy with regard to children, those organs, etc.) But since she was already sent somewhere once by your institution, she is now unable to take advantage of other options as she would wish. I already spoke with Miss Desjobert already about her, but it's a question of money, etc. Therefore I came to ask you if you couldn't "cover the costs" of a stay in a different sanatorium that would be right for her illness.

Dante Elsner, Polish painter, studied at the Krakow Academy of Fine Arts.

Teodor Axentowicz (1859–1938), Polish painter, graphic artist, and draftsman.

Service "prise en charge sanatorium"—the "covering sanatorium costs" service (French).

excuse mes fautes!—forgive my errors! (French).

44.

LETTER →[P 116]

[JANUARY–FEBRUARY 1950]

from Dr. Monsaingeon—During Szapocznikow's illness she met the surgeon Dr. André Monsaingeon (1912–2000), who worked in the Hôpital Paul Brousse, and with whom she kept in touch over the next few years. In 1950 she sculpted a *PORTRAIT OF MRS. MONSAINGEON* → [1] in plaster (no longer extant).

47.

LETTER →[P 120]

[MAY 26, 1950]

Toward the end of May, 1950, Szapocznikow went to Poland once more, traveling through Prague as before.

48.

LETTER →[P 121]

[MAY 28, 1950]

Whitsun, in Polish *Zielone Świątki* (Green Holy Days)—The Christian holiday of Pentecost, which commemorates the descent of the Holy Spirit upon the Apostles, celebrated 50 days after Easter.

Kazimierz "Kachu" Ostrowski (1917–1999), Polish painter associated with the State Higher School of Visual Arts in Gdańsk (now the Academy of Fine Arts). That school was opened in 1945, and until 1954 was located near Gdańsk, in Sopot. Kazimierz was a student there from 1946, and at the end of 1949 and beginning of 1950 he went to Paris (he received a scholarship from the French government), where

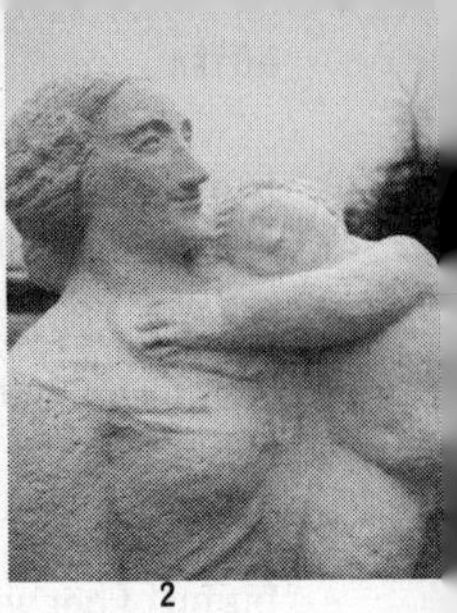
2

he probably met Szapocznikow.

If you haven't already cast it, please throw that figure out—Szapocznikow asks that Stanisławski not cast her sculpture in the two letters that follow, later specifying that she is talking about a figure with a child. It is probably a mother holding an infant to her body. Photographs of two small plaster models have been preserved; in the end a piece on this subject did come to fruition, in stone, known under various names—*Woman with Child, Peace, A Mother's Hope,* MOTHERHOOD → [2]; it is now in Warsaw, near Żoliborz's Comedy Theatre.

49.

LETTER →[P 123]

[MAY 31, 1950]

I also talked to Adam, whose version of things is exactly the opposite of everyone else's here—The views at that time of Adam Leśniewski (cf. note to letter 13), then active in the students' cell of the communist Polish United Workers' Party, are expressed in this excerpt from a letter he sent to Szapocznikow from Zakopane on July 29, 1949: *I want to emphasize to you that it's not just about the fact that the socialist system triggers an enormous amount of talent lying dormant in people who are being elsewhere oppressed, but more importantly, socialism creates new qualitative values that are higher than those that arise in the antagonistic class societies.* [...] And he reproaches Szapocznikow: *You use bourgeois criteria of evaluating art.* [...] *Either you will learn to use and live using different evaluative criteria for art, or you will have to leave us. Of course the reason lies not in views on art, but somewhere deeper, it's just that this is where it manifests itself. The reasons, in my opinion, lie: a. in class background (hence the legacy of the bourgeois tradition); b. in isolation from the labor movement; c. in a poor knowledge of Marxism-Leninism, i.e., the petit-bourgeois revolutionary environment characteristic of a circle of artists; d. in the tremendous pressure of enemy ideology.* [Alina Szapocznikow Archive, http://www.artmuseum.pl/archiwa. php?l=0&a=1&id=2070 through id=2077, date of access March 7, 2012]. After graduation, Adam Leśniewski taught Marxism-Leninism at several universities in Łódź and then did a doctorate in history and was hired by the Department of Modern History at the University of Łódź. In 1969, he and his wife emigrated to Sweden. He was a supporter of the democratic opposition in Poland in the 1980s.

Please say hello to the Lerendus—In 1949, Szapocznikow started working in the stone workshop of Gaston Lerendu near Père-Lachaise Cemetery (Entreprise Générale de Marbrerie Funéraire, 177, rue de la Roquette). She made friends with the owner of the workshop as well as with his sister Simone. Lerendu gave her a small room that was her studio. It is unclear whether she was formally employed there or just periodically charged with certain tasks by Gaston Lerendu.

Did you remember the exhibition of young sculptors?—In the letters from the middle of 1950 we can see clearly that it

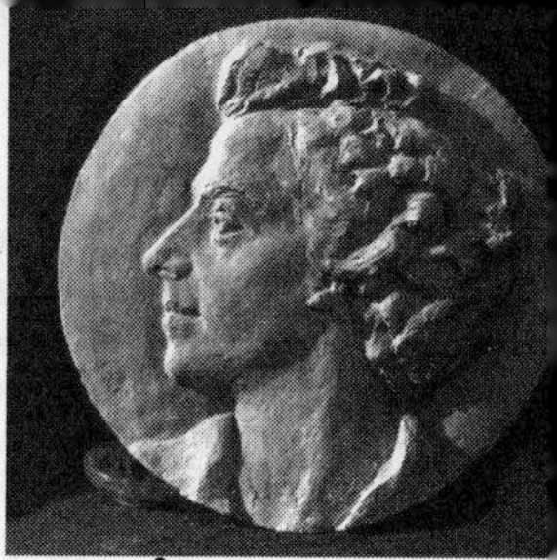

3

is increasingly important for Szapicznikow to participate in artistic life. For the first time she talks about executing concrete projects and about the reception of these early works. According to the list of exhibitions in the catalogue of Alina Szapocznikow's scultpures compiled by Jola Gola, the first exhibition the artist took part in was the "VI Exposition des Artistes Juifs" ("VI Exhibition of Jewish Artists") in 1950, but we have been unable to verify this information. The first exhibition of her work that we can be sure of took place only after the artist had come to Poland, at the end of 1951, in the second National Visual Arts Exhibition, where she exhibited *Portrait of a Boy* (in Jola Gola's *Katalog rzeźb Aliny Szapocznikow,* this appears as number 24, *Boy's Head I*). She made many busts in this period, which were later almost entirely absent from her work.

Vladimir Mayakovsky, *Poems*, published in Warsaw in 1949.

photographs of Ginette—Szapocznikow's most important commission from this period is a *MEDALLION ON THE TOMBSTONE OF GINETTE NEVEU* → [3/1950], the famous French violinist who died in a plane crash on October 28, 1949. The tombstone with Szapocznikow's relief is located in the Père-Lachaise cemetery.

Honoré de Balzac, *Mémoires de deux jeunes mariées* [*Letters of Two Brides*], 1841; translation of this work appeared in Polish in 1951, published by Czytelnik.

It is unclear which book by the Russian writer Ilya Ehrenburg (1891–1967) Szapocznikow has in mind, but it is perhaps *Storm*, the second part of a trilogy on the subject of French society during the Second World War and just afterwards. The Polish translation of this appeared in 1950 (the original in 1947).

s.t.p. et si tu peux (from pouvoir)—please and if you are able (from the verb "to be able") (French).

50.

LETTER →[P 125]

[JUNE 12, 1950]

I dealt with the things for Jerzy—She is probably talking about Jerzy Radkowski (1924–1987), Polish philosopher, sociologist, anthropologist and one of the founders of the monthly magazine *Znak* (in the beginning he was its editor-in-chief). Radkowski went to France in 1946, after becoming involved with Angèle Fumet. In the Ryszard Stanisławski Archive his letter from April of 1950 is preserved, in which he writes *inter alia* of the birth of his daughter Benedicta. In France he went by the name of Georges-Hubert de Radkowski.

Editor K. this is most likely the aforementioned Jan Kott.

Adam Ważyk (1905–1982), Polish poet, writer, essayist, translator, worked for *Odrodzenie*, *Kuźnica*, and *Nowa Kultura*, among others. At that time he was one of socrealism's main advocates, only to, in his 1955 *A Poem for Adults*, take the whole movement to task. Despite being immediately censored, this piece was widely read and circulated.

I stayed with a cousin of mine—During her visits to Warsaw, Szapocznikow would stay with her cousin Halina Daszkiewicz, who lived with her husband Władysław on Belwederska Street.

Mr. Wnuk—Most likely the father of Alina Wnuk (cf. note to letter 14), who, when writing during this period to Ryszard Stanislawski, always included greetings from her parents.

Nowy Świat is completely new—In February 1945 the Bureau for the Rebuilding of the Capital was founded. The combination of modernist ideas originating back before the war and the communist authorities' disdain for the capitalist remnants of the city meant that the activities of the Bureau aimed not to preserve the pre-war architectural tradition, but rather to create a "new, socialist Warsaw" (both in new buildings and in a new urban layout). The opposition of many public figures meant that some parts of the center were rebuilt in the image of their former incarnations, like Krakowskie Przedmieście, which Szapocznikow mentions, Nowy Świat, and Theatre Square. It was the Department of Monumental Architecture of the Bureau for the Rebuilding of the Capital that was charged with these projects. The reconstruction of the Archcathedral of St. John lasted until 1955. Of the new, large-scale investments, Szapocznikow mentions two: the East-West Expressway, built from 1947–9, and the residential district of Muranów, completed in 1952.

They put a tradeswoman done by a young woman sculptor on Mariensztat Square—She is speaking of *Mariensztat Tradeswoman* by Barbara Zbrożyna (1923–1995), a sculpture from 1949.

51.

LETTER →[P 129]

[JUNE 16, 1950]

Wilhelm Sowiński (1892–1955), real name Wilhelm Szenwic, gynecologist and obstetrician.

sauveur—savior (French).

sensibilité—sensitivity (French).

UCP(B)—A Short Course in the History of the *Union-wide Communist Party (Bolsheviks)*. This was basic propaganda material in the USSR and Soviet-bloc countries, published in 1938 by the Central Committee of the Union-wide Communist Party. In Poland, the *Short Course* was sold by the publishing house Książka i Wiedza [Books and Knowledge] in 1949 in a print run of 1.25 million copies.

Charlie is Karol Ferster (1902–1986), Polish painter and draftsman using this nickname.

52.

LETTER →[P 132]

[JUNE 1950]

Mieczysław Porębski (born 1921), Polish critic, art historian. During this period he lived in Warsaw, where he worked at the State Institute of Art and taught at the Academy of Fine Arts. It was at the State Institute of Art (established on November 30, 1949, thanks to the efforts of Juliusz Starzyński, who served as director, now the Institute of Art at the Polish Academy of Sciences) in the Department of Art Theory, that Stanisławski was hired on his return from Paris. Stanisławski and Porębski also collaborated at *Przegląd Artystyczny*; Porębski was the editor-in-chief of that magazine (1952–1957), while Stanisławski was a member of the editorial board at the time.

what's going on with Cinette's patina?—cf. note to letter 49.

my mom wants to give it to that cousin from Palestine—The cousin from Palestine was most likely Lejb Auerbach, who lived in Tel Aviv at that time. A portion of Szapocznikow's family had emigrated from Poland to Palestine before the war. Alina Szapocznikow's father Jakub, *who bought* [that watch] *from him when they didn't have enough for their ticket*, died in Pabianice in 1938.

53.

LETTER →[P 134]

[JUNE 26, 1950]

Pas de nouvelles, bonnes nouvelles—no news is good news (French).

Gustaw Bachner—An employee of the music department of the Bureau d'Informations Polonaises (cf. note to letter 35).

the shepherd—He is likely referring to a sculpture that appears in the catalogue of Alina Szapocznikow's sculptures as *Country Boy* (1950, plaster, approx. 150 cm, no longer extant).

54.

LETTER →[P 136]

[JUNE 26, 1950]

I am seeing a number of artists from the Sopot circle—She is mainly talking about students and teachers at the State Higher School of Visual Arts (moved from Sopot to Gdańsk in 1954). It is worth recalling that it was in this period that the so-called Sopot School came into being, still in existence today. A defining feature of this artistic milieu was its carrying on colorist traditions and the foregrounding of painterly values.

55.

LETTER →[P 137]

[JUNE 26, 1950]

Jerzy Putrament (1910–1986), Polish writer, political activist and ambassador of the People's Republic of Poland in Paris from 1947–1950.

I was at a competition of teams from the Service to Poland brigades—The National "Service to Poland" (SP) Organization was a state paramilitary organization started in 1948 for vocational and military training as well as to promote physical fitness in young people. Its purview was quite wide and included cultural activities; there were, for example, Singing and Dancing Companies within the SP.

57.

LETTER →[P 140]

[JUNE 28, 1950]

M/S *Batory*—A trans-Atlantic liner in service from 1936–1969.

S/S *Maiden of the Sea* [*Panna Wodna*]—The largest coastal vessel in Poland, a German minesweeper before the Second World War.

this is not that kind of puffed up lordly Polishness, but rather an honest Polishness, flowing from the folk—The interest in folk art evinced here by Szapocznikow was characteristic of French artists (like Picasso) sympathetic to communist ideas. Western artists sought in folk art an authenticity uncontaminated by capitalism.

Zofia Stryjeńska (1891–1976), Polish painter who focused on village life, rituals, and folk costumes, presented in a style modeled on folk art. She enjoyed great early success with pieces like the *Polish Dances* series of 1929 (still popular to this day), but with time, and particularly after the Second World War, her work began to be seen as synonymous with a certain superficial take on folk styles, in large part the fault of the artist herself, who gradually ceased to explore new ideas in her work.

The Fédération Nationale Tourisme et Travail was an organization founded in 1943, which set itself the task of making travel available to all. Szapocznikow and Stanisławski did in fact travel around France in 1950 (August–September), but it was a trip they organized themselves. They were aided by Gaston Lerendu, who gave them money to buy an old car. The trip was planned carefully by them and was partly documented by Szapocznikow. Among her notes: *9/14 Thursday Toulon, 2 × en panne* [breakdown, French]*, at 2 we're in St. Tropez. A Czech garagist vows to take care of selling it. We make it to Antibes before 7 eve and find the letters but no cash. We send off express mail letters and telegrams. It's dark, and we look for a place to spend the night. We pitch our tent under the eucalyptus trees. Friday morning 9/15. It turns out that it's lovely. We go to Vallauris, there's a storm. In the afternoon we make potato latkes. Saturday 9/16, at the beach. In the evening we go to Picasso's. He receives us in his garden, where he's playing with his child and his dog. Simple, family atmosphere. He is great and naïve. The sky is sky-blue. We borrow 2000 francs. We buy sandals and meat.* [Alina Szapocznikow Archive]. Stanisławski would recall that unannounced visit to Picasso many years later: *"We wanted to pay you homage [...]", I say, "as befits a gentleman!" To which Alina promptly adds, "We also wanted to borrow three thousand francs!" Just like that, on* *the spot. You know, Alina had a kind of courage that I found embarrassing sometimes* [Rypson, *op. cit.*].

58.

LETTER →[P 143]

[JUNE 29, 1950]

writers' summit—The 5th Polish Writers' Union Congress was held from June 24–27, 1950. Today this meeting is seen as key in the ideological offensive of socrealism. It included a Union member verification process based on political views.

our ambassador—At the time this was Jerzy Putrament (cf. note to letter 55).

Peuples amis—Organ of the organization *L'Amitié Franco-Polonaise* (French-Polish Friendship) founded in 1944 by Jean Fréderic Joliot-Curie (1900–1958).

In even the littlest towns they have a "Book Club"—In 1948 a network was established in Poland of Clubs of International Press and Books (commonly called *"empiks,"* a kind of acronym for the name in Polish [*Klub*] *Międzynarodowej Prasy i Książki*), selling Polish and foreign press (mostly from other Easter bloc countries; Western materials during this period were primarily limited to leftist titles) and hosting reading rooms.

61.

LETTER →[P 147]

[JULY 5, 1950]

at the international department of the Party—The Polish United Workers' Party.

Salon de la Jeune Sculpture—Annual exhibition organized in Paris from 1949–1990, Szapocznikow would take part in it every year, beginning with the fifteenth salon in 1964.

Salon d'Automne—Exhibition held in Paris every year since 1903. It arose in response to the more conservative Paris Salon.

Maison de la pensée [*française*]—Former palais of a Parisian banker (at 2, rue de l'Elysée), transformed into a salon for exhibitions and then a leftist cultural center in 1947. In the 1950s and '60s well-known artists like Matisse, Picasso, and Léger exhibited there.

en plus—in addition (French).

62.

LETTER →[P 149]

[JULY 6, 1950]

Of course, I will try to deal with your request as best I can in Warsaw—Stanisławski was trying to establish contacts in Poland during this period, presumably doing the groundwork for the career he wished to establish when they returned to Poland, as they had already planned to do.

64.

LETTER →[P 152]

[JULY 9, 1950]

get the stone ready for the head of Simone—In 1950,

Szapocznikow did plaster busts of *SIMONE* → [4] and of Gaston Lerendu (no longer extant).

send the photograph of the shepherd to my Łódź address—cf. note to letter 53.

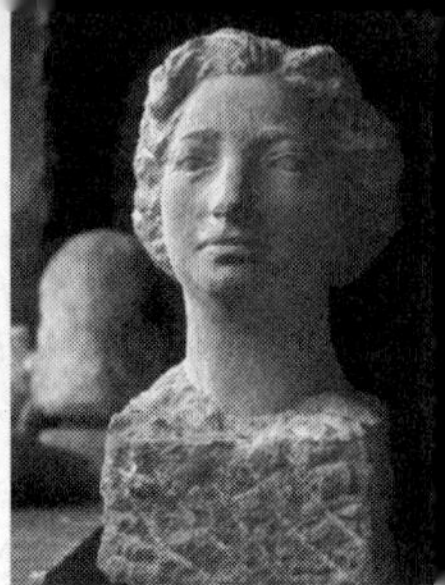

4

66.

LETTER →[P 154]

[JULY 14, 1950]

the exhibition of works from the Grand prix de Rome—The history of the French prize for young artists, the Prix de Rome, whose winners received three-year stipends to the Villa Medicis in Rome, is a very long one, reaching back to 1663. It was last awarded in 1968 (de Gaulle's culture minister André Malraux eliminated the traditional academic competitions after the events of May).

In February 1951, Alina Szapocznikow and Ryszard Stanisławski returned to Poland. This was Stanisławski's first return to his country after he had left it illegally in 1946. They lived in Warsaw, initially in a room at the Central Bureau of Art Exhibitions in Saska Kępa, allotted to them thanks to Szapocznikow's efforts at the Polish Association of Visual Artists. Alina Szapocznikow worked on the sculptural portion of the buildings in the new Marszałkowska residential district MDM (*Marszałkowska Dzielnica Mieszkaniowa*); it was thanks to this that they later got their apartment at Marszałkowska 15. Ryszard Stanisławski began working at the State Institute of Art. He also enrolled at the University of Warsaw, to finish the education that had been interrupted by his departure for Paris, receiving his master's degree in art history in 1952. Alina Szapocznikow, meanwhile, discontinued her studies of art.

69.

LETTER →[P 157]

[DECEMBER 22, 1951]

There are a few miners here from Kleofas—The Kleofas coal mine in Katowice, in existence from the mid-nineteenth century to 2004.

ça va—fine (French).

On July 12, 1952 Alina Szapocznikow and Ryszard Stanisławski were married. The witnesses were Karol Ferster (mentioned in the letters as "Charlie") and Wojciech Fangor. The painter and graphic artist Wojciech Fangor (born 1922) was a longtime friend of Szapocznikow. He included several sections on her in his memoirs. In one he wrote: *We were very different. She was a beautiful, petite, voluptuous girl with thick, wavy, dark hair. I was a dour, lanky man with light, straight hair that she called "goy hair."* "Les extrêmes se touchent" [Opposites attract (French)]. *She liked me perhaps as a necessary contrast to herself. Alina drew on contrasts from without in order to create herself within as a work of art.* [...] *We never really talked about art or discussed our works.*

Just once Alina evinced the opinion that what I was doing was "so h-m-m-m...". We exchanged our thoughts on nature, the people surrounding us, the cultures of other countries, all with a sense of humor and a kind of joy. [May 12, 2004, unpublished text, Wojciech Fangor Archive].

70.

LETTER →[P 158]
[NOVEMBER 1953]

I've only been here three days, and already I would very much like to come home—This letter may have been sent in November of 1953, during Szapocznikow's work reconstructing the sculptures in Gdańsk's Old Town (the rebuilding and reconstruction of old Gdańsk was begun in 1949). Szapocznikow did a female figure during this period that stands at the top of the building at Długi Targ 36.

I saw an awful presentation of Halka—*Halka*, an opera by Stanisław Moniuszko, was put on in 1953 by the Baltic Opera and Philharmonic in Gdańsk.

I miss Piotruś very much—In 1952, Szapocznikow and Stanisławski adopted a boy of a few months of age, Piotr (born July 22, 1952).

Hello to Jadzia—There was a housekeeper that looked after little Piotr living with Szapocznikow and Stanisławski on a permanent basis. In the letter from Gdańsk she speaks of Jadzia, and then for many years the name Zosia appears in the correspondence.

71.

LETTER →[P 160]
[WINTER 1955]

Szapocznikow and Stanisławski went (together or separately) to two places on their vacations: in the summer to the sea (to Kuźnica on the peninsula of Hel, and then to Karwia), and in the winter and at Easter to Zakopane. In Zakopane they stayed at a vacation home for visual artists called Magnolia, run by a woman named Maryta, who is mentioned here.

Jacek Żuławski (1907–1976), Polish painter and graphic artist working at the State Higher School of Visual Arts in Gdańsk, avid sailor and mountaineer.

he is taking me to Pięć Stawów for three days—She is referring to the Valley of the Five Polish Ponds in the Upper Tatra Mountains, *Pięć Stawów* in Polish.

young people from Bim-Bom and some carefree recreation—Bim-Bom was a theater founded by students at the Gdańsk University of Technology, the Academy of Fine Arts, and the Academy of Music. It was active in Gdańsk from 1954–1960, co-founded by famous actors Zbigniew Cybulski, Bogumił Kobiela, and Jacek Fedorowicz, among others. The work of this milieu was seen as a kind of artistic manifesto of the thaw generation.

Ewa and Kazimierz Fajkosz, Zakopane artists.

Janusz Wilden (1906–1991), Polish painter and sculptor, PAVA activist (among other things he was the secretary of the Sculpture Section).

Tadeusz Brzozowski (1918–1987), Polish painter of the Krakow milieu and a member of the so-called Krakow Group, living in Zakopane from 1954.

in Nieborów—The Radziwiłł Palace in Nieborów was incorporated into the Warsaw National Museum. It contains a Center for Creative Work.

the Bronisław Czech Memorial—A ski race held every year in March in Zakopane, dedicated to the memory of Polish skiers murdered during the Second World War.

Kenar school—In 1876, the Tatra Society established a woodworking school in Zakopane, whose directors set themselves the goal, among other things, of supporting the traditions of their native land. In 1954, the school (by then the State School of Art Technique) was directed by Antoni Kenar (1906–1959), who reformed the educational process and emphasized the harmonious relationship between technical skills and students' artistic development, and between folk art and contemporary art. The school was widely known as "the Kenar School," and a few months after his death in 1959, it officially took this name. Kenar and his students took part in the exhibition at the Polish Pavilion in the Venice Biennale of 1956, on which more below.

72.

LETTER →[P 162]

[FEBRUARY 17, 1955]

Walter is Walerian Borowczyk (1923–2005), Polish graphic artist, creator of animated and feature films, living in Paris from 1957 on.

73.

LETTER →[P 163]

[FEBRUARY 1955]

I was writing for Leszek—In 1955, two articles by Stanisławski appeared in the monthly magazine *Polska*, where the artistic director was Stanisławski's friend Lech (Leszek) Zahorski. This is perhaps a reference to one of those.

The opening of the Mexican art exhibition took place at the Zachęta Gallery on February 19, 1955.

74.

LETTER →[P 164]

[SUMMER 1955 OR 1956]

They sing Karolinka—Most likely a reference to the popular folk song "Karolina Went to Gogolin".

76.

LETTER →[P 167]

[MAY 21, 1956]

In May 1956, Alina Szapocznikow went to Paris in conjunction with the international exhibition of contemporary sculpture "Exposition Internationale de Sculpture Contemporaine" organized by the Rodin Museum. The curator of the Polish portion of the exhibition was Mieczysław Porębski. Szapocznikow exhibited her <u>*MONUMENT TO A BURNED-DOWN CITY* → [5/1954]</u>, and perhaps also *First Love* (1954), though the latter does not appear in the catalogue.

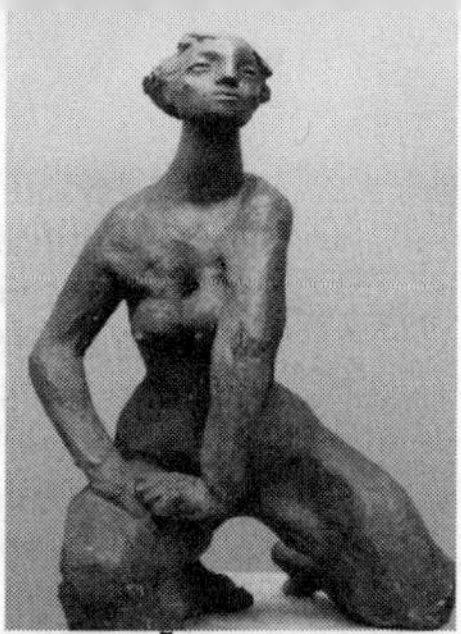
5

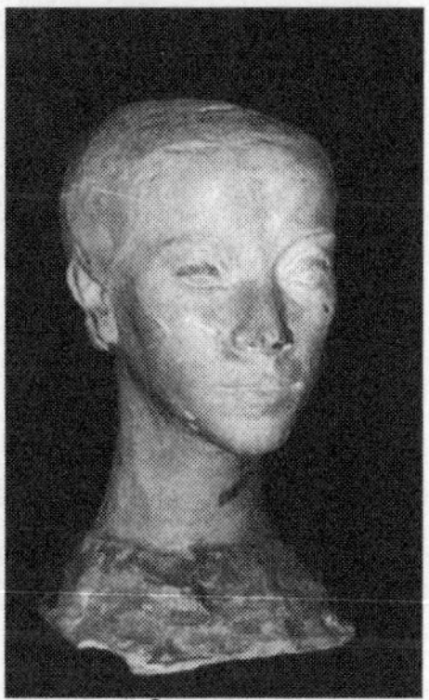
6

cet air parisien—that Parisian aura, Parisian smartness (French).

The Jaśes aren't even here—Wanda and Jan Jasiński.

Max Gerson—Szapocznikow's cousin.

Michel de Gallard (born 1921), French painter. His first solo show was in 1956 at the Galerie Framond in Paris.

Grabowski was seriously ill, apparently he's wandering around somewhere half-paralyzed—Stanisław Grabowski (1901–1957), Polish painter living in Paris from 1924. In 1954, he suffered a stroke, after which he was confined to a rest home in Chartres, occasionally coming to Paris, where he maintained a studio.

Musée d'Art Moderne is being dismantled—The Musée National d'Art Moderne was housed at the Palais de Tokyo from 1947–1977, when it was transferred to the Centre Georges Pompidou. In the 1950s, its east wing was renovated so as to incorporate the Musée d'Art Moderne de la Ville de Paris (inaugurated in 1961); we assume this was what Szapocznikow was referring to here.

I went to see Ms. Goldscheider—Cécile Goldscheider was at the time the director of the Rodin Museum.

soignée—neat (French).

allure—appearance, attitude (French).

jours de vacances—vacation days (French).

si encombrants—so cumbersome (French).

Jan Styczyński (1917–1981), photographer.

the picture of Naya in the wood—Szapocznikow befriended Naya Marquez-Rodilez, the wife of the curator of the Hispanic art exhibition that took place at the Zachęta Gallery in 1956. She made two sculptures of her head—one in wood (now in the collection of the National Museum in Krakow), the other in plaster: <u>*A PONY TAIL: PORTRAIT OF A MEXICAN WOMAN* → [6/1955–56]</u>

tout de même—nonetheless (French).

I am sending a present for Piotrek through Nieciuński—Nieciuński was Stanisławski's superior on the Central Board of the Visual Arts and Exhibitions at the Ministry of Culture and Art, where Stanisławski worked from 1955 as vice director. In the letters written by Szapocznikow during her stay in Paris in May and June of 1956, Nieciuński appears several times as the person through whom she sends Stanisławski a gift for their son, letters, and a check.

Tomorrow I'm going to go and try to get my Italian visa—In the letters from summer 1956, Szapocznikow's and Stanisławski's passport and visa problems come up repeatedly. These were common problems for residents of the People's Republic of Poland who wished to go abroad. The first difficulty was posed by getting a passport; these were only issued to individuals in possession of an invitation from abroad or those sent on official business by the government. Passports were issued for a concrete trip, to a country specified in the passport application, which also contained an outline of the planned itinerary. Permission to leave the country was not always granted, and it was difficult to know in advance how long the application would take to be processed. As historian Marcin Kula notes, *An essential step on the path to departure was "pushing"* [Kula, *op. cit.*, p. 100]. Upon return to Poland the passport had to be surrendered, and then the person had to reapply if he or she wished to leave again. Sometimes it was possible to have the passport extended to some other country, but—as this correspondence shows—this was no easy matter. The next step was getting visas: transit visas and the visa for the destination country (the former were issued for a very short period); this tended to take a lot of time and was also not guaranteed. In addition these visas often had additional restrictions; for example, for some time it was possible to require the person to go through a specific border crossing.

and maybe we will see each other—Ryszard Stanisławski left at that same time for Italy. His trip was in conjunction with the 28th Venice Biennale in 1956, where he was serving as assistant commissioner at the Polish Pavilion.

Michelle and Lech Zahorski were close friends of Szapocznikow and Stanisławski from the time of their first stay in Paris. Lech Zahorski (1923–1993) was born in Warsaw and studied at the École Nationale Supérieure d'Architecture et des Arts in Brussels, and lived in Paris in the 1950s. In 1954, he returned to Poland with his wife, where both worked on theatrical projects; he did set designs, she designed costumes. Lech Zahorski was also a graphic artist, and for many years, among other things, artistic director of the magazine *Polska*. The grandma with the two kids mentioned in the letter is no doubt Michelle Zahorska's mother, Hélène Mossé.

77.

LETTER →[P 170]

[MAY 23, 1956]

Alexander Calder (1898–1976), American sculptor whose solo show at the Galerie Lucie Weill in Paris took place in May, 1956.

Abraham (Abrasza) Zemsz is remembered by many people involved in the Polish community in Paris as a colorful character. Czesław Miłosz wrote of him: *He was studying at the Sorbonne; to be more precise, he was an eternal student, or rather, he was one of those people who cling to a student's existence as an alibi, to avoid bearing the burden of a career, a salary, etc.* [...] *In*

Paris, he was very poor; he lived in a garret somewhere [Czesław Miłosz, *Milosz's A B C's*, translated by Madeline C. Levine]. Zemsz received his master's degree in ethnology and was working on a dissertation he never finished. He helped Szapocznikow when in 1949 she had trouble with the French courts, finding her a very good lawyer (cf. note to letter 12). He later committed suicide.

Cepelia—An acronym for the *Centrala Przemysłu Ludowego i Artystycznego*, or the Center for Folk Industry and Art, a state enterprise established in 1949, giving rise to a network of stores with products made by folk artists or inspired by folk art. Items from Cepelia enjoyed enormous success as gifts for foreigners.

digne à rang—with the dignity due her, according to her rank (French).

78.

LETTER →[P 173]

[MAY 30 OR JUNE 6, 1956]

Jan Danielewicz (1903–1982), well-known pediatric laryngologist.

Jean Cassou (1897–1986), French writer and art critic. From 1946–1965 he was the director of the Musée National d'Art Moderne. An important figure for Stanisławski, who during the period of his studies in Paris at the École du Louvre attended Cassou's lectures (his notes are still preserved in his archive). Years later Stanisławski would recall: *I introduced myself to him—and we became friends, if I may say so. He was a distinguished figure—a writer, a poet.* [...] *We often met in cafés; he introduced me to his family. I was quite close to him, and yet at the same time he was the kind of person who intimidated me enormously in terms of politics. He was a person of the left, but very far removed from the whole murky history of Communism.* [...] *He was a person that exercised an enormous influence on me* [Rypson, *op. cit.*].

Antoine Pevsner (1886–1962), Russian sculptor, one of the creators of constructivism.

Bernard Dorival (1914–2003), French critic and art historian.

Le Mystère Picasso, 1956, directed by Henri-Georges Clouzot, a documentary on Pablo Picasso.

The exhibitions Szapocznikow writes about in this letter are those of Georges Braque; French sculptor Henri Laurens (1885–1954); Swiss painter Paul Klee (1879–1940); Spanish painter Francisco Bores (1898–1972); and Italian painter Berto Lardera (1911–1989).

Jacques Taminiaux (born 1928), Belgian philosopher. In 1955, during the 5th World Festival of Youth and Students in Warsaw, Szapocznikow met a couple of young philosophers from Belgium interested in contemporary art, Taminiaux and Françoise Collin (born 1928). Collin would recall years later: *The most original and most significant event during that festival was the exhibition of Polish artists organized at the Warsaw Arsenal.* [...] *As I was perusing it, I paused before a gouache maintained rather in the spirit of surrealism that reminded me of the works of some Belgian artists, like Delvaux. When I expressed my astonishment, and my interest in this work, I heard behind me in excellent French: "If you'd like, I can take you to that artist and to his studio; it's one of my friends, Jerzy Tchórzewski". The person that had issued this invitation from behind us was a young woman, warm and radiant: Alina Szapocznikow. She took us to her apartment in the Old Town and introduced us to her husband, Ryszard Stanisławski, and their young son. She became our first guide in our discovery of the Polish artists of that time, her friends.* [Statement by Françoise Collin during the conference "Alina Szapocznikow: Works. Documents. Interpretations" organized by the Museum of Modern Art in Warsaw on May 15–16, 2009].

I'm giving you the Jaśes' number, maybe it's better if in the future you call them, not Mossé—At that time calls were almost always made from Poland to France and not the other way around, in an effort to save those traveling "to the West" from spending "valuable" francs on phone calls. Characteristic of correspondence at that time (not only of the letters between Szapocznikow and Stanisławski) is arranging by letter times for phone calls. Szapocznikow benefited numerous times from the hospitality of the Jasińskis mentioned in these letters ("the Jaśes", cf. note to letter 76). Mossé is Michelle Zahorska's mother, Hélène Mossé.

M.E.N. Menilmontant 45–97—This is a phone number, somewhat erroneously recorded here (the correct version being MÉN 45.97). The three letters, which at that time was how French phone numbers began, were often an abbreviation of the name of the neighborhood, as in this case, Ménilmontant.

Bronisław Korwin Czarnocki—Wound up in Italy after the Second World War, in which he had fought with the Polish Armed Forces in the West. He settled permanently in Venice, marrying a wealthy Venetian woman from the Lucheschi family.

Emmanuel Auricoste (1908–1995), French sculptor.

Stanisław Lorentz (1899–1991), Polish art historian serving as director of the National Museum in Warsaw from 1936–1982 (with a break during the war).

Paul Niclausse (1879–1958), French sculptor, professor at the École Nationale Supérieure des Beaux-Arts, where Szapocznikow studied under him in the late 1940s and early 1950s.

what's going on with Brussels—In 1956, Alina Szapocznikow took part in the competition for the Polish Pavilion at EXPO 58 in Brussels, organized by the Polish Association of Visual Artists and the Association of Polish Architects. As Team 13, Walerian Borowczyk, Roman Cieślewicz, Jerzy Czyż, Duszan Poniż, Alina Scholtz, and Szapocznikow tied for first place with Team 17, but a different project altogether ended up being the one actually executed.

as for that seated one, I don't think anything will come of it, and I don't know what to do—it's just an unnecessary nuisance. In any case we'll see after the vernissage—She must be referring to *FIRST LOVE* → [7/1954]. During Szapocznikow's stay in Paris, there were ongoing talks about the purchase of that sculpture by the Musée de l'Art Moderne de la Ville de Paris. These were brokered by Jean Cassou, who was at that time the director of the Musée National de l'Art Moderne. The transaction did take place, in the end, and the piece is still in the collection of the first of those institutions. Copies of that sculpture also exist, one being held by the Muzeum Sztuki in Łódź, and the other in a private collection.

call Czyż—Jerzy Czyż, Polish architect, cf. above.

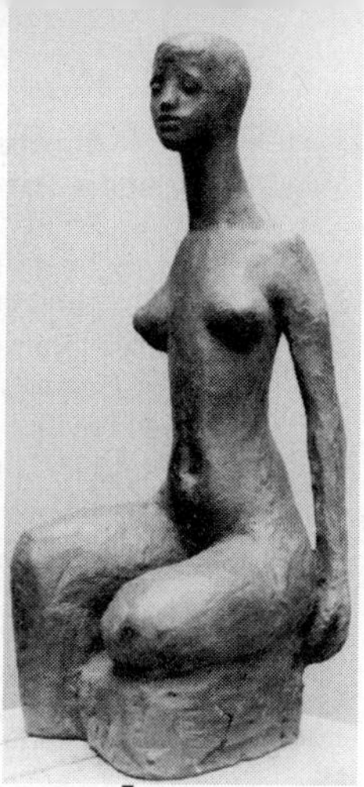

7

79.

LETTER →[P 177]

[JUNE 9, 1956]

I'll have to make plans with Zosia and Romek for next time, and also with Olek—This is Szapocznikow's son Piotr's babysitter, as well as, most likely, Roman Cieślewicz and Aleksander Stanisławski, Ryszard's brother, who was then living in Warsaw. Roman Cieślewicz (1930–1996) was the Polish graphic artist and alumnus of Krakow's Academy of Fine Arts who had moved, in 1955, to Warsaw, where he met Szapocznikow and Stanisławski. He was Szapocznikow's second husband (they were married in February, 1967 in Paris).

The pavilion was in a million pieces when we got here—The reference is to the Polish Pavilion at the Venice Biennale. In 1956, it hosted a group show featuring works by Adam Marczyński, Zbigniew Pronaszko, Marek Włodarski, Antoni Kenar, Jerzy Nowosielski, and Tadeusz Dominik. The exhibition's curators were Juliusz Starzyński, the Pavilion's commissioner, and his assistants, Ryszard Stanisławski and Aleksander Wojciechowski.

The Italians have [...] *a gargantuan painting by Guttuso:* The Beach—*The Beach* (1955–6) by Renato Guttuso (1911–1987), now housed at the National Gallery in Parma.

The Soviet Pavilion seems to be a real revelation, that is, a total sensation—The Union of Soviet Socialist Republics exhibited at the Venice Biennale in 1956 for the first time since 1934. They chose to show traditional paintings, like the artist Stanisławski mentions, Aleksandr Gerasimov. German Nedoshivin was the commissioner of the Soviet Pavilion and at the time the director of the Tretyakov Gallery.

Vera Mukhina (1889–1953), Soviet sculptor, leading representative of socialist realism.

Karol Tchorek (1904–1985), Polish sculptor, fabricator of monuments and plaques to mark sites where Poles were executed during the Nazi occupation from 1939–1945.

Constantin Brâncuşi (1876–1957), Romanian sculptor working in Paris from 1907.

François Pompon (1855–1933), French sculptor specializing in animals.

Luigi Cini, professor of Slavic literatures at the University of Venice. An active member of the Society of Italian-Polish Friendship, frequent assistant commissioner at the Polish Pavilion at the Venice Biennale (first in 1952, and then in the 1960s and 70s).

80.

LETTER →[P 180]

[JUNE 1956]

Stanisławski mentions the exhibitions of French painter Eugène Delacroix (1798–1863); Italian painter Giorgio de Chirico (1888–1978); Spanish painter and sculptor Juan Gris (1887–1927); Dutch painter Piet Mondrian (1872–1944); Belgian painter and sculptor Hendrik Emil (Rik) Wouters (1882–1916); French painter and graphic artist Jacques Villon (real name Gaston Duchamp, 1875–1963); and Italian painter Filippo De Pisis (1896–1956).

81.

LETTER →[P 182]

[JUNE 12, 1956]

pneumatic post—The reference is to a pneumatic system of sending letters through underground pipes using compressed air. The pneumatic post operated in Paris until 1984.

Robert Wogensky (born 1919), a French painter who did wall paintings and tapestry designs.

I got a telegram from Warsaw—The telegram concerned the competition for the Polish Pavilion at EXPO 58 (cf. note to letter 78).

I have a sortir et retour *visa* [then also *aller et retour*]—I have a visa to leave and to return (French).

the question of the sale of the sculpture—She is talking about the sale of *First Love* to the Musée de l'Art Moderne de la Ville de Paris (cf. note to letter 78).

82.

LETTER →[P 184]

[JUNE 14, 1956]

Germaine Richier (1902–1959), French sculptor. Sarah Wilson, citing the research of her student Amy Chmieleski, writes of the connection of her work to Szapocznikow's œuvre: *The links that can be made between Richter's* L'Homme-Forêt *and Szapocznikow's* People-Trees *(1957) are convincing; these are works marked by the "existential" aura of their times* [S. Wilson, "Alina Szapocznikow in Paris...," in *Alina Szapocznikow: Awkward Objects*, *op. cit.*, p. 217].

Stanisław Gajewski (1912–1995) was ambassador of the People's Republic of Poland in Paris from 1954–1961.

André Malraux (1901–1976), French writer, art theorist, first minister of culture under Charles de Gaulle (from 1959–1969). He published, among other things, the three-volume *Le Musée imaginaire de la sculpture mondiale* (1952–1954), which was most likely the book Szapocznikow had in mind.

Marino Marini (1901–1980), Italian sculptor.

Maybe you could get Moore?— English sculptor Henry Moore (1898–1986). In 1956, the second volume of the monograph dedicated to Moore was published by Lund Humphries, encompassing all drawings and sculptures by the artist since 1948.

I'm including the letter from Taminiaux that I received today—Jacques Taminiaux writes in this letter about the planned exhibition of Polish art in Brussels: [The society] *of Belgian-Polish friendship will meet next week to talk about the exhibition of young Polish artists.* [...] *I would like you to speak with Ryszard and suggest some names. It is very hard for me to decide on the basis of the few reproductions I have. I need a list of 15 young artists whom you highly rate: seven or eight less or more non-figurative, seven or eight less or more figurative. You no doubt know what I mean by that. The Belgian painters from the Belgian-Polish friendship society are in large part figurative, and in addition are not the best. Many of them were actually proponents of socrealism, thus it is necessary to be capable of handling sensitive issues* [Ryszard Stanisławski Archive]. The exhibition, curated by Ryszard Stanisławski, was organized in autumn of that year at the Galerie Georges Giroux under the title "Dix peintres polonais: Brzozowski, Fangor, Gella-Melerowicz, Gierowski, Gleb, Mazurkiewicz, Mikulski, Pagowska, Stern, Tchorzewski" (October 27–November 10, 1956).

Un grand bonjour de ton vieux Julien et pour toute la famille—a big hello from your old pal Julien [Lustre] and for the whole family (French).

84.

LETTER →[P 187]

[JULY 1, 1956]

Teresa Pągowska made a very bad impression here and did a very bad job—Teresa Pągowska (1926–2007), Polish painter. This probably concerns the fact that the artist remained in Italy after her visa had expired. Taking advantage of Italian people she had befriended, she spent four months there, which she later recalled as her first important artistic journey.

85.

LETTER →[P 191]

[JULY 2, 1956]

"Lucek" is Lucjan Motyka (1915–2006), Polish United Workers' Party and state activist. He worked at the Ministry of Art and Culture beginning in 1951; from 1955–1957 he was undersecretary of state, and from 1964–1971 the Minister.

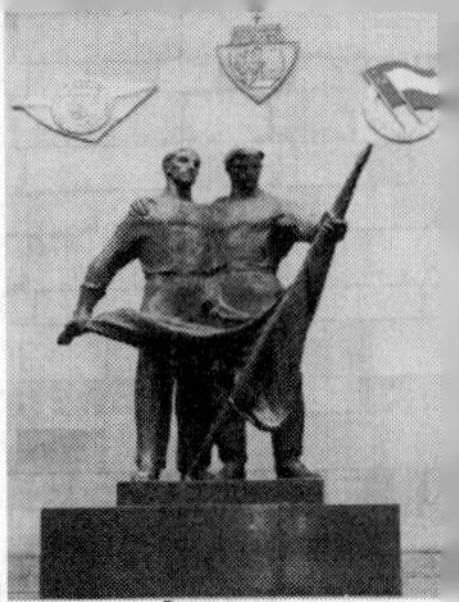

8

on Szucha—The Ministry of Foreign Affairs is located at 23 Szucha Avenue in Warsaw.

88.

LETTER →[P 196]
[JULY 4, 1956]

to poste restante, bureau de poste principale, Roma—to the general delivery window at the main post office in Rome (French).

for sending people out on official passports without funding, and that they should be ashamed of themselves, etc. He led me to believe that he was talking about Teresa and me—cf. note to letter 84.

in view of the fact that I am not without resources (friends, a cousin, and you)—Writing about her cousin, Szapocznikow probably has in mind Max Gerson, with whom she corresponded at that time. On July 20, 1956, he wrote to her from London: *I'll happily counsel you on all things* and recommended her to his two Parisian acquaintances [Ryszard Stanisławski Archive].

they wrote about it in Trybuna—The daily *Trybuna Ludu* [Tribune of the People], the official publication of the Central Committee of the Polish United Workers' Party, published from 1948–1990, printed two notices concerning this exhibition, the first an informational piece entitled "The International Exhibition of Contemporary Sculpture", which listed the Polish artists taking part in the exhibition, including Szapocznikow and her *Monument to a Burnt City* (*Trybuna Ludu*, no. 174, June 23, 1956, p. 2). One month later a photograph of that piece appeared with the caption "The work of Polish sculptor Alina Szapocznikow at the International Exhibition of Contemporary Sculpture at the Rodin Museum in Paris" ("Dzieło polskiej rzeźbiarki w Paryżu", *Trybuna Ludu*, no. 206, July 25 1956, p. 4).

Gaffka—The name of a person renting out a room to people on summer holiday in Karwia.

I collected the rest of the money for the monument—She is referring to payment for the *MONUMENT TO POLISH-SOVIET FRIENDSHIP* → [8/1954], which Szapocznikow did for the Palace of Culture and Science. That building, erected in the very center of Warsaw on the initiative of Joseph Stalin from a design by Lev Rudnev and built by Soviet and Polish workers, was, as emphasized, proof of the friendship between the two nations. The Palace of Culture and Science was opened in 1955, and the unveiling of the monument took place a year later, as was the custom in the People's Republic of Poland, on July 22, that is, the National Day of the Rebirth of Poland. The monument was located in the main lobby of the building until 1992, when it was ordered scrapped.

Mr. Lustre and Michelle—Michelle is the daughter of the Lustres (cf. note to letter 1), born in 1940.

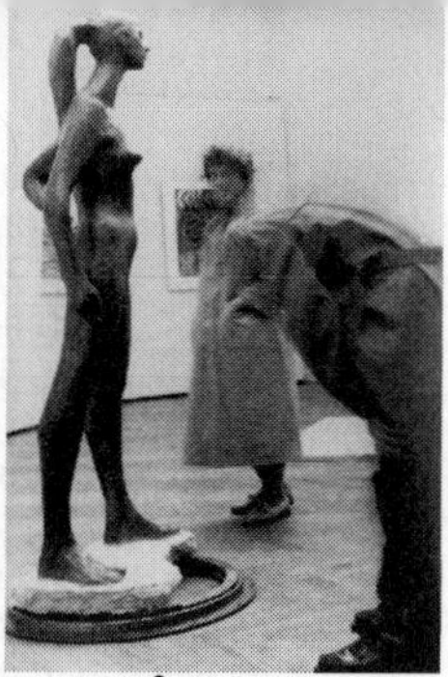
9

89.

LETTER →[P 200]

[JULY 5, 1956]

s'according—come to an agreement (a word of Szapocznikow's creation from French *s'accorder*).

I will be, I think, unveiling the monument to friendship at that time—cf. note to previous letter.

Cesia—Stanisławski's collaborator on the Central Board of Visual Arts and Exhibitions at the Ministry of Art and Culture.

Are Stanisław Zamecznik, Juliusz Starzyński and Olo Wojciechowski still with you?—Juliusz Starzyński (1906–1974), Polish art historian, then director of the State Institute of Art, was the chief commissioner of the Polish Pavilion in Venice. Aleksander Wojciechowski (1922–2006), Polish art historian, also employed by the State Institute of Art, was, along with Stanisławski, one of his deputy commissioners. The exhibition designer was Stanisław Zamecznik (1909–1971), the Polish architect specializing in innovative exhibition layouts and concepts.

C.B.V.A.—The Central Bureau of Visual Arts and Exhibitions at the Ministry of Art and Culture.

Are people all worked up about the incidents in Poznań there, too?—The brutally suppressed workers' protests on the streets of Poznań, begun on June 28, 1956 with a strike by workers at the Cegielski Metal Industry plant that turned into a broader rebellion against totalitarian authorities. Soldiers were deployed against the demonstrators, and several dozen people were killed. In Italy the events in Poznań were widely known: Italian cities were covered with posters expressing solidarity with the Polish workers [Joanna Sosnowska, *Polacy na Biennale Sztuki w Wenecji 1895–1999*, Warszawa, 1999, p. 100.].

93.

LETTER →[P 210]

[JULY 20, 1956]

meet with the plasterer so that he can cast that standing figure for me—"That standing figure" is most likely one of the most important pieces Szapocznikow did during this period, *DIFFICULT AGE* →[9/1956].

The Good Person of Szechwan, Bertolt Brecht's 1940 play.

Halina Mikołajska (1925–1989), Polish actress that from 1955 was with the newly formed Polish Army House Theater (from 1957 the Dramatic Theater), where she acted in *The Good Person of Szechwan*.

in honor of July 22—The most important national holiday in People's Republic of Poland, the National Day of the Rebirth of Poland, which existed until 1990. It was celebrated on the anniversary of the signing of the Manifesto of the Polish Committee of National Liberation in 1944.

95.

LETTER →[P 213]

[JULY 2, 1957]

A friend of Zula's—In one of the appointment book preserved in the Ryszard Stanisławski Archive we found an entry for Zula Polasińska, whose address was in Sopot.

Mr. Honig cares for us just like a father—Camille Honig, writer, literary editor of the California publication *The Jewish Voice*, founder of the International Martin Buber Society. Szapocznikow did a portrait bust of him in 1957 (bronze, height 50 cm).

I don't want to go to Moscow, but I'm afraid to phone the committee without talking it over with you first—In 1957 the 6th World Festival of Youth and Students was held in Moscow (the previous one had taken place in Warsaw in 1955). The committee is the Polish Festival Organization Committee. Szapocznikow ultimately did not take part in the festival. She did go to Moscow in 1959 for the "Exhibition of Polish Industry".

How are things with Poleszczuk?—Ryszard Stanisławski's work on the Central Board of Visual Arts and Exhibitions at the Ministry of Art and Culture did not suit him. He tried to get transferred to the Ministry of Foreign Affairs and was corresponding with Romuald Poleszczuk, director of the Press and Information Department of the Ministry of Foreign Affairs about this until in April 1957, he left the Ministry of Art and Culture of his own accord.

96.

LETTER →[P 214]

[JULY 5, 1957]

Mrs. Ostaszewska, Kasia's mom—The Ostaszewskis and their daughter Kasia were Szapocznikow and Stanisławski's neighbors when they lived on Old Town Square in Warsaw.

97.

LETTER →[P 217]

[JULY 8, 1957]

Jan Brzechwa (1898–1966), real name Jan Wiktor Lesman, a classic writer of children's literature in Poland.

after the opening of the exhibition—From September 6–26, 1957 Alina Szapocznikow had her first exhibition in Poland, along with Jerzy Tchórzewski, in Warsaw's Zachęta Gallery (then operating as the Central Bureau of Art Exhibitions). Jerzy Tchórzewski (1928–1999), painter, graduate of Krakow's Academy of Fine Arts, living in Warsaw during this period, would recall years later: *I think it was at the beginning of 1957 that Alina and I went to Zachęta with the impudent proposition of organizing a shared exhibition in its hallowed halls.* [...] *Szancerowa—the woman at Zachęta—*[Gizela Szancerowa, Zachęta's director] *picked up our idea, much to our surprise. I now think that they happened to need an exhibition of "moderns" at that moment.* [...] *After years of extreme artistic poverty, heck, even after the famous Arsenal exhibition, suddenly Zachęta exhibited painting and sculpture that were modern in the full meaning of that word. The crowded vernissage, as Jerzy Ludwiński described it in* Plastyka *(a supplement to* Życie Literackie*), "delighted some and disgusted others. One way or another, everyone reacted strongly."* [Jerzy Tchórzewski, *Świadectwo oczu. Wspomnienia z lat 1946–1957*, Kraków: Wydawnictwo Literackie, 2006, pp. 263–4].

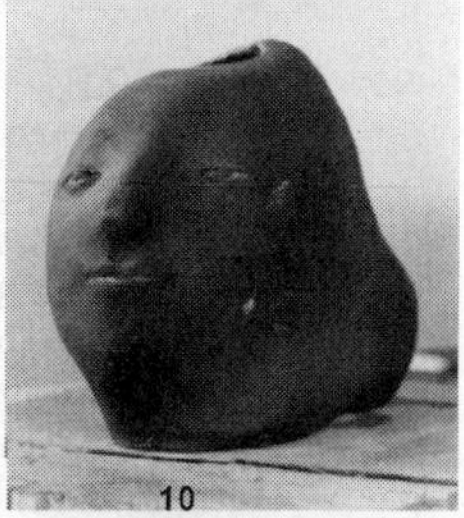

10

When I saw here and in Karwia these little groups of soldiers, I realized that we can't send Zosia—The Hel peninsula was fortified during the interwar period, and for several decades an army garrison was stationed there; during the era of the People's Republic of Poland a considerable portion of the peninsula was off-limits to civilians.

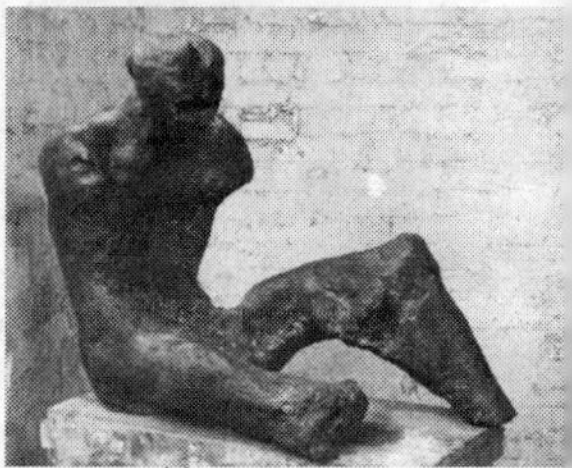

11

and then get started on that ceramics thing—From 1956–57 Szapocznikow made a series of ceramic works, like *POT I* → [10/1956], some of which were shown at the Zachęta exhibition mentioned above.

Welcome Hela Lustre warmly and invite her over, and when I get back, I'll do the rest—Helena Lustre did not end up visiting at that time. She came to Poland in 1958.

98.

LETTER →[P 218]

[1957]

some lodging options—Probably regarding an apartment for Stanisławski. During this period their marriage had fallen apart, and Szapocznikow had become involved with Roman Cieślewicz. The formal divorce was granted on August 21, 1958. In April 1958, Stanisławski moved into Dąbrowski Square 7.

101.

LETTER →[P 221]

[JUNE 21, 1958]

In 1958 Alina Szapocznikow took part in, among other shows, the "Internationale Beeldenteentoostelling in de Open Lucht" ("Plein-Air Exhibition of Contemporary International Sculpture") organized in Arnhem, Holland, which took place at Sonsbeek Park, hence the name Sonsbeek '58. She exhibited *EXHUMED* → [11] there, a sculpture from 1955.

102.

LETTER →[P 222]

[JUNE 25, 1958]

I came from Brussels on Monday night on Sabena—The Belgian national airline Sabena (in operation 1923–2001).

César (1921–1998), full name César Baldaccini, French sculptor. From the 1950s on he made sculptures that were assemblages of metal fragments. He was collaborating at that time with a factory producing metal furniture called Matériel Malma in Villetaneuse. He belonged to the group Nouveaux Réalistes founded in 1960 by critic Pierre Restany and painter Yves Klein.

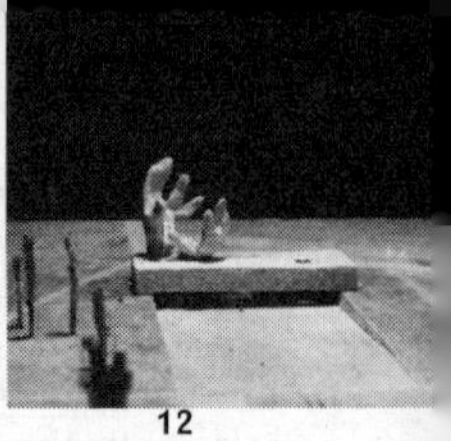

12

Cordegardie—Szapocznikow is probably thinking of the Kordegarda, a gallery founded in 1956 and situated in the former guardhouse of the Potocki palace, since 1949 the seat of the Ministry of Culture and Art.

put the sculptures into the bagnole *etc.*—in the car (French).

The Stadler Gallery was founded in Paris in 1955 by the collector Rodolphe Stadler (1927–2009).

que je suis l'amie de Marie la polonaise sa femme! Ça alors—that I'm a friend of Marie, that Polish woman his wife! Goodness me... (French).

Gualtieri di San Lazzaro (given name Giuseppe Papa, 1904–1974), founder of the important *revue* and Parisian gallery XXᵉ Siècle. Maria Papa Rostkowska (1923–2008). Her first husband was Polish sculptor Ludwik Rostkowski Jr; she emigrated to France in 1957, marrying San Lazzaro in 1958.

comble—the height of (French).

quand je dis que je suis logée par César—when I said I was staying with César (French).

mais pour la prochaine fois—but for next time (French).

The Lustres want to come for August—After returning to Paris from that trip to Poland, Helena Lustre wrote Ryszard Stanisławski: *Everything we managed to see and visit in Warsaw really interested us, thank you very much for being such a good friend and making our stay so nice.* (Ryszard Stanisławski Archive). No letters sent from the Lustres to Alina Szapocznikow have been preserved.

the Sonsbeek catalogue—cf. note to letter 101.

the Auschwitz competition—In 1957, the International Auschwitz Committee organized a competition for an International Monument to the Victims of Fascism, to be erected at the former concentration camp of Auschwitz-Birkenau; with Henry Moore as head of the jury. Among the 426 proposals from all over the world was one proposed by a team whose members included, in addition to Szapocznikow, Jerzy Chudzik, Roman Cieślewicz, and Bolesław Malmurowicz (MAQUETTE → [12]). Their design obtained a distinction and was one of seven that moved on to the second round. In the end, the monument did not come into being until 1967, and was designed by Pietro Cascella and his associates Jerzy Jarnuszkiewicz, Julian Pałka, and Giorgio Simoncini.

Leszek Kołakowski (1927–2009), Polish philosopher, essayist and writer, at the time (from 1954–68) a lecturer at Warsaw University.

Hans Ludwig Cohn Jaffé (1915–1984), German art historian living in Holland.

105.

LETTER →[P 226]

[DECEMBER 9, 1962]

your business cards could be quite quick, but just in

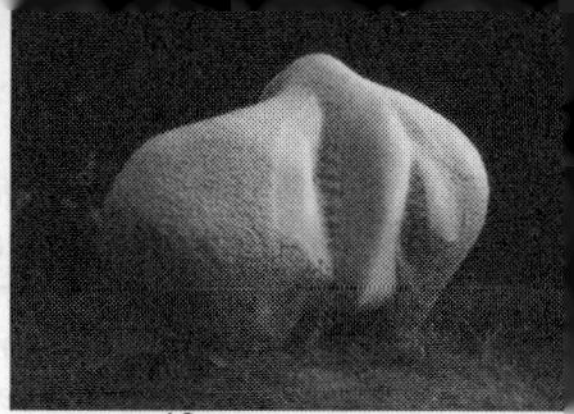

13

Półtawski (you know that typeface)—She is speaking of a Polish type designed in the 1920s by Adam Półtawski.

106.

LETTER →[P 228]

[JULY 14, 1963]

In the summer 1963, Szapocznikow and Cieślewicz spent several weeks abroad. Szapocznikow took part in the "Forma Viva" International Sculpture Symposium in Portorož (in the former Yugoslavia), where she made *BIOLOGICAL SCULPTURE* → [13/1963]. She was probably supposed to see Stanisławski. Cieślewicz started working in West Germany (in Essen, for the firm Krupp). Recommended by Eugenio Carmi, he then worked in Italy as a graphic artist for the steel company Italsider, where he made decorative *panneaux* for five steelworks.

Following this departure, Szapocznikow and Cieślewicz did not return to Poland. They went to Paris with the intention of settling there permanently. Years later Piotr Stanisławski would recall: *Alina decided to leave around Easter. We knew that we were going for a longer time. But we couldn't say that officially, because we wouldn't have gotten our passports* [Excerpts from conversations with Piotr Stanisławski..., *op. cit.*, p. 27.]

107.

LETTER →[P 229]

[DECEMBER 20, 1963]

We wish you and Urszula—After his divorce from Szapocznikow, Stanisławski entered into a relationship with Urszula Czartoryska, and they were married in February, 1966. Urszula Czartoryska (1934–1998) was an art historian and critic. After earning a degree in art history at the Catholic University of Lublin, in 1956 she moved to Warsaw, where she started work as an editor at the magazine *Fotografia*.

108.

LETTER →[P 230]

[JANUARY 9, 1964]

Grand Palais de la Découverte—Parisian science center located in the Grand Palais, founded in 1938. The tunnel beneath the English Channel would not open until 1994.

The Chase of the Golden Meteor (French *La Chasse au Météore* [*Le Bolide*], 1901)—A novel by Jules Verne that appeared in Polish for the first time in 1908 under the title of *Pursuit*, and later (in 1949) as *Meteor Hunters*.

the Susse foundry—In Paris, Szapocznikow worked with the long-standing *fonderie* Susse Frères. The company, originally a stationer's, specialized in bronze casting starting in the 1830s.

with payment conditionnelle—payment on condition of sale (French).

the costs get into the millions in old francs—On January 1, 1960 a currency reform took place in France, introducing a new franc equal to 100 of the old francs.

if I should withdraw from the exhibition in Rome—In this period Szapocznikow was corresponding with Federico Quadrani from the Galleria Odyssia in Rome, who liked the sculptures she had exhibited at the Venice Biennale in 1962. No exhibition ended up coming out of this correspondence, however.

Romek has more work by the day—After coming to Paris, Roman Cieślewicz worked with numerous publishing houses, including Tchou, Julliard, and J.-J. Pauvert, for whom he did graphic design for their books. He also did assignments for the weekly magazine *Elle*, where he later became artistic director.

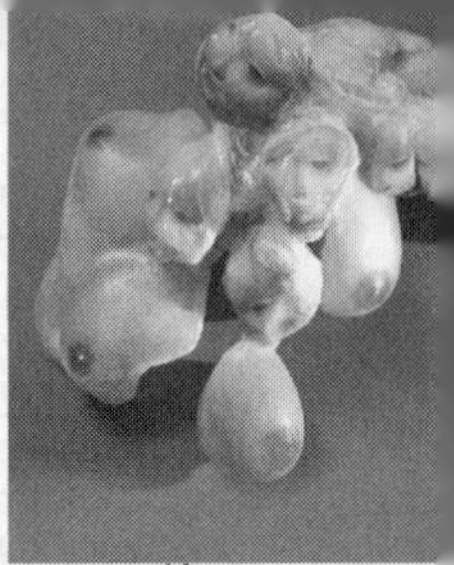

14

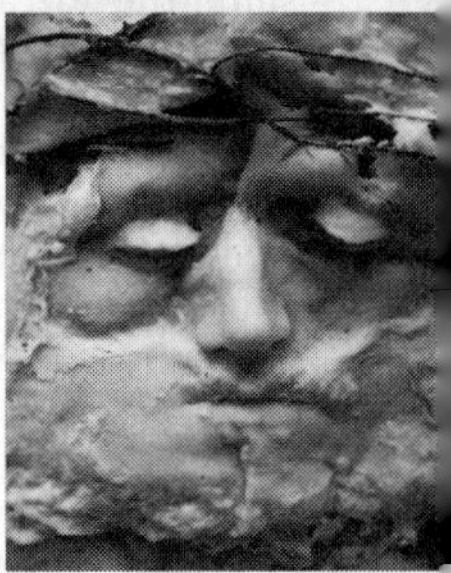

15

109.

LETTER →[P 232]

[APRIL 10, 1964]

classement—report card (French).

récitation—learning by heart and reciting (French).

Dad! I am writing this letter—Piotr Stanisławski's letter is written in French: *Mon cher Papa! J'ecrit cette lettre aprés le vacance de «paques» où je casse la jambe en faisant ski! Je descendu pendant deuxieme jour à Chatel. La place de cette accident est marque sur la carte postale en bleu. L'autre côte de moi ètè monsieurs Pion et Michel. Je sorte dè la piste et je tombe dans la neige mole. Je crie, tout suit monsieur Pion ètè venu Michel ètè parti chercher tobogan. Czykałem pół godziny. Je attendu demi heur. Aprés jè ètè parti à chalet. A deux heur jè ètè parti a hôpital. Mon radio ètè fait. La grande ose ètè casse, en hôpital je mange bien. Merci pour les livres pour chocolate et pour l'animal magnetique et la bille. Je t'embrasse milles fois. Pierre S*

110.

LETTER →[P 234]

[MAY 3, 1964]

Arkady Fiedler, *Robinson's Island*, first Polish edition 1954.

at a printing boarding school—It was during Piotr's first stay at the boarding school, described here, that Szapocznikow first interacted with the Polish Pallottines (the Society of the Catholic Apostolate formed in 1835 in Rome). In Osny, near Paris, they first founded an orphanage, then a boarding school and printing press for the publishing house they ran. A second center is located in the heart of Paris on the rue Surcouf. Here during the 1960s, Father Józef Sadzik (1933–1980), publisher and writer, played a key role, making the Parisian headquarters of the Pallottines one of the most important centers of Polish émigré life there. The Pallottines commissioned two sculptures from Szapocznikow—in 1969 *MADONNA OF KRUŻLOWA (MOTHERHOOD)* → [14] and in 1972 *HEAD OF CHRIST* → [15].

Jan Lebenstein (1930–1999), Polish painter, graphic artist, draftsman, a graduate of the Warsaw Academy of Fine Arts. In 1959, he received the Grand Prix at the 1st International Biennale of Young Artists in Paris, which carried a prize of an arts residency in that city. He then decided to remain in France. In 1964, he had solo shows in, among other places, the Palais des Beaux-Arts in Brussels (Jean Cassou wrote the introduction to the catalogue) and at the Galerie Lacloche in Paris. In 1969, Szapocznikow did a plaster cast of Lebenstein's face.

Olga Scherer-Wirska (1924–2001), Polish writer, translator, literary historian, Slavicist, lived in the United States after the war, and moved to Paris in 1957. She was with Lebenstein in the 1960s.

André Breton (1896–1966), French writer, poet, and art critic, leader of the Surrealist movement.

who was chosen to go to Venice from Poland?—At the Venice Biennale in 1964 at the Polish Pavilion works by Tadeusz Kulisiewicz (graphic artist) and Zofia Woźna (sculpture) were shown. The commissioner of the pavilion was Ksawery Piwocki, Luigi Cini his assistant.

That large sculpture with the tubes I am sending to the Jeune Sculpture salon—The XVI Salon de la Jeune Sculpture in 1964 was the first exhibition of that annual series in which Szapocznikow took part. She then participated in all future years. In 1964, she most likely exhibited two works: *SCULPTURE WITH A TURNING WHEEL* → [16/1963-63] ("that big sculpture on tubes") and *ANIMAL* → [17/1963].

111.

LETTER →[P 236]
[JUNE 25, 1964]

I went to see Dad at Elle—cf. note to letter 108.

112.

LETTER →[P 237]
[JULY 17, 1964]

I got your letter [...] *at my new address*—Szapocznikow and Cieślewicz lived at that time at 32, rue Bertillon. They then moved to Malakoff, a suburb of Paris. Szapocznikow, after arriving in Paris, worked at her studio near the Père-Lachaise cemetery, as she had done before. After moving to Malakoff, she had a workshop near her house.

With regard to the exhibition—in this and in the following letters, she is talking about the sculptures for the exhibition "Profile IV. Polnische Kunst Heute" ("Profile IV: Polish Art Today") at the Städtische Kunstgalerie in Bochum and the Kulturhaus in Kassel, whose curators were Ryszard Stanisławski and Mieczysław Porębski (November 8, 1964–January 17, 1965). Aside from Szapocznikow, also exhibiting were Jerzy Bereś, Stefan Gierowski, Władysław Hasior, Jan Lebenstein, Aleksander Kobzdej, Lucjan Mianowski, Jerzy Nowosielski, and Jan Tarasin. Ultimately, Szapocznikow exhibited her bronze cast of *UNMARRIED* → [18/1963, PLASTER CAST] (which later disappeared), *MACHINE EN CHAIRE I* → [19/1964], *ARMORED II* → [20/1964] (1964) and *BIOLOGICAL SCULPTURE II* → [21/1964].

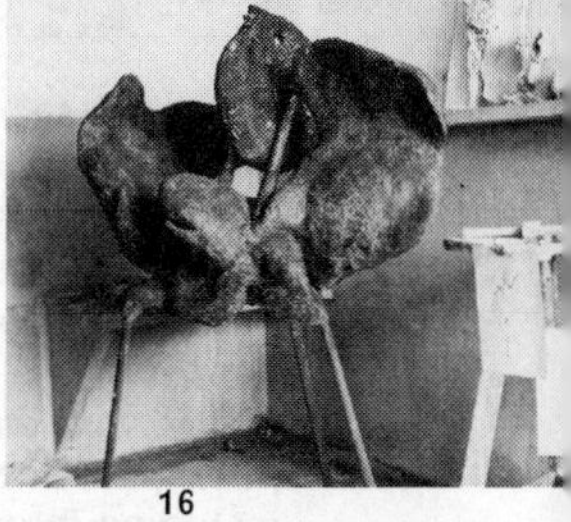
16

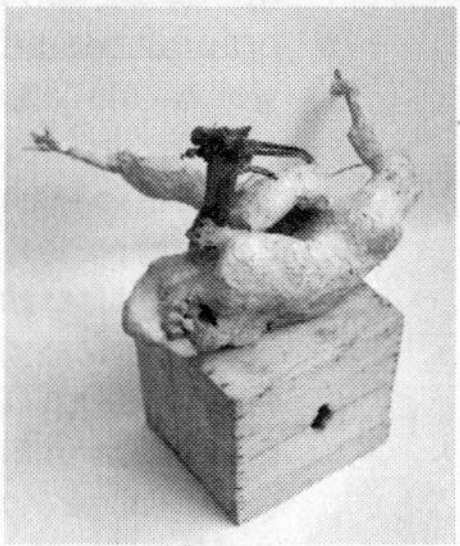
17

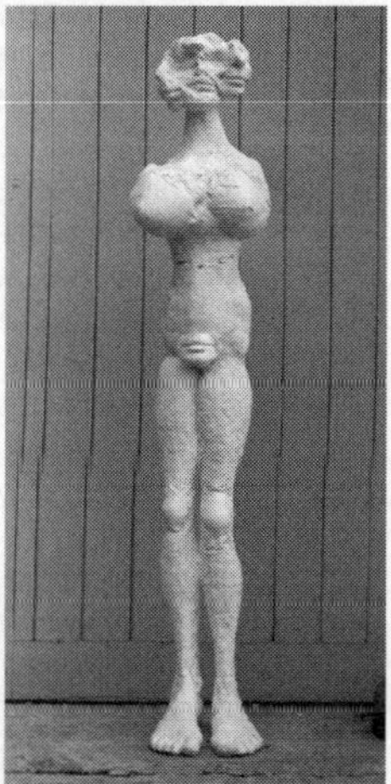
18

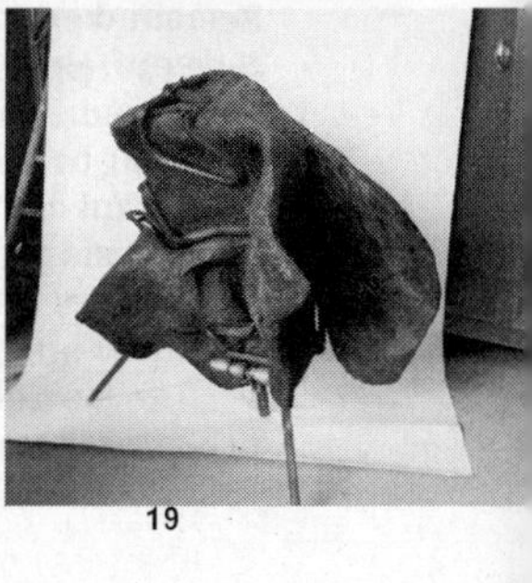
19

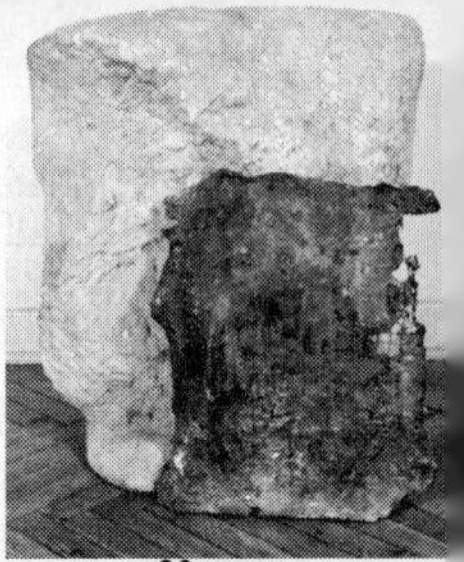
20

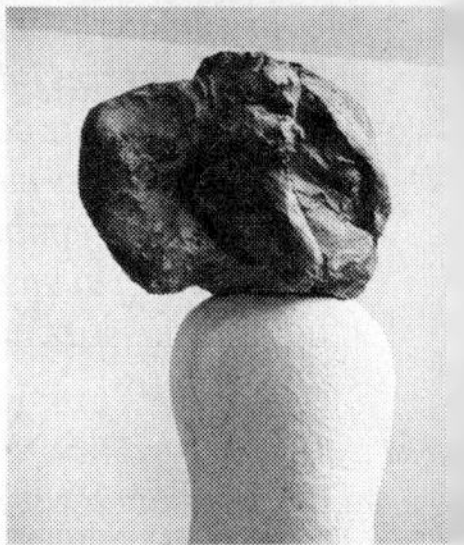
21

"Bronze hand" is most likely a fragment of a design done for the competition organized in 1957 for the Monument to the Heroes of Warsaw. Szapocznikow's team (which also included Jerzy Chudzik, Roman Cieślewicz, and Bolesław Malmurowicz) was awarded a distinction. The cast of the hand in bronze was done in 1963.

take what you need from my studio—Leaving Poland, Szapocznikow and Cieślewicz did not clear out their apartment or her studio on Brzozowa Street. In public statements and official documents, Szapocznikow would state, in fact, that she "went often" to Paris, not that she was living there.

Unmarried, *170 cm, is currently in Opole for the plein-air exhibition*—Szapocznikow took part in the "Polish Plein-Air Sculpture 1964" exhibition at the Opole Silesian Museum.

After the biennale I participated in: *Bronzetto 63, Carrara 63, Sympozjon Portorož 63, Salon Jeune Sculpture Paris 1964*—"biennale" is the 31st Venice Biennale, where Szapocznikow was exhibiting at the Polish Pavilion along with Tadeusz Brzozowski, Eugeniusz Eibisch and Stanisław Horno-Popławski. The curator of the Pavilion was Stanisław Teisseyre. "Bronzetto 63" is the XV Biennale d'Arte. The V Concorso Internazionale del Bronzetto in Padua (previously, in 1961, she had taken part in the fourth edition of this biennale). "Carrara 63" was the Biennale internazionale di scultura in Carrara; here Szapocznikow errs, as the third edition of this took place in 1962. For the Portorož 63 Symposium see the note to letter 106; the XVI Salon de la Jeune Sculpture in Paris took place in 1964 (cf. note to letter 110).

I think we are going to Vienna, where Romek is supposed to have a poster exhibition—Roman Cieślewicz's exhibition in Vienna did not take place until 1965, at the Galerie in der Biberstrasse.

113.

LETTER →[P 240]

[AUGUST 2, 1964]

Herta Wescher (1899–1971), German art historian. She wrote, among other subjects, on what came to be called the "*nouvelle*" or "*seconde École de Paris*", that is, the painters living and working in Paris who come onto the scene after the Second World War, such as Pierre Soulages, Nicolas de Staël, Jean Fautrier, Serge Poliakoff).

cours Nadeau—the Nadeau courses (French). She is referring to the French-language course that Piotr Stanisławski was taking.

Mrs. Michelle Zahorska is at the same campsite, and in a few days she is going with Dorian to Bulgaria—After separating from her husband, Michelle Zahorska returned in 1961 to Paris (cf. note to letter 76). Michelle and Lech Zahorski had two children—Beata and Dorian.

114.

LETTER →[P 242]

[AUGUST 21, 1964]

Dad! Thanks for your letter—Piotr Stanisławski's letter is written in French: *Mon cher Papa! Merci pour la lettre. Pendent le vacances l'eau d'Atlantique était très bonne. J'ai vue pendent le vacances le film qui s'apelle le «Trou» c'est un film qui raconte une histoire des prisoniers français qui creuxsent deux trous pour se delivrer, mais quand ils comencent a desendre les gardiens de prison ont decouvert leurs trous. Mes vacances de cette anne était vraiment très jolis. Les filmes étaient gratuites; j'ai joue aussi sûr les flipers avec le copain. Je m'amuse bien avec le cousin de Dorian qui s'apelle Jean-Luc et qui est mechant et gentille et il change tout le temps. Ma jambe va très bien j'ai ne pas mal, seulement une fois par semaine j'ai un peu mal au genou. Tout va bien. Maman se sent bien, Papa aussi, et moi aussi. Je T'embrasse bien fort et tante Ursule, ton fils Piotrek*

The Hole (*Le Trou*)—French-Italian film from 1960, directed by Jacques Becker.

jeune homme—young man (French).

because everything was registered under all three last names, and the mail is forwarded regularly from Sextius Michel—After arriving in Paris, Szapocznikow and Cieślewicz settled first at 15, rue Sextius-Michel. The "three last names" she mentions are Szapocznikow, Cieślewicz and Stanisławski (Piotr).

Jean-Louis Bloch-Lainé—French photographer then working with fashion photographer Peter Knapp, artistic director of *Elle*. He later specialized in photographing food.

cours Nadeau cours révision et préparatoire pour lycée—Nadeau courses, review and preparation for high school (French).

the big sculpture with the revolving wheel from the Salon was bought by the museum—She is speaking of *Sculpture with a Turning Wheel* (1963–1964). That piece, shown for the first time at the XVI Salon de la Jeune Sculpture at the Rodin Museum, was purchased by the Musée d'art Moderne de la Ville de Paris.

115.

LETTER →[P 244]

[SEPTEMBER 26, 1964]

Peter Leo, director of the then Städtische Kunstgalerie Bochum (today's Museum Bochum-Kunstsammlung and Kunstmuseum).

Biological Sculpture *is a mixture of bronze with stone*—there were three versions of this sculpture. The first, made only of stone, appeared in 1963 at the Portorož Symposium. The remaining two, combining stone and bronze elements, appeared in 1964.

limite d'âge—age limit (French).

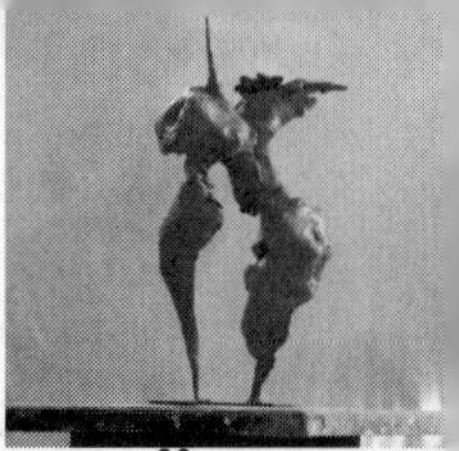
22

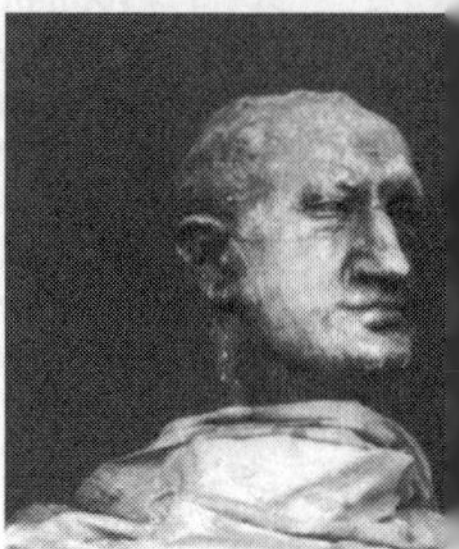
23

116.

LETTER →[P 246]
[OCTOBER 2, 1964]

Duo—At the end of 1959 and beginning of 1960, a version of this sculpture was fabricated in cement, and cast in bronze in 1960 (*DUO* → [22]). This was purchased from the artist in 1967 by the Regional Museum in Toruń.

because that has nothing to do with Desa—Sales of works of art in communist Poland were made through the State Enterprise DESA (an acronym for *Dzieła Sztuki i Antyki*, or "Works of Art and Antiques"), founded in 1950. In 1959, a separate entity was formed, the DESA Bureau of Foreign Trade, under the Ministry of Foreign Trade, which was responsible for dealing with works of art sold internationally. The sales procedures, and above all, the forms of payment for the works, were strictly delimited, and the possibilities of utilizing the foreign currency earned were very restricted. Ordinance 2 of January 4, 1962 stated, for example, that works fabricated or taken abroad (i.e., for an exhibition) may be sold directly, but the contract must be registered with the Bureau of Foreign Trade, as *foreign means of payment* [...] *may be spent by the artist abroad in an amount equal to up to 50% of the sum total earned from a given sale, not more, however, than 12,000 zlotys from all transactions conducted over the course of any given trip of the artist abroad.*

Armored *(unique cire perdue)*—*Armored* was a sculpture made up of two parts—of the base block made of sandstone and the bronze attached to it, cast by the "lost-wax" method (*cire perdue* in French). The first version of *Armored* was made in 1962, and then it was redone.

because with the two possible exchange rates it's hard for me to give them in zlotys—The Polish zloty was not a freely exchangeable currency, and the official rate was very low. There was also the "Pekao" rate (from the name of the state savings bank Powszechna Kasa Oszczędności PKO), according to which calculations falling under the category of "internal export" were made, that is, the sale of goods by the state for hard currency. Foreign currency could also be purchased on the black market, but the price was high, and it was illegal to take it out of the country.

118.

LETTER →[P 248]
[JANUARY 16, 1965]

James Oliver Curwood, *Les cœurs les plus farouches*, original title *Isobel: A Romance of the Northern Trail*, 1913.

Leopold Infeld (1898–1968), Polish theoretical physicist, associate of Einstein, gained international fame before the Second World War. From 1938 he lived in Canada; in 1950 he returned to Poland. In 1953, Szapocznikow made a *PORTRAIT* → [23] of him in plaster. In 1964, his *Sketches from the Past*

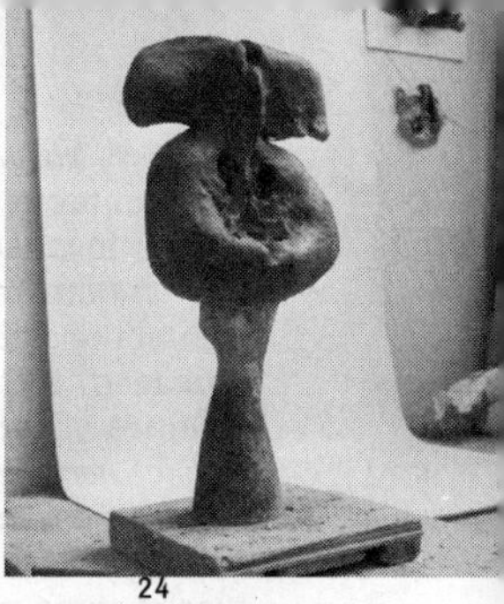
24

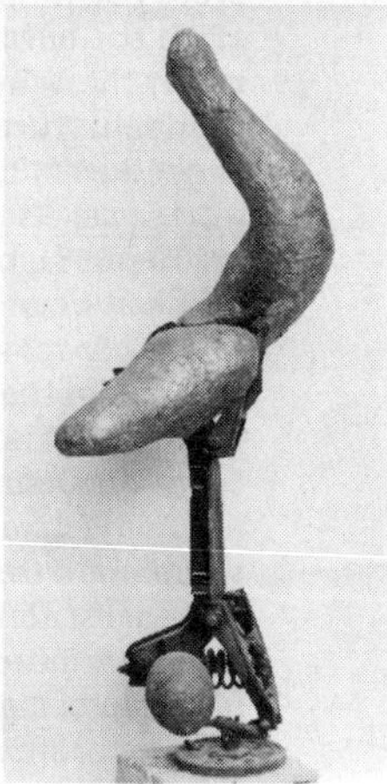
25

appeared, published by PIW, the State Publishing Institute.

Today's news of Churchill's death throes—Winston Churchill died on January 24, 1965 in London.

119.

LETTER →[P 250]
[FEBRUARY 22, 1965]

your postcard came from Amsterdam—From 1960 to 1966, Stanisławski worked with the DESA Bureau of Foreign Trade as a permanent expert on contemporary art and was frequently sent abroad in that capacity. In February 1965, he went to Eindhoven for the opening of an exhibition of Polish tapestries at the Stedelijk Van Abbe Museum in order to—as he stated in his report—discuss "matters relating to the use of this exhibition" (Ryszard Stanisławski Archive). He stopped in Amsterdam along the way.

Sławomir Mrożek (born 1930), Polish playwright, writer of prose and satire, illustrator.

Kazimir (Kazimierz) Karpuszko (1925–2009), art collector, dealer, and curator, born in Poland, lived in the United States after the war.

Pierre Restany (1930–2003), French art critic and curator. His acquaintance with Szapocznikow began in 1960, when he came to Poland for the Annual Congress of AICA (the Association Internationale des Critiques d'Art), held that year in Warsaw. After moving to Paris, Szapocznikow remained in constant contact with him. Restany wrote several pieces on her work.

Dobrochna Strumiłło-Olkiewicz (1932–1993), Polish art historian then working at DESA.

I am supposed to exhibit at Réalités Nouvelles and at the Salon de Mai, and then on my own—Szapocznikow did take part in 1965 in the XX Salon des Réalités Nouvelles, where she exhibited *Faruk* (PHARAOH → [24/1964]) and the XXI Salon de Mai, where she exhibited GOLDFINGER → [25/1965] (titled *Sculpture* then). Her solo show did not take place until 1967. When Szapocznikow writes about important meetings, she probably has in mind a meeting arranged by Marcel Duchamp with William and Noma Copley. In 1954, they founded a foundation in Chicago that awarded an annual prize in the field of art (the responsibility of William Copley) and one in the field of music (the responsibility of his wife). We do not know whether this meeting occurred, but the artist did receive the prize at the end of 1965. (See letters 125 and 126.)

121.

LETTER →[P 253]
[APRIL 1, 1965]

Stefan G. is Stefan Gierowski (born 1925), Polish abstract painter, graduate of the Krakow Academy of Fine Arts, lived in Warsaw from 1949.

Mrs. Radziejowska adds that I should do something about

that Perry woman—Zofia Radziejowska was then the head of the trade unit of DESA. Beatrice Perry (1921–2011) ran the Gres Gallery in Washington, and in 1962 she took four sculptures by Szapocznikow (including WOMAN-ROSE → [26/1958–59]) with the goal of selling them to American collectors. They arrived damaged, and in fear of further damaging them, the gallery never returned them to Szapocznikow. Attempts were made to recover them for several years, but it appears that these failed, and today they are considered lost.

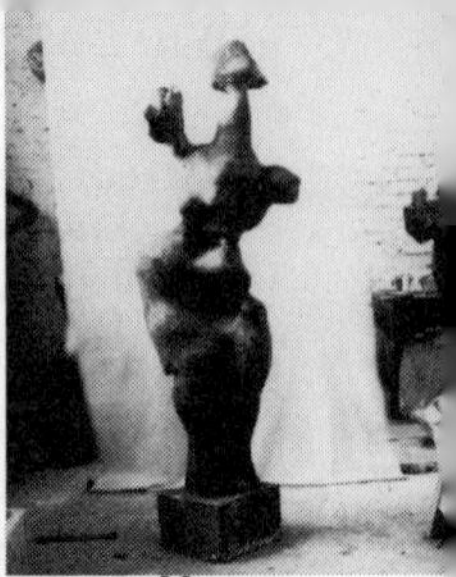

26

you as the commissioner of "Sopot Similitudes"—This took place beginning in 1948 at the Sopot Festival of Visual Arts. In 1965, the curator of the festival exhibition, entitled "Similitudes," was Ryszard Stanisławski. Szapocznikow exhibited four sculptures there: *Machine en chaire I* (1964), *Biological Sculpture II* (1964), *Goldfinger* (1965), and MAN WITH INSTRUMENT → [27/1965]. The invitation was signed by Stanisław Teisseyre (1905–1988), painter and long-time president of the Polish Association of Visual Artists.

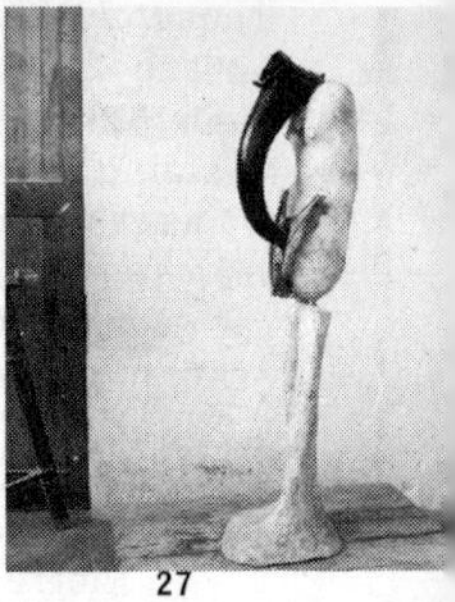

27

Szymczak was on vacation—Zygmunt Szymczak was then director of the Bureau of Art Exhibitions in Sopot.

Giza is the aforementioned Gizela Szancerowa, director of the Central Bureau of Art Exhibitions, Zachęta.

Wojciech Wilski (1914–2011), then the director of the Visual Arts Department at the Ministry of Art and Culture, later of the Central Bureau of Art Exhibitions, Zachęta.

We saw the movie King Kong *recently*—There were two films featuring the giant gorilla made prior to 1965, the original from 1933, and the second from 1962, the latter a Japanese science-fiction film entitled *King Kong vs. Godzilla*, directed by Ishirō Honda.

I saw GOLDFINGER, it is really neat—*Goldfinger* was the third film of the James Bond series, whose world premiere took place in 1964. It came out in French cinemas in February of 1965. It was probably the advertising campaign for this film that inspired Szapocznikow to later make a sculpture by the same name (for more on this, see Agata Jakubowska, "Alina Szapocznikow's *Leg* and *Goldfinger*: Between Reality and Illusion," in *Alina Szapocznikow: Awkward Objects*, *op. cit.*).

122.

LETTER →[P 255]

[APRIL 8, 1965]

consular passports—See note to letter 16. Every time the bearer of this type of passport wished to come to Poland, he or she was required to apply for a visa.

my files have been bogged down by starting back in canteen times—namely by you and your visits to the miners—See note to letter 35.

I received a sculpture studio in Sopot—In 1965, the Art School Department of the Ministry of Art and Culture offered Szapocznikow a job at the Academy of Fine Arts in Poznań or Gdańsk; at the end she turned them down. Stanisław Horno-

Popławski (1902–1997) was a sculptor and teacher (from 1949 at the Academy of Fine Arts in Sopot, then in Gdańsk).

Romek is supposed to become the art director—Cieślewicz did assume the artistic directorship of *Elle*, but not until 1966.

Tadeusz Breza (1905–1970), Polish writer and literary critic, cultural attaché from 1955–65, in Rome from 1955–9, then in Paris.

he is supposed to do a book on Eisensztajn—Cieślewicz was doing a number of commissions around this time for the French publisher Éditions Julliard (founded in 1942); we have been unable to pinpoint this particular project, probably on Sergei Eisenstein (1898–1948), Russian avant-garde film director.

the credits he's doing for Wajda—Cieślewicz did the poster for the 1965 movie *Ashes*, directed by Andrzej Wajda.

carte de séjour—temporary residency permit (French).

in connection with my past—See note to letter 12.

123.

LETTER →[P 257]

[MAY 23, 1965]

Georges Boudaille (1925–1991), French art critic and director of the visual-arts section of *Les Lettres françaises* from 1958–72.

I was even supposed to participate this year in a symposium in California—She is referring to the International Sculpture Symposium organized in 1965 at California State University at Long Beach, for which she had been invited to apply. Each of the artists that received this invitation was then asked to send in photographs of four pieces, on the basis of which the jury would make a final selection of 11 participants. Szapocznikow did not make it to this final round.

Giuseppe Marchiori (1901–1982), Italian art critic, whom Szapocznikow met in 1958 during his stay in Poland. Marchiori initiated Szapocznikow's first show abroad, an exhibition of drawings at the Falsetti Gallery in Prato in 1960. In 1965, Szapocznikow did, in fact, take part in the fourth Carrara Biennale.

124.

LETTER →[P 258]

[DECEMBER 22, 1965]

especially Romek, because of the Biennale—The first International Poster Biennale was organized in Warsaw in 1966 (from 1968 it would be organized by the Poster Museum, then a division of the National Museum in Warsaw). Cieślewicz was one of the IPB laureates, receiving the prize for his poster design for Warsaw's Dramatic Theatre for its presentation of Franz Kafka's *The Trial*.

very connected with Aubusson textiles—Some of the most respected mills were located in Aubusson; they executed many designs by well-known artists. In the 1960s there was a kind of renaissance of textiles, one manifestation of which was the 1962 Lausanne International Tapestry Biennale. The Polish presence at this first edition, which included Magdalena Abakanowicz (born 1930), was distinctive.

Jean Picart Le Doux (1902–1982), French textile designer.

Bogusław Płaza, then vice-director of the Bureau of International Cultural Cooperation at the Ministry of Art and Culture.

Paris is defending itself as best it can against op. pop. stop, super op. [...] *Did you all see the new* SECOND REALISM *and* SUPER POP—*that the Americans did?*—Cieślewicz jokingly refers to contemporary trends in art and their reception in the French capital. It was, among other things, a period of intense flourishing of pop and op art (the latter in particular after the exhibition "The Responsive Eye" at the Museum of Modern Art in New York in 1965).

I've already applied for the '67 exhibition—Probably the Second Polish Poster Biennale in Katowice. Cieślewicz exhibited a poster for Adam Mickiewicz's *Forefathers' Eve*, put on by the National Theater in Warsaw.

Urszula's paper on my photocherches—Urszula Czartoryska, working as a photography critic, had occasionally written on Cieślewicz's photomontages; here probably the reference to her article "Mechaniczne obrazy w plastyce" [Mechanical Images in the Visual Arts], *Projekt*, no. 5–6 (1965). "Photocherches" is a neologism for photographic searching (from French *chercher*, to look for.)

125.

LETTER →[P 260]

[JANUARY 25, 1966]

while you were in Głuchów—She almost certainly means Stanisławski's stay in Gołuchów (not Głuchów); there was a house for artistic residencies located in the vicinity of the castle there, which was a branch of the National Museum in Poznań.

the letter he promised from the Golovanoffs' house—Nina Golovanoff ran a boarding house in Janvry where Piotr Stanisławski stayed for a few months.

Anton Makarenko (1888–1939), Soviet educator, founder of the communist education system, advocated the benefits of collective and group activites.

For now Romek is the one that has skipped ahead—Cieślewicz, along with Antoine Kieffer, did the layout for the French edition of *Vogue* in 1966.

Jerzy Stajuda (1936–1992), Polish painter and art critic. In the late 1950s and early 1960s, he published in many periodicals, including in *Przegląd Artystyczny*, *Przegląd Kulturalny*, *Polska*, *Ty i Ja*, and *Współczesność*. The latter publication published two texts by Szapocznikow originally written as letters to Stajuda.

Alberto Giacometti (1901–1966), Swiss sculptor and painter. In one of the aforementioned letters for *Współczesność*, Szapocznikow describes her acquaintance with Giacometti and the visit he paid to her studio—this would be, as it turned out, the last time they spoke ["Z Paryża pisze Alina Szapocznikow," *Współczesność*, no. 5 (1966), p. 8]. Giacometti was known for often destroying his own work.

Cérès Franco, gallerist and collector, a Brazilian woman who, after studying in the United States, settled in Paris in 1951, where in 1952 she started the gallery L'œil de Bœuf.

We recently went to a cocktail hour at Ceres' in honor of Penrosa—This is almost certainly an error and should read "Pedrosa:" Mario Pedrosa (1900–1981), Brazilian art and literary critic, whom Stanisławski would recall years later: *He was a wonderful art critic, a member of the Secretariat of the Trotskyists Fourth International, who hit the art scene like a meteor* [interview with Ryszard Stanisławski by Adam Szymczyk and Andrzej Przywara, *Muzeum to są również ludzie* [A Museum Is Also People], http://www.obieg.pl/rozmowy/1419, date of access March 8, 2012].

"Ewa Garszt." is no doubt Ewa Wilczur-Garztecka (1920–2007), Polish art critic and co-founder, along with her husband, Juliusz Wilczur-Garztecki, of the Klub Krzywego Koła [Crooked Circle Club] (1955–1962).

Jean—the Brazilian-Romanian-Slav, is probably Jean Boghici, a gallerist with part-time residency in Brazil who was then working with Cérès Franco.

Corneille (1922–2010), real name Guillaume Cornelis Beverloo, Dutch painter and one of the founders of the group Cobra.

Honorio Morales (born 1933), Argentine painter.

126.

LETTER →[P 262]

[FEBRUARY 9–10, 1966]

Julian Pałka (1923–2002), Polish poster artist and exhibition designer.

Michel Ragon (born 1924), French art and architecture critic.

René Salanon was chief conservator at the Bibliothèque des Arts Décoratifs at the Musée des Arts Décoratifs located in the Pavillon de Marsan in a western wing of the Louvre.

Józef Mroszczak (1910–1975), Polish graphic artist, founder and long-time organizer of the International Poster Biennale.

Strangle Bojko for a good cause!—Szymon Bojko (born 1917), Polish art historian and critic.

the publishing house that the Polish priests run—The publishing house Éditions du Dialogue, run by the Pallottines in

Paris from 1966 (ending in the 1990s), initially directed by Father Józef Sadzik (1933–1980). Polish artists living abroad, including Roman Cieślewicz and Jan Lebenstein, worked there with the Pallottines (cf. note to letter 110).

They are anti-Wyszyński and anti-Piasecki—Stefan Wyszyński (1901–1981) was from 1948 the Roman Catholic Archbishop of Warsaw and Primate of Poland and elevated to Cardinal in 1953. Bolesław Piasecki (1915–1979) was before the Second World War one of the leaders of the nationalist ONR [*Obóz Narodowo-Radykalny*, National Radical Camp]. In the People's Republic of Poland he collaborated with the communist authorities, and in 1947 founded the PAX Association, a Catholic lay organization collaborating with the Polish United Workers' Party.

Skira—Italian publisher specializing in art books.

Marcel Duchamp (1887–1968), French artist who settled permanently in the United States from 1942.

Barnet Hodes, American lawyer and art collector.

Eleanor Hodes, American art collector.

Darius Milhaud (1892–1974), French composer who emigrated to the United States after the outbreak of the Second World War.

Jean (Hans) Arp (1887–1966), painter, graphic artist, sculptor of Alsatian origin.

Alfred Barr, Jr. (1902–1981), American art historian, in 1929 named first director of the Museum of Modern Art in New York.

Roberto Matta Echaurren (1911–2002), known as Matta, Chilean painter.

Max Ernst (1891–1976), painter, graphic artist, poet of German origin.

Walter Hopps (1932–2005), American, worked in galleries and museums, at the time director of the Pasadena Museum of Art in California (today the Norton Simon Museum).

William S. Lieberman (1924–2005), curator at major American museums, at the time of this letter curator at the Museum of Modern Art in New York, later at the Metropolitan Museum of Art.

Man Ray (1890–1976), real name Emmanuel Radnitzky, American photographer.

Roland Penrose (1900–1984), English artist and organizer of artistic life, with Herbert Read co-creator of the Institute of Contemporary Art in London.

Herbert Read (1893–1968), English poet, art critic and theorist, co-creator of the Institute of Contemporary Art in London.

A. James Speyer (1913–1986), American architect and curator at the Art Institute of Chicago.

I have the feeling that Speyer put me up for it [...] *his sister has a salon here*—James Speyer's sister was the gallerist Darthea Speyer.

Please convey our sincere congratulations to Ewa on her wedding—The wedding of Stanisławski's eldest daughter, Ewa.

He (P.R.) is a correspondent at Vytvarna Prace *in Prague*—From 1964–8, Pierre Restany was the French correspondent for the Czech magazine *Vytvarne Prace, Vytvarne Umeni.*

I've been invited to the symposium in Hořice—One of the typical phenomena of artistic life in the 1960s was the international sculpture symposium organized peridiocally in different places in Central and Eastern Europe, like St. Margarethen in Austria, Vyšné Ružbachy in Slovakia, and Portorož and Vrnjačka Banja in Yugoslavia. These were occasions for sculptors to create larger works of their own design (while in making monuments, for example, the person or organization commissioning the work often determined, at least in part, its design). Szapocznikow participated in symposiums in all of the aforementioned places. The symposium in Hořice was founded in 1966. We have not been able to obtain any information about her stay there.

because of AICA—The Annual AICA (International Association of Art Critics) Congress took place in Czechoslovakia in 1966.

Romek was working till four in the morning all last week with different Avedons, Penns and others—Cieślewicz became artistic director of *Elle* in 1966. While working there, he carried out sessions with renowned photographers like, as mentioned here, Richard Avedon and Irving Penn. At the beginning of 1967, in a letter to Wojciech Fangor, Szapocznikow wrote: *Romek is flourishing and blossoming more and more in Paris. He's ousted Knapp and a few others and is the undisputed king there now, surrounded by secretaries—he reigns and swells with influence and money that unfortunately he irrationally throws away on financing my art, which, like anything else that is different and interesting, no one here wants* [Wojciech Fangor Archive].

That cousin from Israel—Szapocznikow kept in touch with three of her cousins—Max Gerson and Lejb Auerbach (in 1952, the latter emigrated from Tel Aviv to Canada), mentioned above, and with Marek Helman.

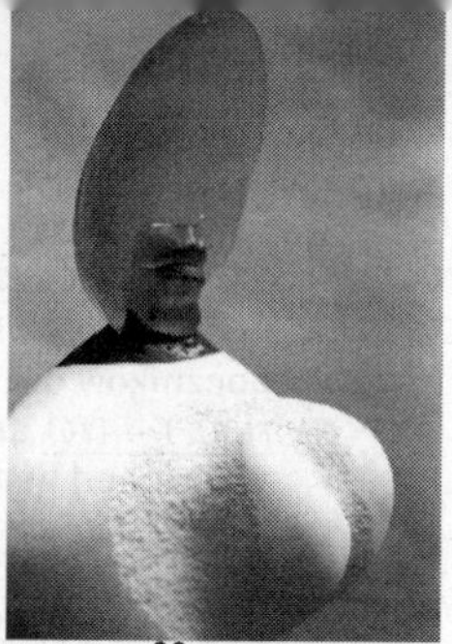

28

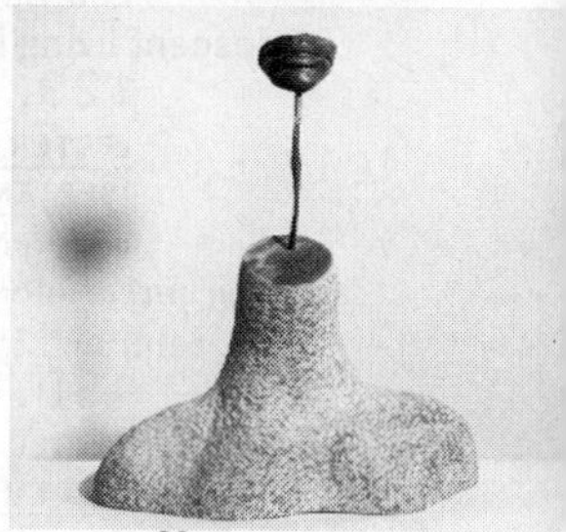

29

127.

LETTER →[P 267]

[MARCH 15, 1966]

a fan of my "fine arts" has funded this wonderful trip—During this stay in Carrara, Szapocznikow sculpted, among other things, the marble portion of *SELF-PORTRAIT I* → [28/1966] and *TORSO* → [29/1966–67]. She worked in stonemasonries owned by Carlo Nicoli. That fan was probably Peter Kaufmann, a Swiss collector.

sono tanto felice!—I am so happy! (Italian).

Moore bought a little house from a peasant—The sculptor Henry Moore had his studio in Forte dei Marni.

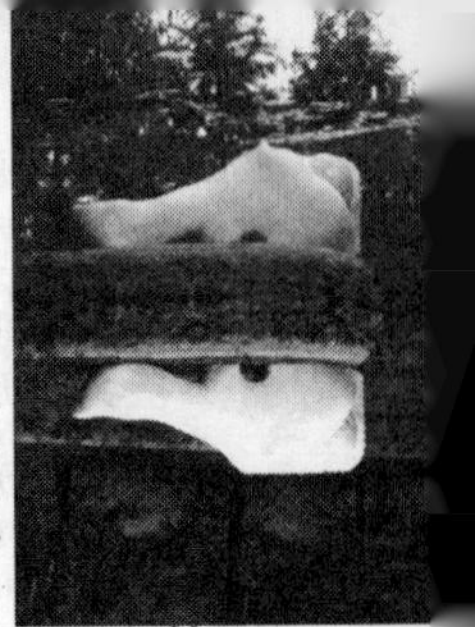
30

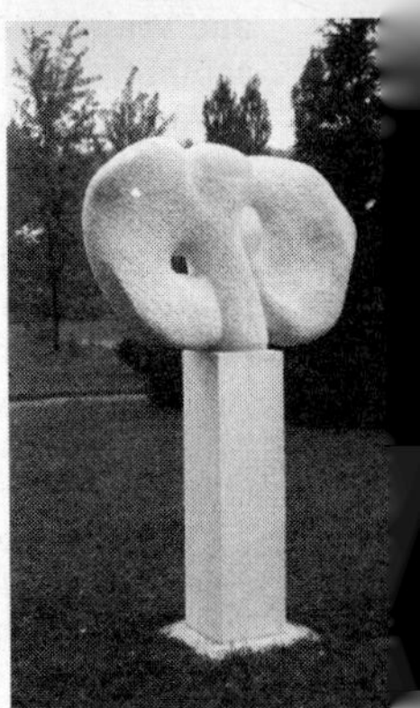
31

128.

LETTER →[P 268]

[JULY 23, 1966]

Mom already finished one marble sculpture here—Szapocznikow did two pieces in Vrnjačka Banja: *PLEIN-AIR SCULPTURE I* → [30] and *II* → [31], like Ernst Neizvestny (born 1926), mentioned here, who did *Centaur* and *Stone Tears*.

Elle est très belle, et maintenant elle a commencé une seconde sculpture—She looks very lovely, and she has just begun a second sculpture (French).

Lea Lublin (1929–1999), Argentine artist of Polish descent living in Paris from the 1960s.

129.

LETTER →[P 270]

[SEPTEMBER 19, 1966]

your letter from Poznań bearing the news of the death of your father—Ryszard Stanisławski's father Romuald died on September 12, 1966.

130.

LETTER →[P 271]

[DECEMBER 4–5, 1966]

Dear Dad. Thank you very much for the three books—Piotr Stanisławski's letter is written in French: *Je te remercie beaucoup des trois livres et des ces deux disques. A l'ecole ca va, sauf en anglais. la matiere où j'ai des meilleures notes c'est les mathematiques. Pour les vacances de Noël je vais aller à Val d'Iser. Je serai la bas dans une colonie du lycée Montaigne à Paris. Mes parents sont en train de chercher un apartement, car celui où nous habitons maintenant est trop petit pour nos besoins. Le temps ici n'est pas merveilleux. Il pleut souvent et le soleil est caché presque toute la journée. Comment vous vous portez? Chez nous tout va bien. J'aie un petit rhume, mais a part ca rien à signaler. Sur ca je vais finir ma lettre car 7 h. sonne. Je vous embrasse bien fort, Piotr*

Val d'Isère—A well-known ski resort in southeastern France.

my exhibition with Houston Brown—Szapocznikow's first solo show since her departure from Poland in 1963 was on view at the Florence Houston Brown Gallery in Paris from April 11–May 6, 1967. Later that year, this exhibition was also presented at Warsaw's Zachęta Gallery from July 7–30 (separate catalogue), as well as in Stockholm at the Gallery Latina and in Copenhagen at the Gallery Marya. The curator of this exhibition was Pierre Restany, who included the following in the catalogue: *The artist appears to be slowly freeing herself after her long-standing torments from the horror of the war and the camps: she is beginning to wake up to life, to the objective and peaceful consciousness of the world.* [...] *It seems to me that it is thanks to Paris that Alina has come to this dual phenomenon of cleansing and crystallization that we can see in her latest pieces. Of*

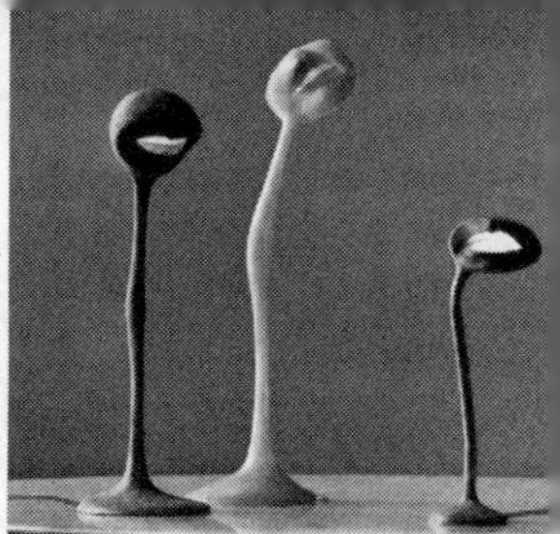

32

course, she will require a considerable amount of time to fully tear away the curtains to her inner world. [...] *In 1967, in Paris, in the midst of some developmental cycle—which was no doubt delayed due to the burden of psychological obstacles that had to be overcome—Alina Szapocznikow stood before my eyes in the too sparse a row of Césars and Delahayes, among the most outstanding artistic talents of the post-war generation* [Pierre Restany, "Forma między ciałem a grą" (Form Between Body and Game), in *Alina Szapocznikow. Sculpture*, exh. cat., Zachęta Gallery, Warsaw, 1967].

131.

LETTER →[P 273]

[DECEMBER 16, 1966]

BICC—The Bureau of International Cultural Cooperation, housed in the Ministry of Art and Culture.

I got a letter today from Giza saying that she had gone to the BICC about that Restany thing—In her letter of December 13, 1966, Gizela Szancerowa wrote to Szapocznikow: *As you can of course imagine, the subsidizing of any costs related to Mr. Restany's stay in Warsaw is not up to me. In order to get the matter onto the right track as soon as possible, I have gone to the BICC with a proposal to covering a few days of Mr. Restany's stay in Warsaw, and I hope that the matter will be resolved according to your wishes. Meanwhile, we will be delighted to organize Mr. Restany's talk in our conference room at Zachęta* [Alina Szapocznikow Archive]. The next letter (dated January 30, 1967) informs Szapocznikow that the BICC agreed to cover only room and board, and not Restany's travel costs. Nonetheless, in July 1967, the French critic did visit Poland and give his talk at the Zachęta Gallery on July 10.

push this with Markowski—Eugeniusz Markowski (1912–2007), Polish painter. After the war, he worked as a journalist and diplomat in Italy and Canada, returning to Poland in 1955. From 1956–1970, he was director of the Bureau of International Cultural Cooperation at the Ministry of Art and Culture.

I have made a couple of interesting things out of plastic with light—In 1966, Szapocznikow started making small lamps, the shades of which were composed of casts of mouths or breasts. The first of these lamps, titled *Lampe de chevet* [Nightlight], appeared in the exhibition called "L'objet" at the Galerie Lacloche. Among other models, she apparently cast the mouth of Julie Christie, who was in the David Lean film *Doctor Zhivago* (1965) that Szapocznikow mentions (*ILLUMINATED LIPS I* → [32/1966]).

Romek got a new journal to work on—In 1967, Cieślewicz did the layout for a new contemporary-art journal called *Opus International*, edited by Jean-Clarence Lambert, and with Jean-Jacques Lévêque on the editorial staff, published by Georges Fall.

133.

LETTER →[P 275]
[AUGUST 18, 1967]

I'll do the photographs of the sculpture once I'm done with it—Szapocznikow did a piece from local stone entitled *A* → [33/1967] at the symposium in Vyšné Ružbachy. It is still in the local quarry.

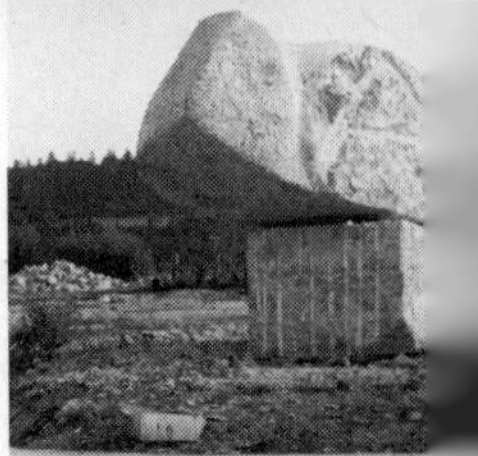

33

I'm enormously curious to know how you displayed my works at the Museum—Stanisławski became director of the Muzeum Sztuki in Łódź in 1966. The basis of the Museum's holdings was the 1931 International Collection of Modern Art by the group a. r., comprising 111 works by representatives of the international avant-garde defining a clear profile for that institution. From the moment he took up the directorship (a function he continued to exercise until 1991), he attempted to abide by this tradition, expanding the collection and generating a program of exhibitions that would demonstrate the connection between the achievements of the pre-war avant-garde and art that was his contemporary. Two pieces by Szapocznikow were held by the Muzeum Sztuki in Łódź: *CORRIDA II* → [34/1960], which she mentions (purchased from her at the time), as well as the newly acquired *MULTIPLE PORTRAIT (QUADRUPLE)* → [35/1967], which is what Szapocznikow has in mind when she writes of the necessity of showing off "the transparency of the mouth." They were shown in an exhibition newly arranged by Stanisławski. The remainder of Szapocznikow's works now held by the Muzeum Sztuki in Łódź were acquired after the artist's death.

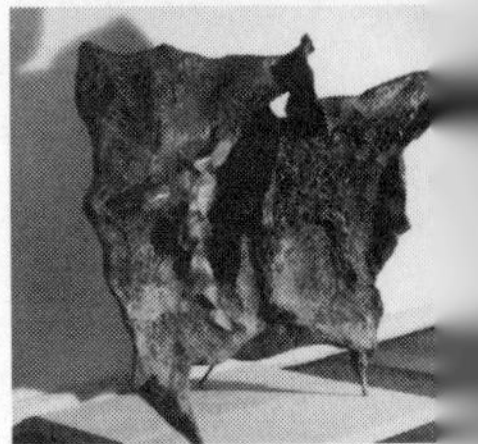

34

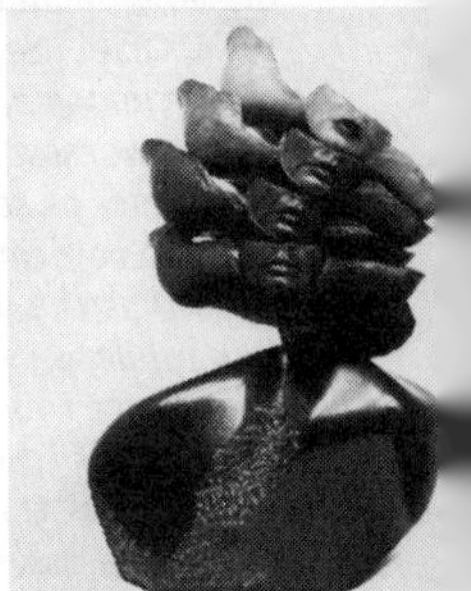

35

Le Falstaff—A restaurant in Paris.

if Piotrek has a sister or a brother—Olga Stanisławska, the daughter of Urszula Czartoryska and Ryszard Stanisławski, was born on November 2, 1967.

134.

LETTER →[P 276]
[AUGUST 29, 1967]

Szapocznikow's *COFFEE TABLE* → [36/1966] was sold in 1967 to the Swiss collector Peter Kaufmann for $1,400. Kaufmann had been the director of the Globus department stores in Zurich since 1961. In 1967, a new branch of Globus was opened, and a range of works were exhibited on that occasion, including *Coffee Table*.

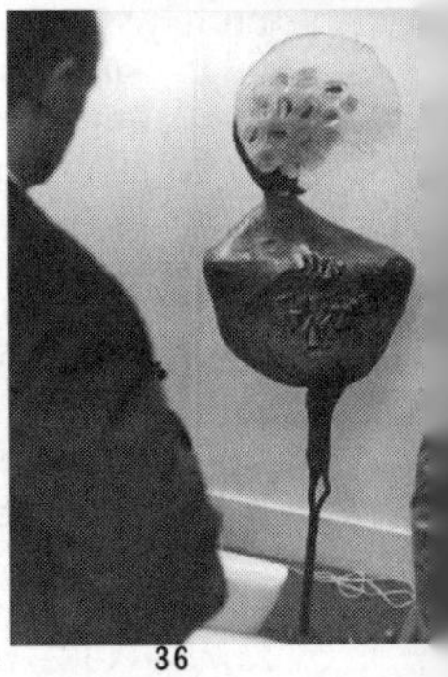

36

to the so-called "Roundagon"—In 1966 a new branch of the bank PKO was opened in the center of Warsaw in a modernist building now known as the Rotunda.

the money will definitely be there, because what the Toruń Museum sent was transferred to me—See note to letter 116.

PAVA, or ZPAP in Polish, is the Polish Association of Visual Artists. Alina Szapocznikow joined PAVA in 1951 after arriving in Poland, and she paid dues until 1970. In the People's Republic of Poland, PAVA, an organization in existence

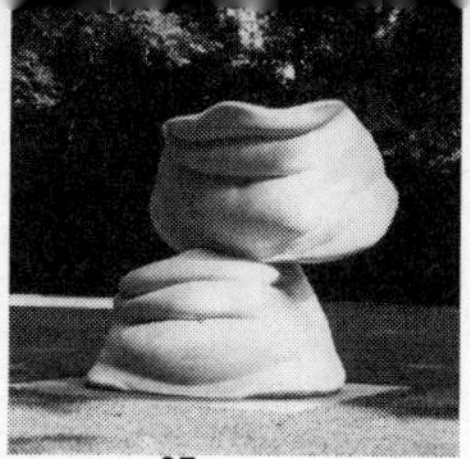
37

since 1911, like other official organizations subordinated to the authorities, played an extraordinarily crucial role. In practical terms, one could not function as an artist without being a member, not least because of the restrictions on purchases of art supplies and access to studio space.

open up a savings book for a car in my name—In the People's Republic of Poland, automobiles produced domestically were difficult to obtain. They could only be purchased either with vouchers that became a kind of reward from employers or the communist authorities, or—considerably more expensive—on the car market. At some point savings books were introduced which, after the acquisition of the appropriate capital, made it possible to "sign up for a car."

Ronchamp (Giacometti, Le Corbusier)—The construction of Le Corbusier's chapel of Notre Dame du Haut at Ronchamp was completed in 1955.

135.

LETTER →[P 279]
[OCTOBER 9, 1967]

follow the results of the drawing in the papers— Names were drawn from among the holders of car savings books (cf. note to letter 134); winners were entitled to a priority purchase.

136.

LETTER →[P 280]
[MAY 13, 1968]

Domus—Italian monthly primarily dedicated to architecture and design published since 1928, bilingual (Italian-English). Pierre Restany collaborated on the magazine beginning in the 1960s. *Domus* published an article on the Muzeum Sztuki in Łódź (Pierre Restany, "Le Musée d'art de Lodz, Pologne: l'index d'un humanisme sans frontière," *Domus*, no. 461 (1968), pp. 49–54).

Projekt—Founded in 1956, this magazine was dedicated to the applied arts, and in particular, to the art of the poster. Józef Mroszczak was a co-founded, and Danuta Wróblewska and Szymon Bojko were long-time contributors.

Alina: Italy, Yugoslavia—In the summer (August) of 1968, Szapocznikow was working in Carrara, from where she wrote to Wojciech Fangor: *They offered me an enormous block of marble, and Romek absolutely wants to pose. Aside from that, we go for swims in the sea, check out the Apennine Mountains, along with the television, with the latest events from our brother countries*—having in mind the Warsaw Pact invasion of Czechoslovakia. This is when *BIG BELLIES* → [37/1968], the marble sculpture she mentions later on in the letter, comes into being. Szapocznikow also took part in the first International Drawings Exhibition at the Moderna Galerija in Rijeka.

Everything depends on our passports. We have a letter from Boguś P. from November 67 saying "Things are underway."

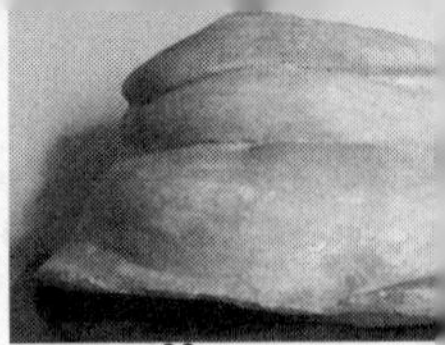
38

While we call the consulate about every 10 days—nothing.—The information provided by Cieślewicz might suggest that neither of them had been in Poland for a long time, while in fact Szapocznikow went to Poland in March, 1968 in conjunction with the work of the group designing for Wrocław a Memorial to the Return of the Western and Southern Lands to the Nation. Szapocznikow worked on that team with Alicja Listowska, Hieronim Listowski, and Janusz Matecki. A team assembled by Henryk Morel (1937–1968) ended up winning, although the monument was never completed.

I am sending you Lebenstein's catalogue—Most likely the catalogue from the Jan Lebenstein exhibition that took place at the Galerie Desbrières in Paris. Cieślewicz did the layout of many catalgoues, including two for exhibitions by Alina Szapocznikow—the aforementioned show at the Florence Houston Brown Gallery in Paris in 1967, and the exhibition at the Ivan Lechien Gallery in Brussels that took place in late fall of 1968.

In addition to the Lebenstein, Cieślewicz mentions the exhibitions of Barbara Kwaśniewska (born 1931, painter, living in Paris since 1958), Leopold Buczkowski (1905–1989, writer, painter), and Teresa Pągowska as well as the following exhibitions in which Szapocznikow appeared: XX Salon de la Jeune Sculpture, II Salon "L'art pour la paix au Viètnam" in Aubervilliers, and "L'Objet 3" at the Hilton Hotel at Orly. We have not been able to find information on her participation in the Salon de la Jeune Peinture.

and I'm now putting together the biggest collage in the world—The reference is probably to the experimental poster, printed continuously on a roll of paper 99 centimeters wide, which Cieślewicz did in 1967.

Even Ms. Darthea Speyer has started up a huge new gallery, probably to spite Mr. Sonnabend next door—Darthea Speyer was a cultural attaché at the U.S. embassy in Paris from 1950–65, responsible for an international exhibitions program whose goal was the promotion of American art. Its first exhibition was titled "Twelve Americans." In May, 1968, she founded the Galerie Darthea Speyer, which remained in operation until 2010.

Ileana Sonnabend (1914–2007), art dealer in Paris and New York, born Ileana Schapira in Bucharest. Her first husband was Leo Castelli. She set the same goals for her Galerie Ileana Sonnabend, which she founded with her second husband, Polish-born Michael Sonnabend, in 1962.

We spend our days at a factory for these totally sensational plastics—In 1968, Szapocznikow started on a series of work using polyurethane, which she had acquired from the Société Chimique de la Corneuve. In this section of the letter, she is talking about pieces representing a portion of the belly. A *PLASTER MODEL* → [38/1968] for this can be found in the collection of the Museum of Modern Art in Warsaw. Polyurethane casts, of which there were, in fact, over a dozen (there are, in the artist's archive, receipts issued to the Parisian company Sièges Bienaise from one year later). They are now known as *BELLY CUSHIONS* → [39/1960]. And the sculpture she mentions representing two bellies, one atop the other (the two executed in white marble from her model in Querceta, height 240 cm), is in the collection of the Rijksmuseum Kröller-Müller in Otterlo, Netherlands.

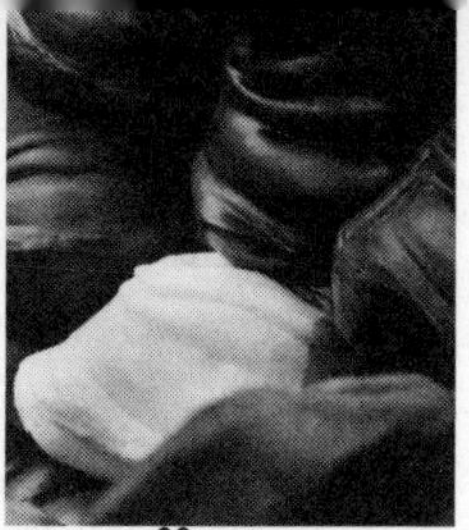

39

You'll see the first [model] *in* Opus—The sixth issue of the magazine *Opus International*, which appeared in April, 1968, was devoted to Polish art, and included an article by Jean-Jacques Lévêque on the work of Szapocznikow.

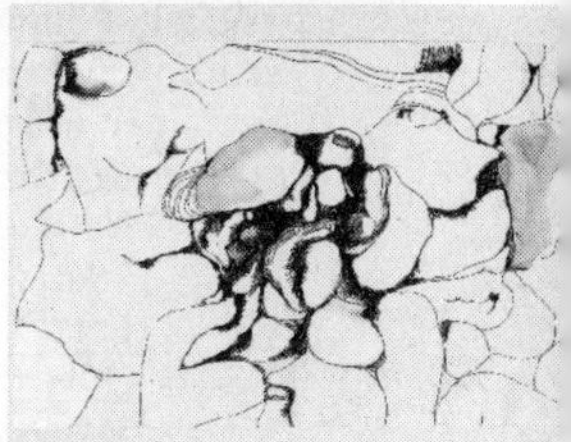

40

I'll go there, then swing over to the biennale—No doubt the Venice Biennale is meant

Too bad you didn't give Modus *the pictures of my sculpture at the museum*—This is clearly a slip, and Szapocznikow is still speaking of *Domus*.

What is the deal with São Paulo, and how how should I get going with it?!—Ryszard Stanisławski was a commissioner for the Polish section and a member of the international jury at the São Paulo International Biennial, where César was awarded one of the prizes. Szapocznikow never participated in that Biennale.

Rysiu, I hope that in Rijeka you award me a prize for my very beautiful drawing—She was not awarded any prize at the aforementioned International Drawing Exhibition in Rijeka until 1972, for her series of drawings *PAYSAGE HUMAIN* → [40/1971].

137.

LETTER →[P 282]

[OCTOBER 16, 1968]

I am leaving for Brussels—This short trip to Brussels was most likely connected with the exhibition Szapocznkow was about to open at the Ivan Lechien Gallery (November 12–December 3, 1968).

You can stay with us and sleep in Piotrek's room—In October of 1968, Stanisławski was traveling for work through Zurich, Milan, Venice, and Paris.

138.

LETTER →[P 283]

[DECEMBER 20, 1968]

Andrzej Strumiłło (born 1927), Polish painter, graphic artist, photographer.

François Pluchart, *Du Cubisme à l'Abstraction réaliste*, Paris, 1967.

I can start on the poster and the catalogue now—In the end Cieślewicz did not do any project for the Muzeum Sztuki in Łódź during this period.

Unizm—A theory elaborated by Władysław Strzemiński in the 1920s (its founding publication, *Unism in Painting*, appeared in 1928). Together with his wife, the sculptor Katarzyna

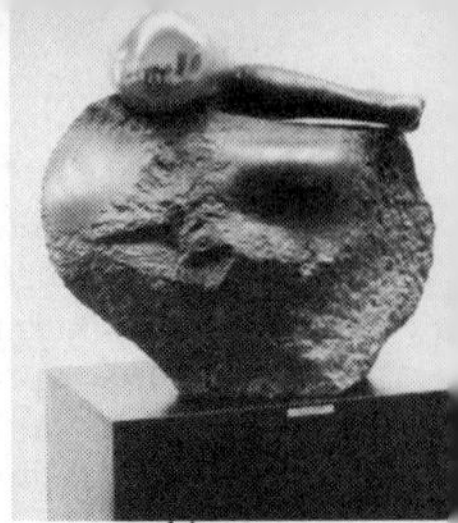
41

Kobro, Strzemiński broadened the foundations of unism to sculpture and architecture.

139.

LETTER →[P 284]

[JULY 1969]

Szapocznikow came back to Poland in the summer of 1969 for the last time. She stayed with Stanisławski, in his apartment on Dąbrowski Square, because after the political crisis in Poland in March, 1968, she lost her apartment and studio on Brzozowa Street. A portion of her sculptures remained in Warsaw, in what had been her studio, which was subsequently occupied by the sculptor Tadeusz Łodziana (1920–2011).

140.

LETTER →[P 285]

[JULY 18, 1969]

"Maigret" series—A series of extraordinarily popular mystery novels by Georges Simenon (1903–1989) featuring Commissaire Jules Maigret.

Dad! Thank you for your very kind words…—Piotr Stanisławski's letter is written in French: *Cher Papa! Merci pour le mot très gentil que tu m'as envoyé par lettre. J'espère te voir ici au moins un jour. J'ai déjà reçu le premier cadeau d'aniversaire, de ma mère, et c'est une Zorka 4 qui me parait très bien. Je m'amuse beaucoup ici et j'ai enormement d'amies et amis. Hier je suis allé avec maman voir Urszula. Olga est magnifique bronzée au cheveux d'or. En t'attendant, je t'embrasse bien fort. Piotrek*

141.

LETTER →[P 286]

[JANUARY 24, 1970]

starting to get ready for my long stay in Amsterdam—In the spring of 1970, Szapocznikow was working at the Stedelijk Museum in Amsterdam as she prepared an exhibition of new pieces called *Envahissement de Tumeurs* [*Invasion of Tumors*]. As Cieślewicz wrote to Stanisławski: *She has got a big studio there on the canal, but she will probably come back to Paris soon, because she gets plaster cheaper here, and she can escape from the stench of polyurethane more easily—there everything is in the same place* [letter from May 5, 1970, Ryszard Stanisławski Archive].

You could make me slides or at least black-and-white photographs of Corrida, Leg, *and* Portrait—Szapocznikow mentions three statues from the collection of the Muzeum Sztuki in Łódź: in addition to the aforementioned *Corrida*, purchased in the same year from the artist, *Multiple Portrait (Quadruple)* (1967), and *LEG* → [41/1967] (bought in 1974 from Roman Cieślewicz).

142.

LETTER →[P 287]

[SEPTEMBER 28, 1971]

It appears from your letter that you will be in Lausanne when I am in Geneva—From October 7–30, 1971, Szapocznikow's last solo show during her lifetime took place at the Aurora Gallery in Geneva, organized by that gallery's diretor, Claudine Martin. From October 2–4, 1971, Stanisławski was attending a conference at CITAM (Centre International de la Tapisserie Ancienne et Moderne) in Lausanne.

No further letters between Szapocznikow and Stanisławski remain. In 1972 Szapocznikow suffered a relapse of the cancer that had first struck in early 1969. She died on March 2, 1973, in Praz Coutant in the French Alps, and was buried at the Montmartre Cemetery in Paris.

PHOTOGRAPHS FROM THE ARCHIVE

From the editors
The following photographs are taken from the Ryszard Stanisławski Archive (p. 361: images no. 1 and 2; p. 364; p. 368: no. 2; pp. 370–1) and from the Alina Szapocznikow Archive (the remaining images). Our sincerest gratitude to Olga Stanisławska and Piotr Stanisławski for granting their consent.

 ALINA SZAPOCZNIKOW AT THE 1961 INTERNATIONAL SCULPTURE SYMPOSIUM IN ST. MARGARETHEN, AUSTRIA, WITH *PULP I*

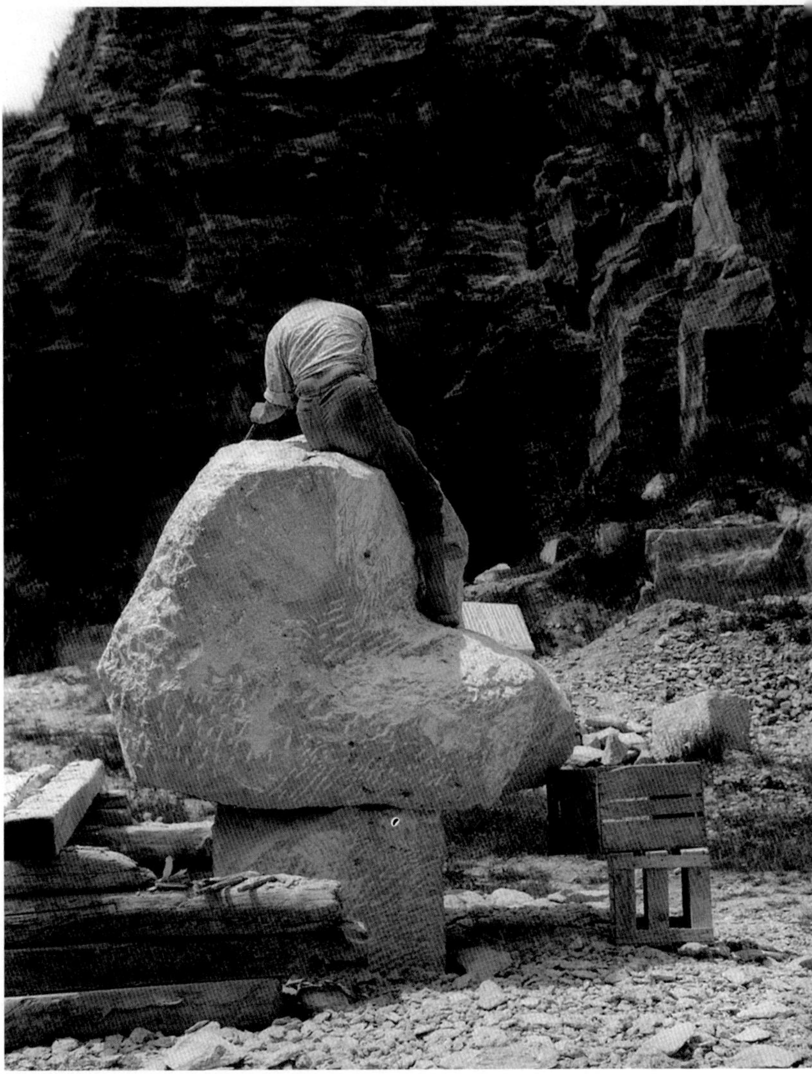

 AT THE 1963 INTERNATIONAL SCULPTURE SYMPOSIUM IN PORTOROŽ, YUGOSLAVIA, WITH *BIOLOGICAL SCULPTURE*

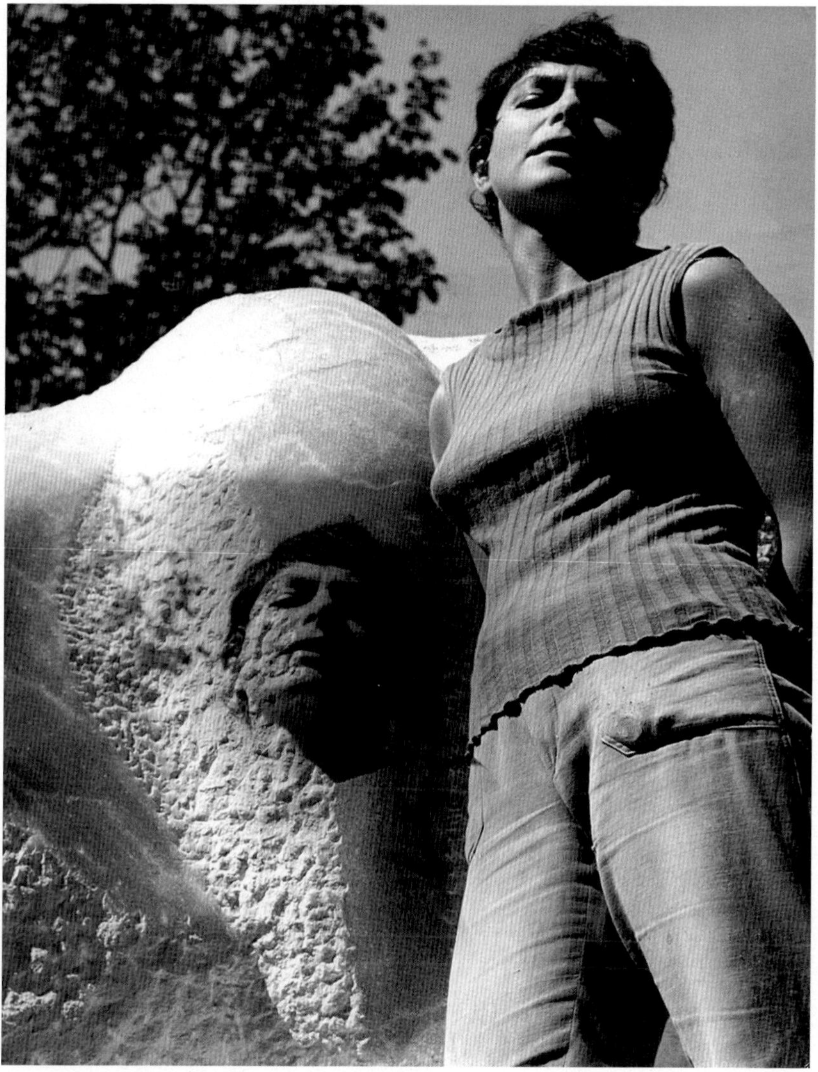

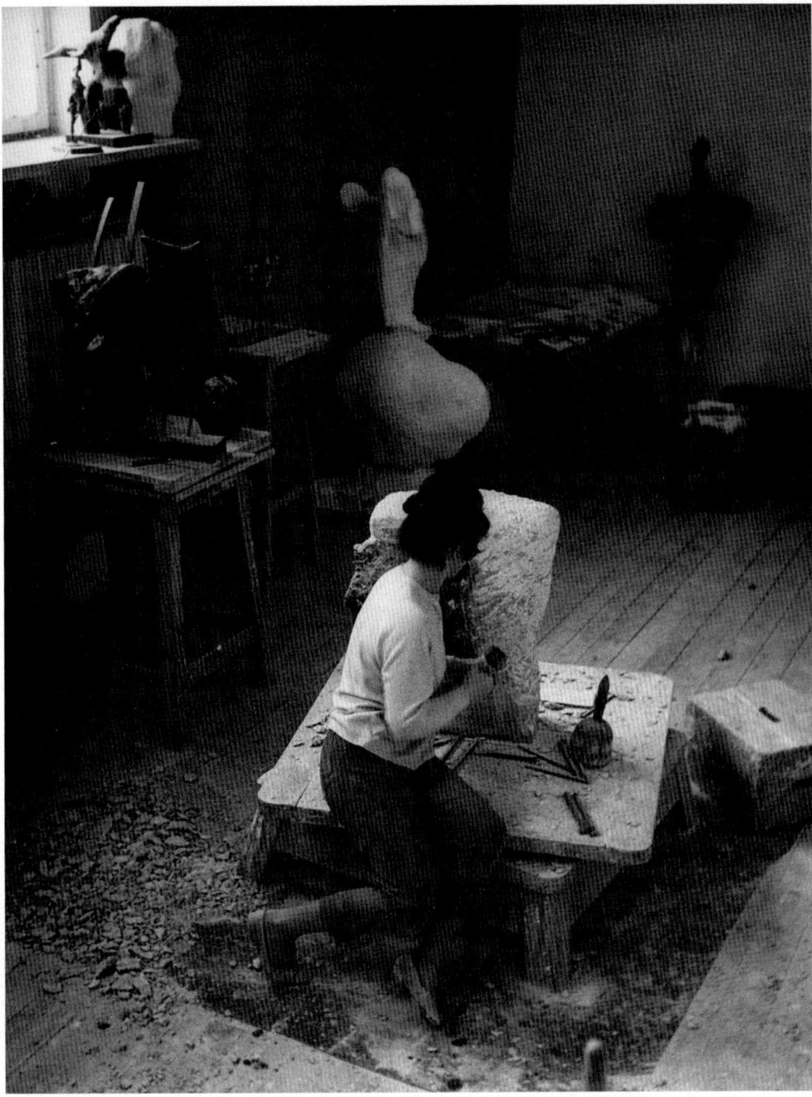

 1. VIEWERS WITH *BIG BEACH*, IVAN LECHIEN'S COGEIME GALLERY, BRUSSELS, 1968; 2. IN HER STUDIO IN MALAKOFF, OUTSIDE PARIS, WITH *UNMARRIED*, C. 1965

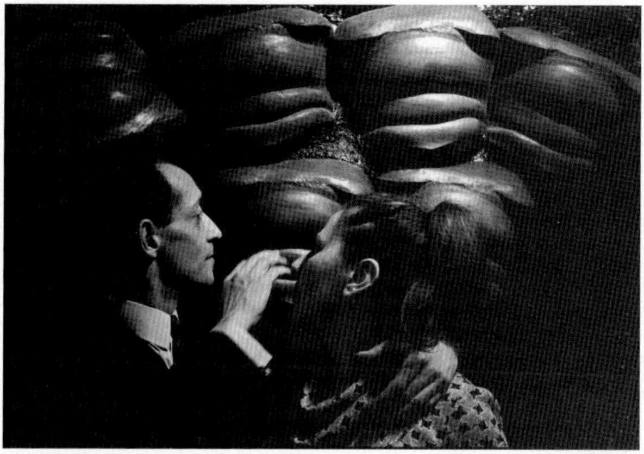

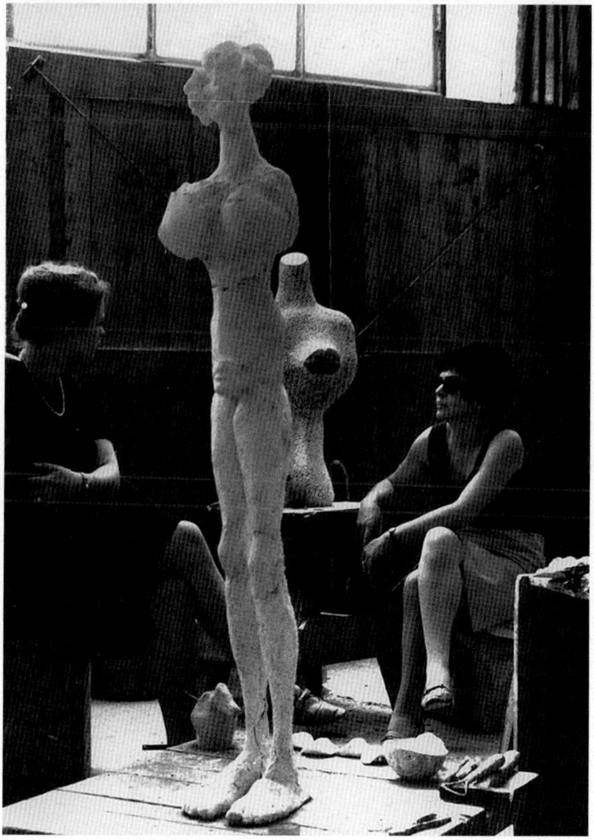

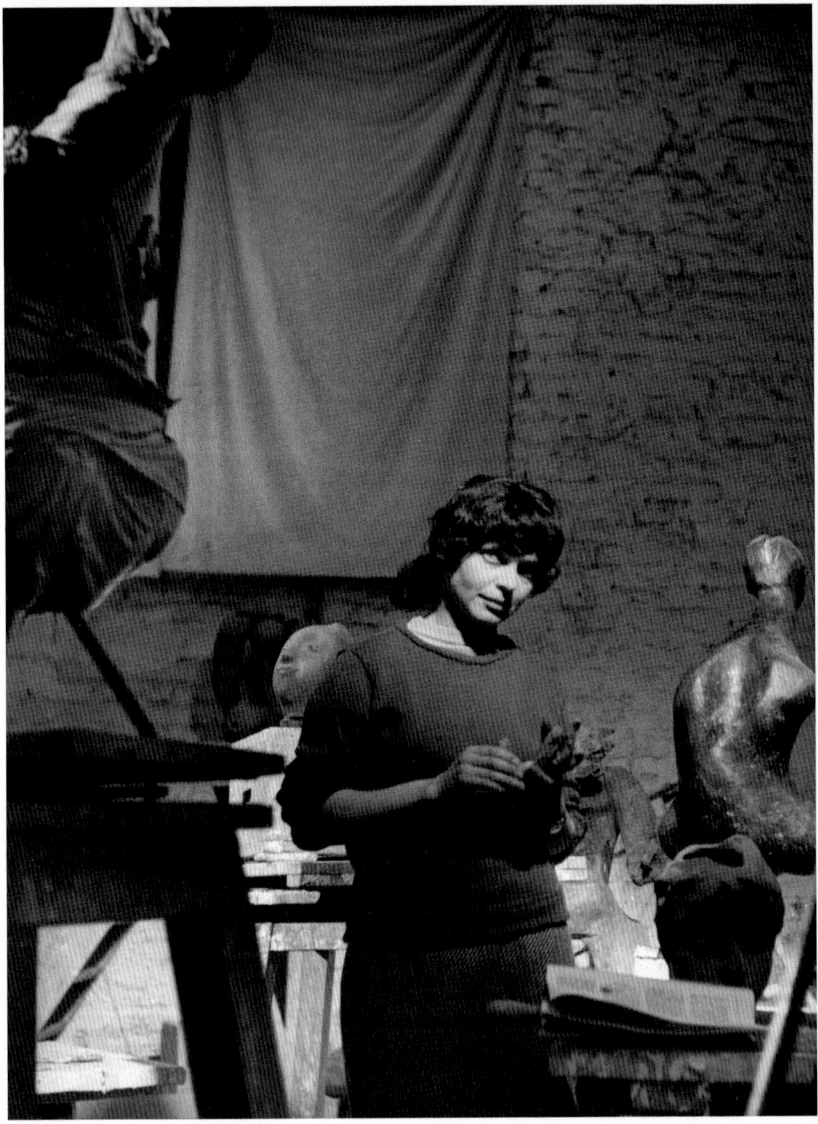

RYSZARD STANISŁAWSKI WITH *MONSTER I*, AND ROMAN CIEŚLEWICZ WITH *DIFFICULT AGE*, ZACHĘTA GALLERY, WARSAW, 1957

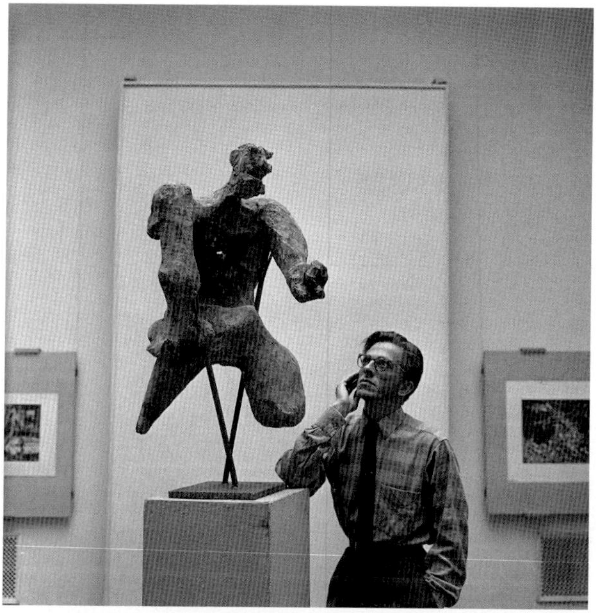

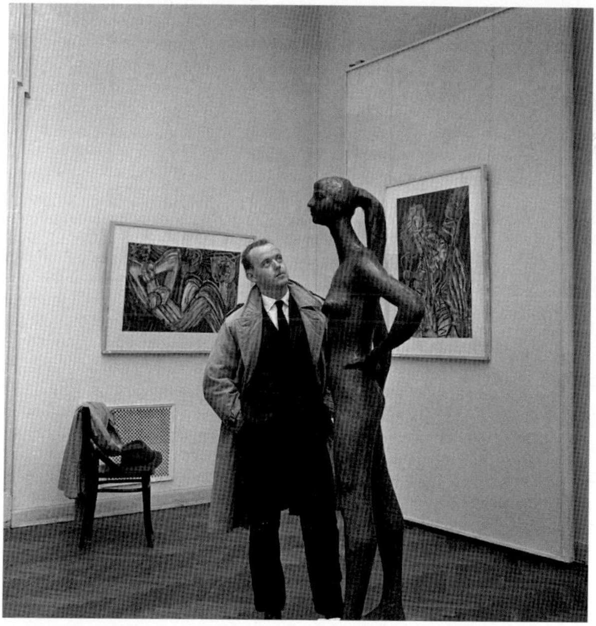

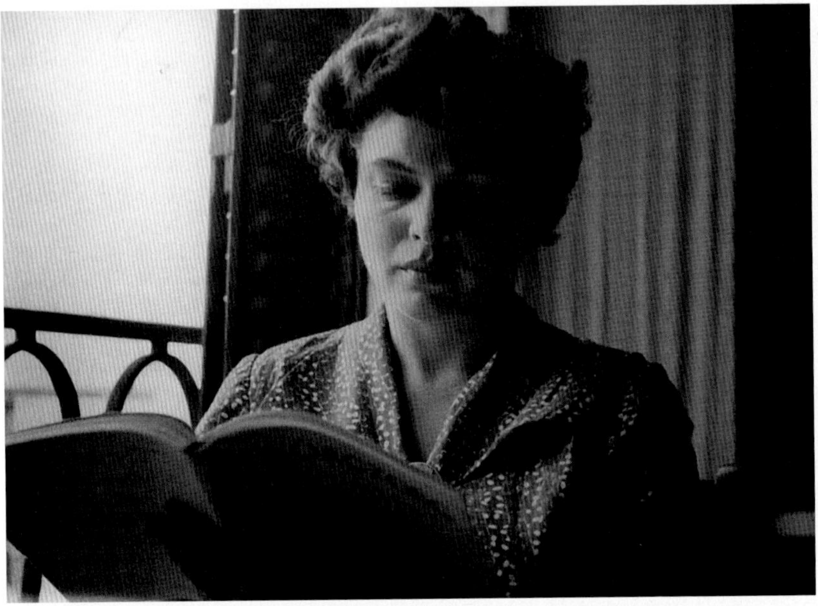

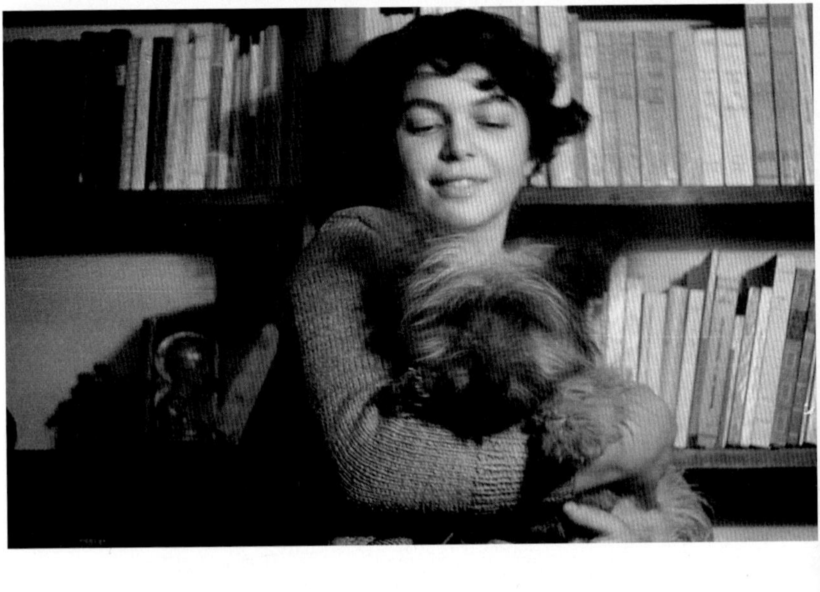

 1. AT THE 1961 INTERNATIONAL SCULPTURE SYMPOSIUM, ST. MARGARETHEN, AUSTRIA; 2. RYSZARD STANISŁAWSKI, STANISŁAW ZAMECZNIK, ALINA SZAPOCZNIKOW, WOJCIECH FANGOR, WARSAW, 1954; 3. AT A FOLKFEST IN FRANCE, 1949–50

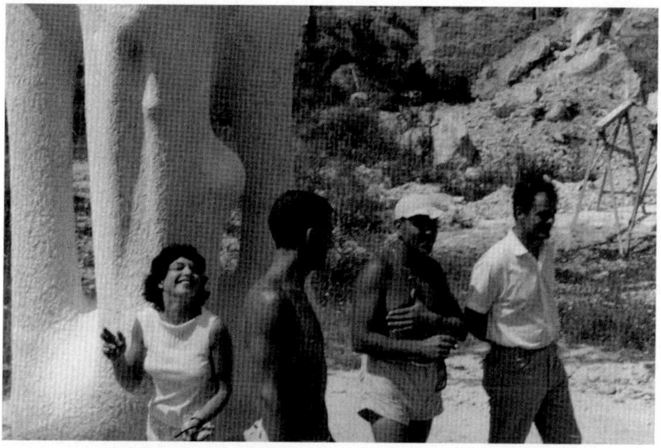

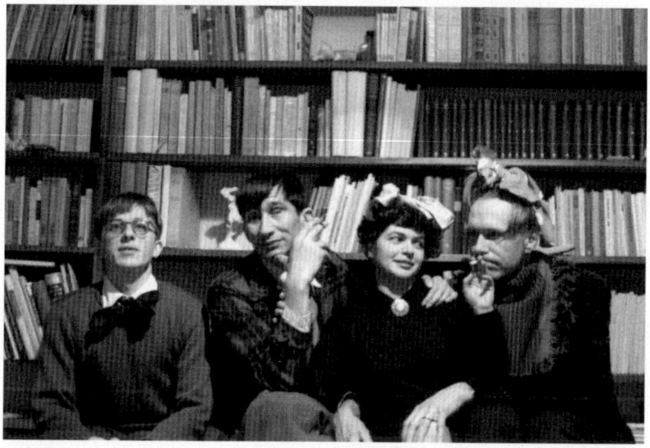

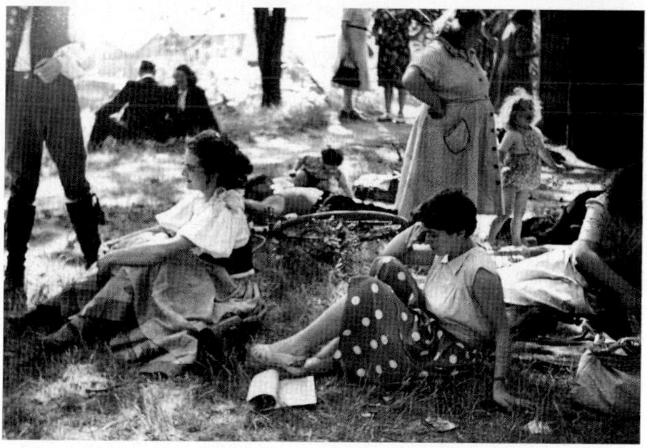

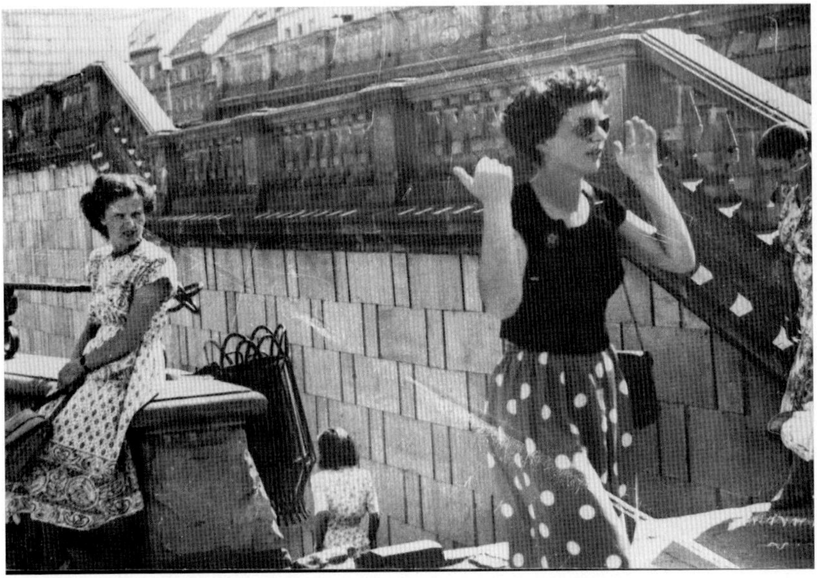

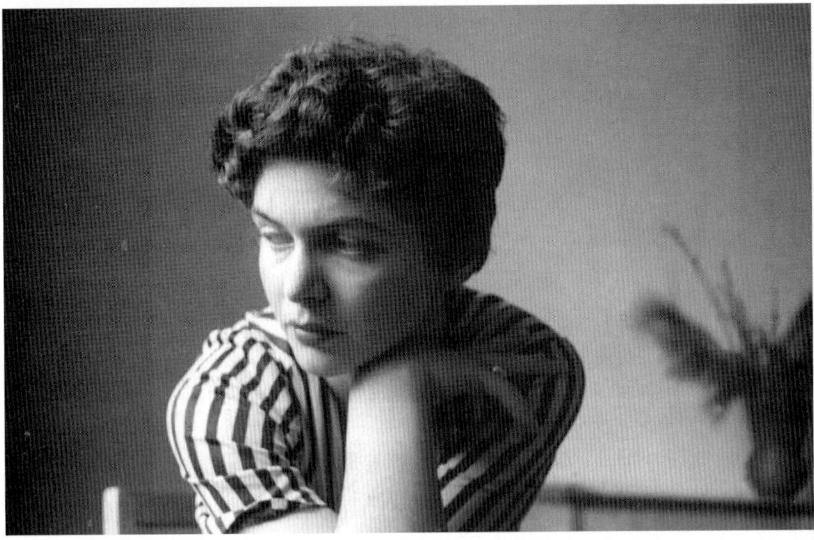

1. STANISŁAWSKI WITH ISSUES OF *PRZEGLĄD ARTYSTYCZNY* MONTHLY, C. 1953; 2. SZAPOCZNIKOW AND STANISŁAWSKI, WARSAW, 1950S; 3. RYSZARD STANISŁAWSKI, 1952

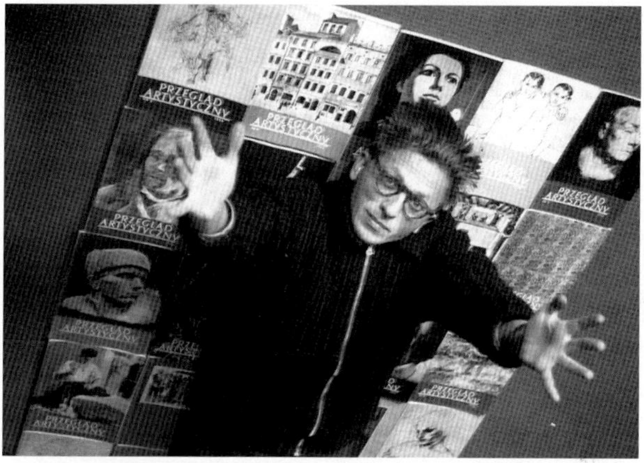

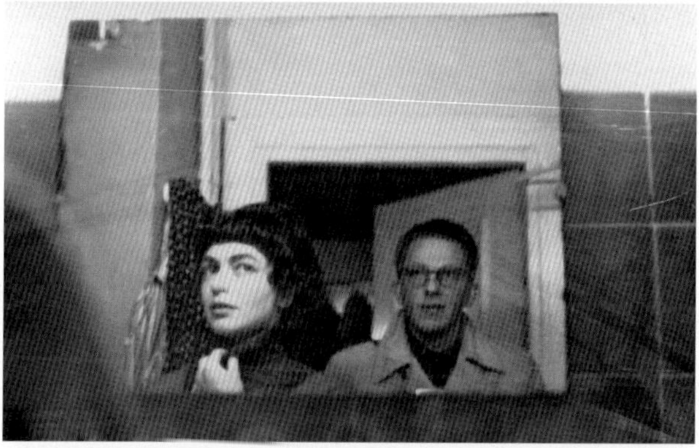

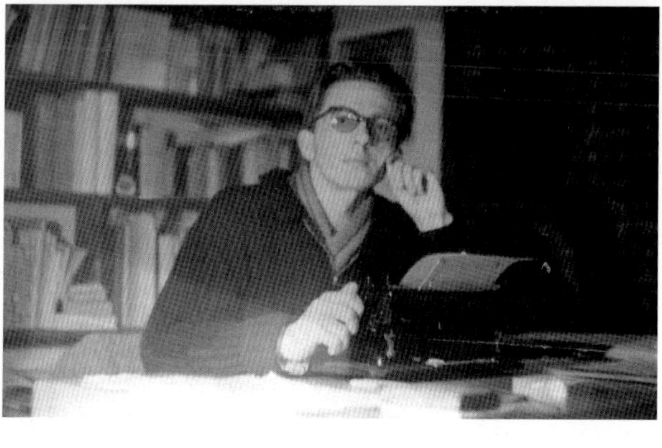

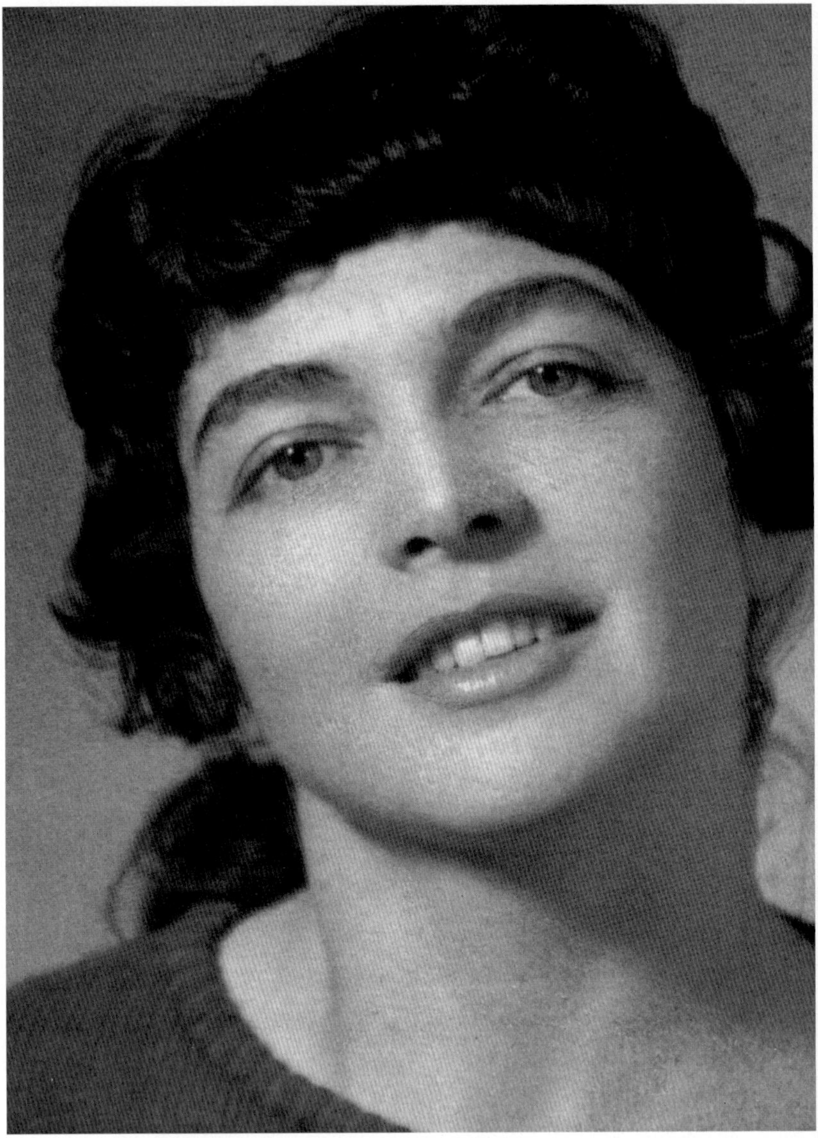

 1. RYSZARD STANISŁAWSKI, C. 1953; 2. SZAPOCZNIKOW AND STANISŁAWSKI TRAVELING IN FRANCE, 1950; 3. SZAPOCZNIKOW AND STANISŁAWSKI IN ZAKOPANE, 1956

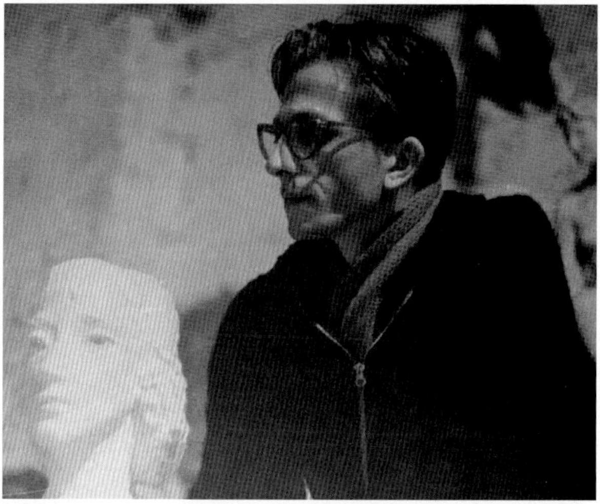

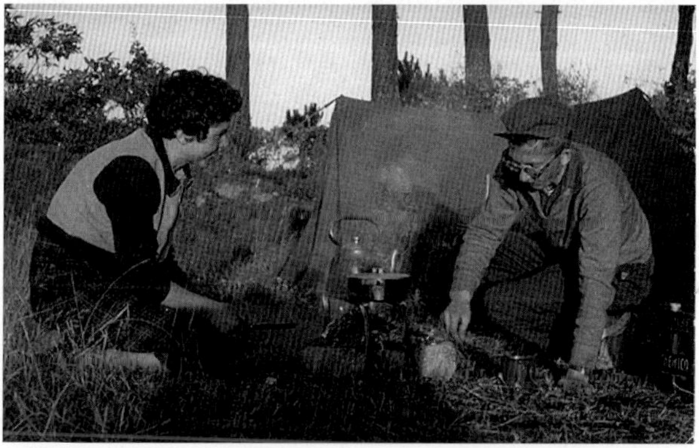

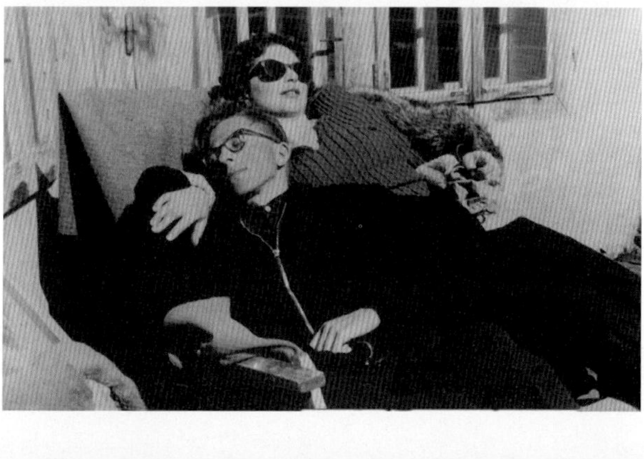

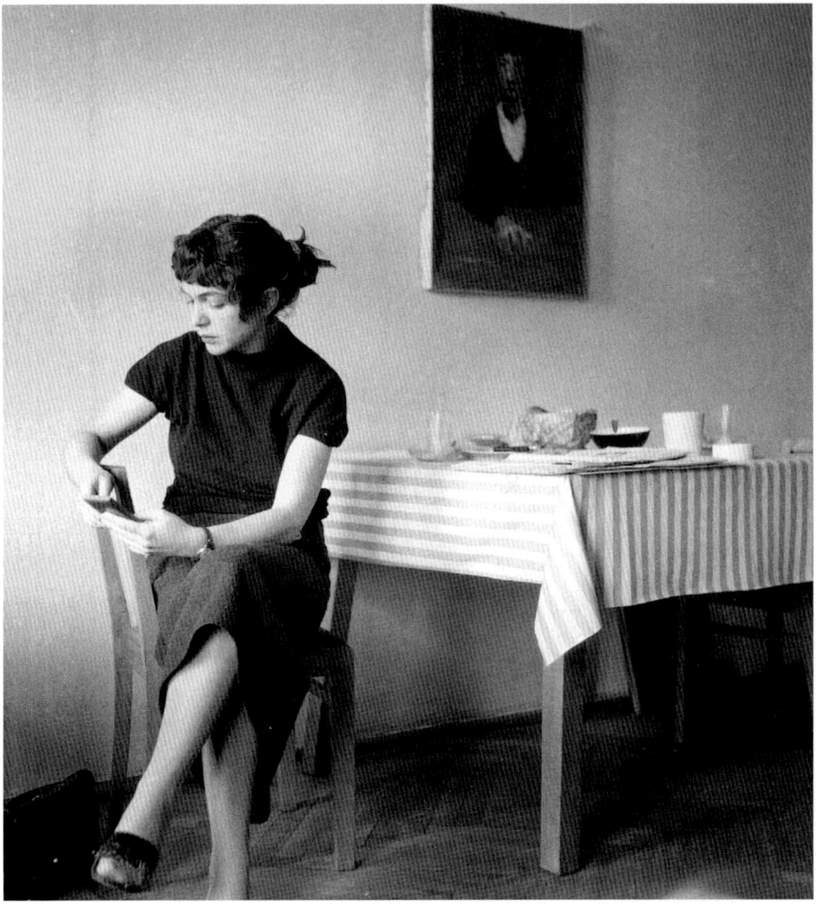

1. WITH HER SON PIOTR IN THE RUINS OF WARSAW, 1952; 2. ALINA SZAPOCZNIKOW, RYSZARD AND PIOTR STANISŁAWSKI, 1953; 3. STANISŁAWSKI WITH PIOTR, WARSAW, 1958; 4. SZAPOCZNIKOW WITH PIOTR, WARSAW'S OLD TOWN, 1950S/60S

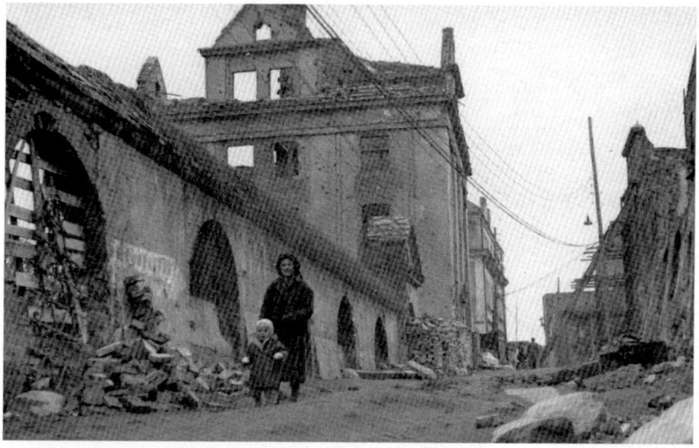

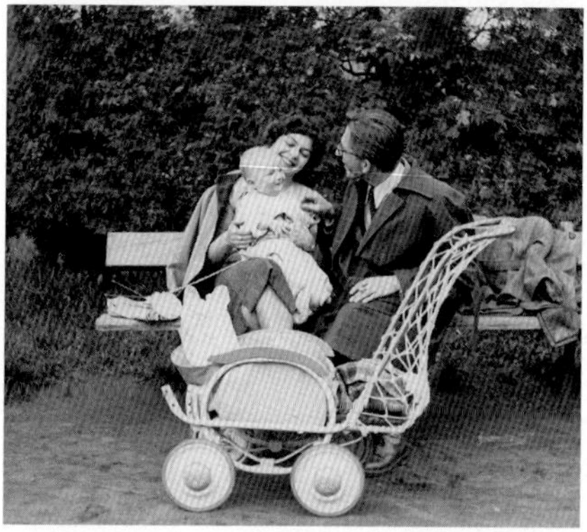

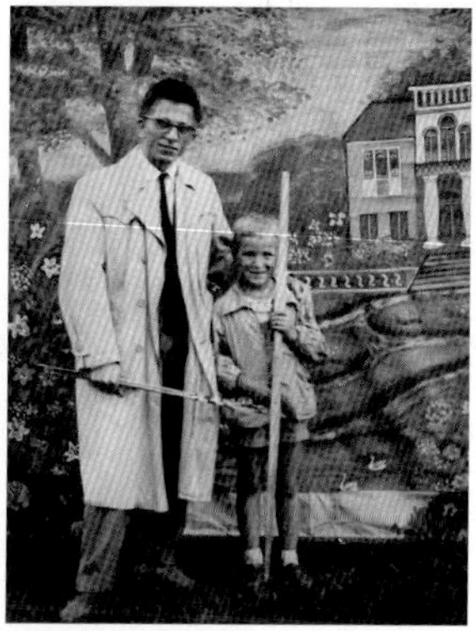

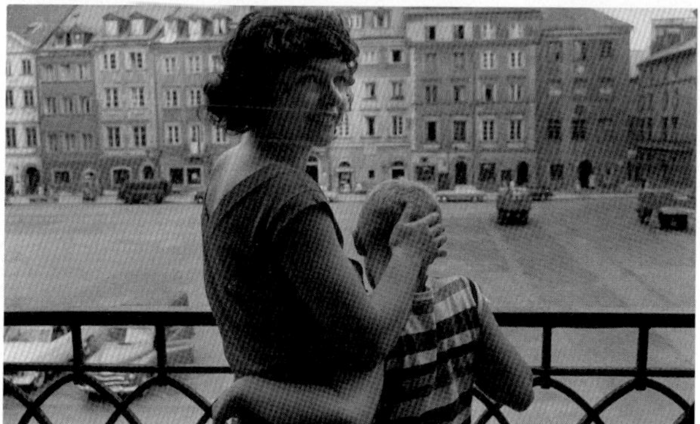

1. IN HER STUDIO IN WARSAW, 1962; 2. PORTRAIT, 1951

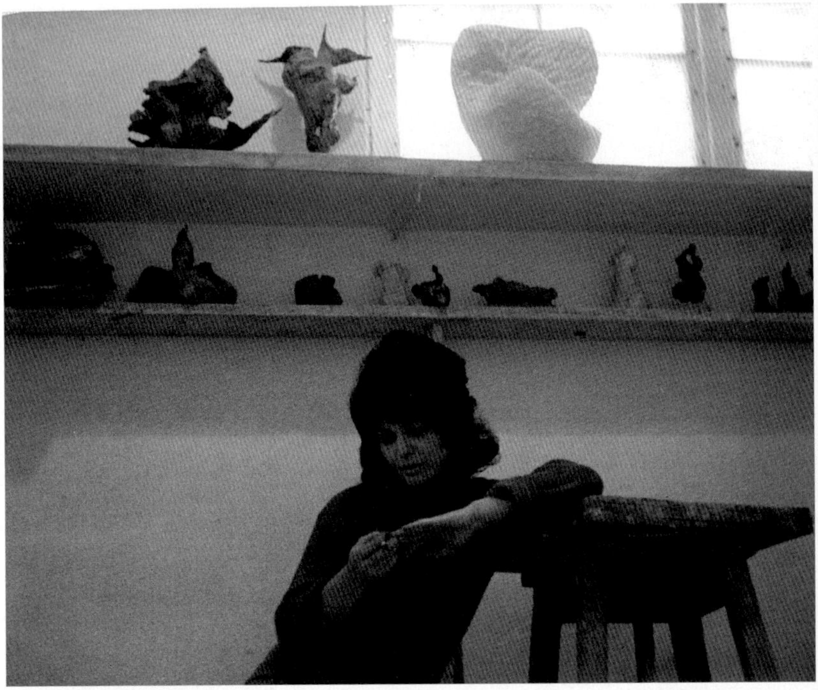

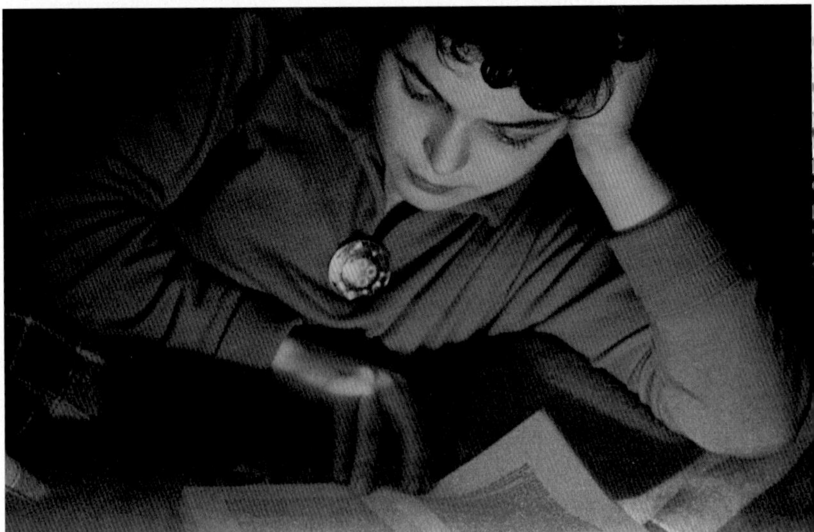

ROMAN CIEŚLEWICZ, ALINA SZAPOCZNIKOW AND PIOTR STANISŁAWSKI, WARSAW, 1960S

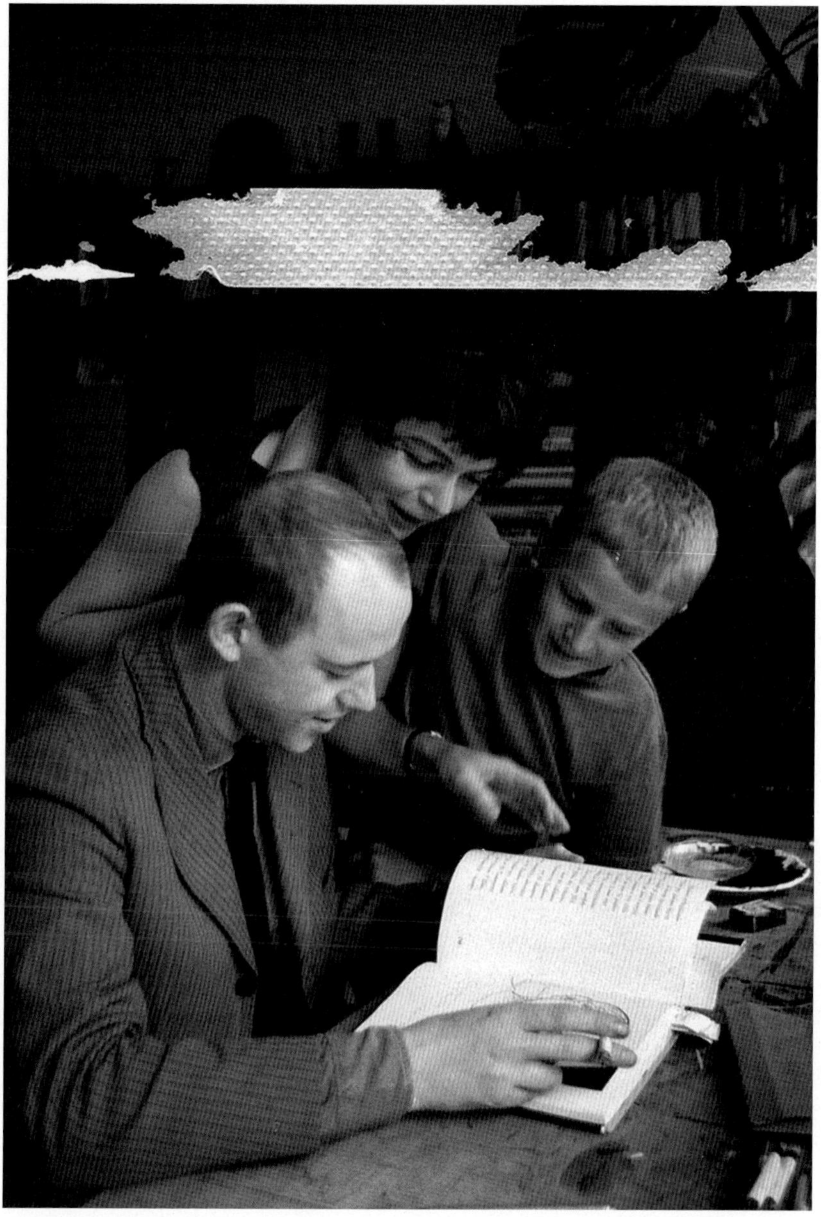

1. IN HER STUDIO IN WARSAW, WITH *WOMAN IN A HEAD SCARF*, 1952;
2. PORTRAIT, 1950S

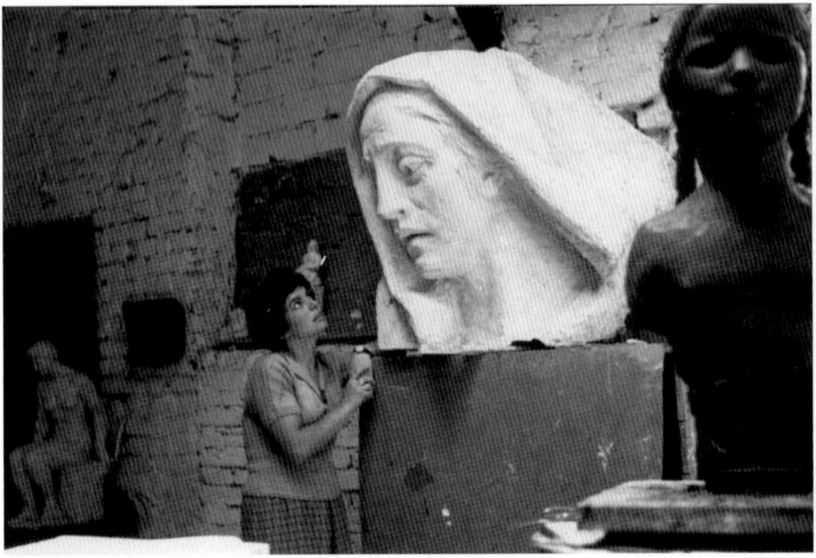

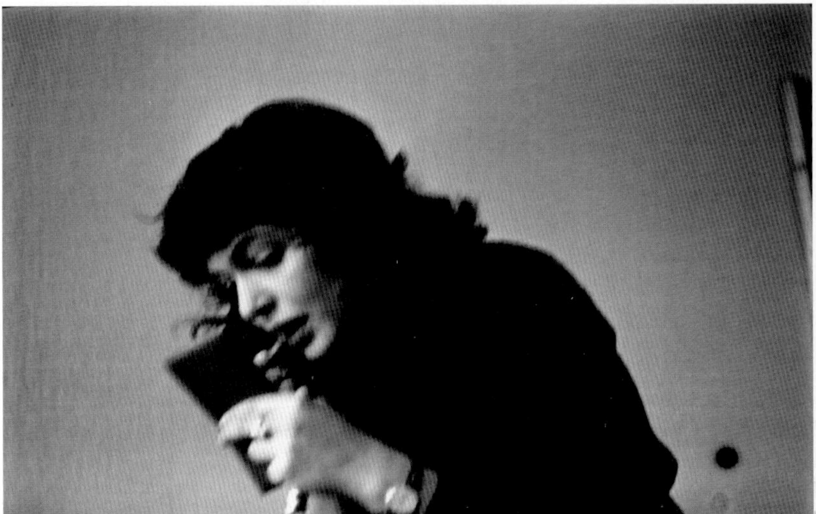

1. SZAPOCZNIKOW WORKING AT THE STONE WORKSHOP OF GASTON LERENDU, PARIS, 1950S; 2. VIEWERS WITH *MULTIPLE PORTRAIT (QUADRUPLE)*, FLORENCE HOUSTON BROWN GALLERY, PARIS, 1967; 3. VIEWERS WITH *PORTRAIT OF BARBARA KUSAK*, MUZEUM SZTUKI IN ŁÓDŹ, 1975

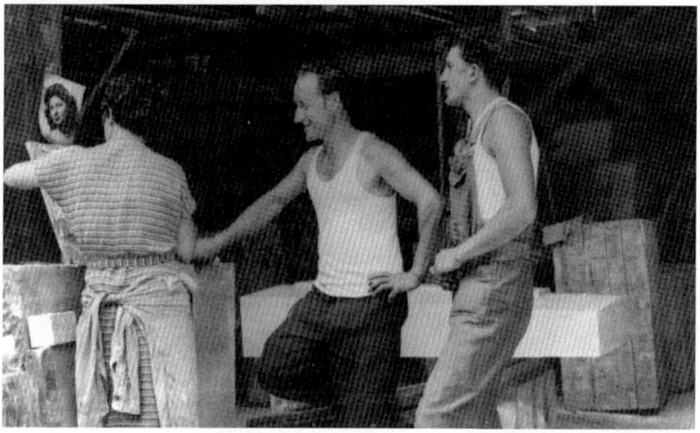

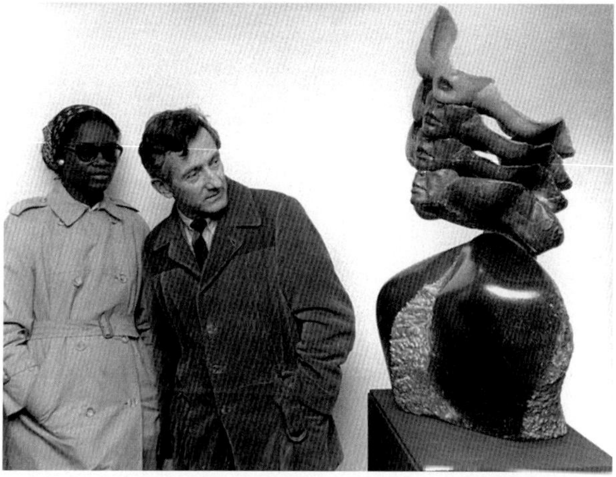

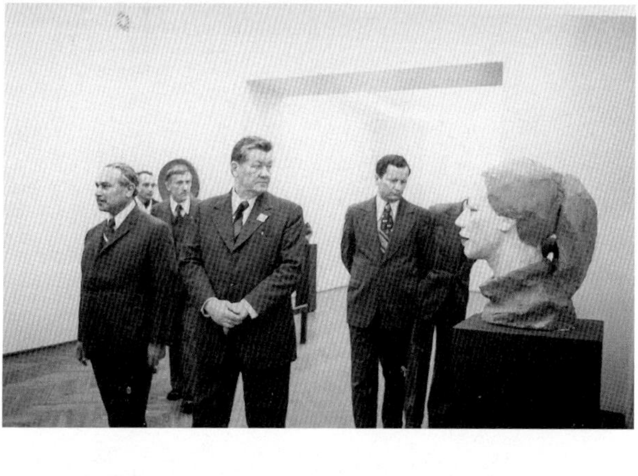

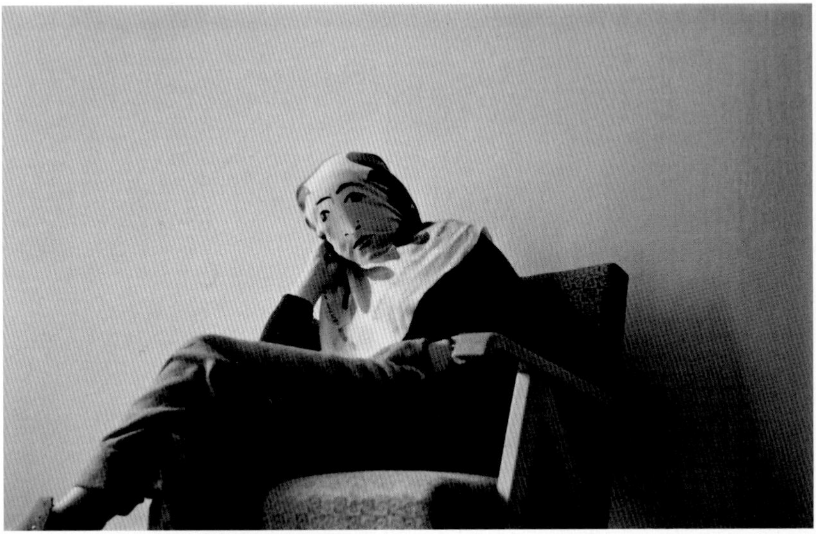

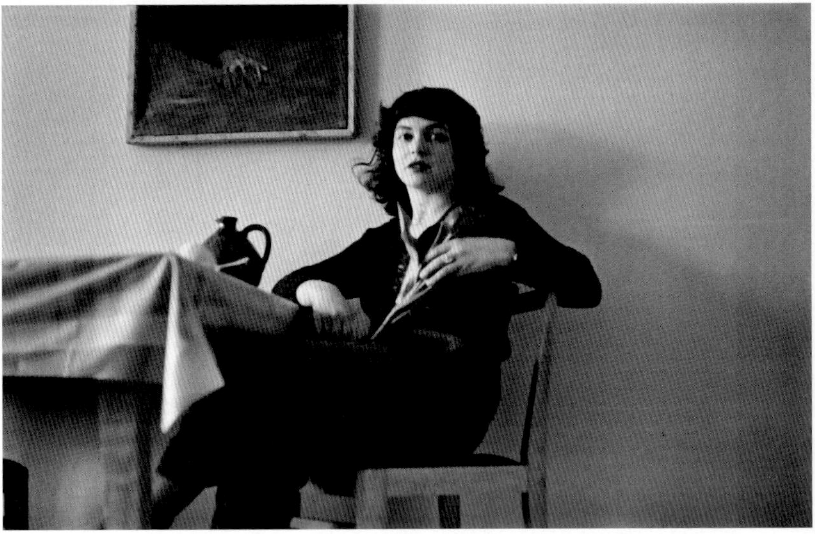

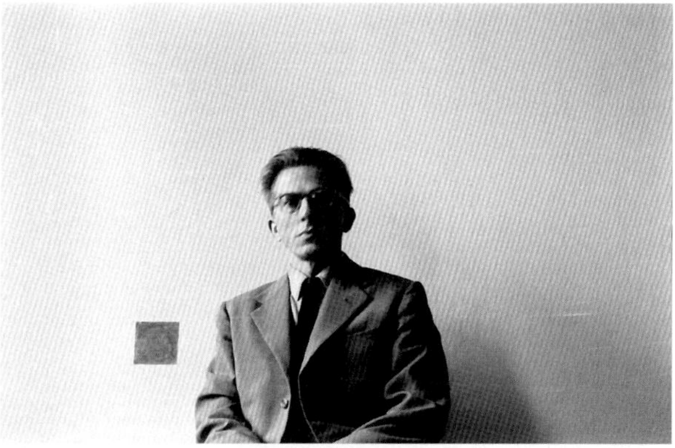

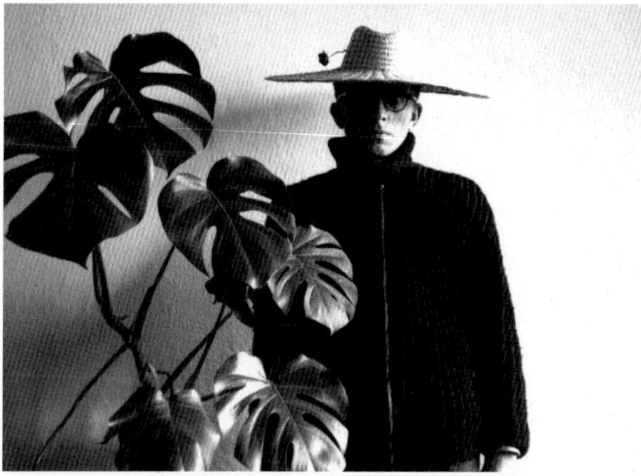

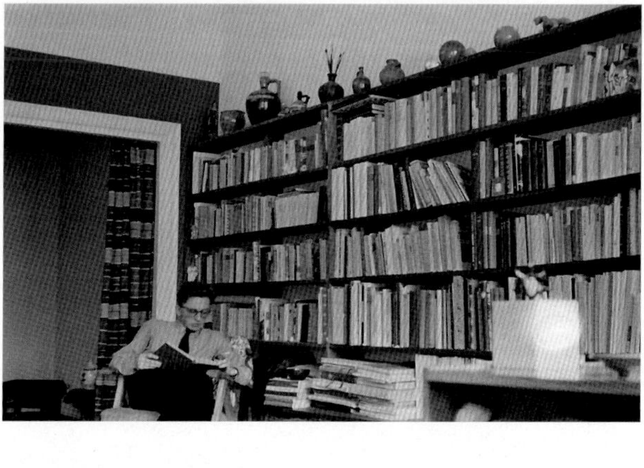

Page numbers in boldface type refer to letters, lightface to the introduction or notes.

Abakanowicz, Magdalena **258**, 338
Andrzej **37**
Anzelm **174**
Aristotle **26**
Arp, Jean (Hans) **260**, **264**, 340
Auerbach, Lejb **133**, 311, 341
Auricoste, Emmanuel **174**, **178**, **182**, 320
Avedon, Richard **266**, 341
Axentowicz, Teodor **114**, 307

Bachner, Gustaw **134**, 311
Baldaccini, César **222**, **280**, 327–8, 343, 347
Balzac, Honoré de **124**, 309
Barr, Alfred H., Jr. **264**, 340
Baudelaire, Charles **21**, **57**
Becker, Jacques 333
Bellini, Giovanni **193**
Bercholc **48**
Bereś, Jerzy 331
Berlikowski, Witold **49**, **57**
Beverloo, Guillaume Cornelis *See* Corneille
Bloch-Lainé, Jean-Louis **243–4**, 333
Blum, Helena 297
Boghici, Jean **261**, **265**, 339
Bojko, Szymon **262**, **280**, 339, 345
Borejsza, Jerzy 292
Bores, Francisco **174**, 319
Borowczyk, Walerian (Walter) **162–3**, **223–4**, 316, 320
Borzym, Józef **279**
Boudaille, Georges **257**, **262**, **273**, 337
Boulanger, Nadia 303
Brâncuşi, Constantin **178**, 322
Brandys, Kazimierz **66**, 300
Braque, Georges **52**, **174**, 298, 319
Braun **262**
Brecht, Bertolt 325
Breton, André **235**, 331
Breza, Tadeusz **255**, 337
Brunelleschi, Filippo **193**
Brzechwa, Jan **217**, 326
Brzozowski, Tadeusz **160**, 316, 323, 332
Buczkowski, Leopold **281**, 346

Calder, Alexander **170**, 318
Camus, Albert **15**, **37**, 290, 294
Candida **265**
Carmi, Eugenio 329
Cascella, Pietro 328
Cassou, Jean **174**, **182**, **185**, **189**, **192**, **197**, **200**, **222**, 319, 321
Castelli, Leo 346
Cellini, Benvenuto **193**
César *See* Baldaccini, César
Cesia **201**, **210**, **213**, 325
Cézanne, Paul **94**
Chaleriere **35**
Chałubiński, Tytus **41**, 296
Charlie *See* Ferster, Karol
Chirico, Giorgio de **180**, 322
Chmieleski, Amy 322
Chopin, Frédéric **105**, 304
Christie, Julie 343
Chudzik, Jerzy 328, 332
Churchill, Winston **248**, 335
Cini, Luigi **178**, **224**, 322, 331
Cieślewicz, Roman 7, 8, **177**, **187**, **193–4**, **198**, **219**, **223–4**, **239–40**, **242–3**, **246–7**, **251**, **255–61**, **264–6**, **270**, **272–5**, **277**, **279**, **281–4**, **286–7**, 320–1, 327–9, 330–3, 337–8, 340–1, 343, 345–8, 357, 367 (photographs)
Clouzot, Henri-Georges **174**, 319
Collin, Françoise 319, 320,
Copley, Noma **260**, **263–5**, 335
Copley, William **260**, **263–5**, 335
Corneille **261**, **265**, 339
Curwood, James Oliver **248**, 334
Cybulski, Zbigniew 315
Czarnocki *See* Korwin Czarnocki, Bronisław
Czartoryska, Urszula 7, 9, **224**, **226–7**, **229–32**, **235**, **239**, **242–3**, **246**, **248–9**, **251**, **254**, **257–9**, **261**, **264–5**, **267–9**, **271**, **273–5**, **279**, **283**, **285–6**, 329, 338, 344, 348
Czech, Bronisław **161**, 316
Czyż, Jerzy **175**, **182–3**, 320–1
Ćwierciakiewicz **262**

Danielewicz, Jan **173**, **191**, **197**, **201**, 319
Daszkiewicz, Halina **125**, 310
Daszkiewicz, Władysław **125**, **259**, 310
Daudet, Alphonse **50**, **52**, 297
Denise **96**
De Gaulle, Charles 314
Degas, Edgar **121**
Delacroix, Eugène **180**, 322
Delahaye, Jacques-Charles 343
Delvaux, Paul 320
De Pisis, Filippo **180**, 322
Desjobert **113**, **116–7**, 307
Dominik, Tadeusz 321
Donatello **193**
Dorival, Bernard **174**, 319
Dostoyevsky, Fyodor **21**
Duchamp, Gaston *See* Villon, Jacques
Duchamp, Marcel **260**, **263**, 335, 340
Dunikowski, Xawery (Ksawery) **38**, **40**, **52**, **59**, 295, 297–8
Dygat, Antoni 290
Dygat, Stanisław **15**, **19**, 290, 292

Ehrenburg, Ilya **124**, 309
Eibisch, Eugeniusz 332
Eile, Marian 298
Einstein, Albert 334
Eisenstein, Sergei **256**, 337

Eisensztajn *See* Eisenstein, Sergei
Elsner, Dante **114**, **170**, 307
Ernst, Max **264**, 340
Ewa **218**

Fajkosz, Ewa **160**, 316
Fajkosz, Kazimierz **160**, 316
Fall, Georges 373, 343
Fangor, Wojciech 8, 9, **198**, 314–5, 323, 341, 345, 359 (photograph)
Fautrier, Jean 332
Fedorowicz, Jacek 315
Ferster, Karol (Charlie) **130**, 310, 314
Fiedler, Arkady **234**, 330
Folman 306
Fra Angelico **193**
Franco, Cérès **260–2**, **265**, 339
Fumet, Angèle 309

Gaffka **198**, 324
Gajewski, Stanisław **184**, **197**, 322
Gallard, Michel de **167**, **182**, 317
Gałczyński, Konstanty Ildefons **59**, 299
Gamza **250**
Gauguin, Paul **32**
Gella-Melerowicz, Teresa 323
Gerasimov, Aleksandr **178**, 321
Gerson, Max **167**, **196**, 317, 324, 341
Ghiberti, Lorenzo **193**
Ghirlandaio, Domenico **193**
Giacometti, Alberto **260**, **277**, 339, 345
Gierowski, Stefan **253**, 323, 331, 335
Giotto **193**
Giroux, Georges 323
Gleb, Tomasz 323
Głogowska **114**
Gola, Jola 9, 292, 302, 309
Goldscheider, Cécile **167**, 317
Golovanoff, Nina **260**, **265**, 339
Gorky, Maxim **21**, 292
Gotlieb **286**
Grabowska-Konwent, Anna 9
Grabowski, Józef 297
Grabowski, Stanisław **167**, 317
Gretchen **52**
Gris, Juan **180**, 322
Guttuso, Renato **178**, 321

Hansen, Oskar 303
Hasior, Władysław 331
Helman, Marek 341
Henio; Heniuś **94**, **114**
Herzog, Émile *See* Maurois, André
Hilton, Rita 297, 301–2
Hodes, Barnet **263**, 340
Hodes, Eleanor **263**, 340
Hoffman, Paweł 292
Honda, Ishirō 336
Honig, Camille **213**, **215**, 326
Honoré, Mme. **122**, **168**
Hopps, Walter **264**, 340
Horno-Popławski, Stanisław **255**, 332, 336–7
Houston Brown, Florence **271**, 342, 346, 369 (photograph)

Infeld, Leopold **248**, 334
Irka (from Poland) **27**

Jadwiga (from Katowice) **214**, **217**
Jadzia (housekeeper) **159**, 315
Jaffé, Hans Ludwig Cohn **223**, 328
Jakubowska, Agata 5, 8–10, 289, 292, 336
Jakubowska, Małgorzata 9
Janoušková, Věra 290–1
Jarnuszkiewicz, Jerzy 328
Jasińska, Wanda **167**, **174–5**, **199**, **202**, **208–9**, 317, 320
Jasiński, Jan **22**, **167**, **174–5**, **199**, **202**, **208–9**, 293, 317, 320
Jean-Luc **242**, 333
Ježerský, František **97**, 305
Joliot-Curie, Jean Fréderic 313
Julek **91**

Kafka, Franz **262**, 337
Kantor *See* Kantorowicz
Kantorowicz **39**, **48**, 295
Karpuszko, Kazimir (Kazimierz) **250**, 335
Kaufmann, Peter **267**, **277**, 341, 344
Kenar, Antoni **161**, 316, 321
Kieffer, Antoine 338
Kika **167**
Klee, Paul **174**, 319
Knapp, Peter 333, 341
Kobiela, Bogumił 315
Kobro, Katarzyna 347–8
Kobzdej, Aleksander 331
Kołakowski, Leszek **223**, 328
Kordiasz **198**
Korwin Czarnocki, Bronisław **175**, **199**, **200**, **204**, **206–7**, 320
Kossak-Szczucka, Zofia **42**, 296
Kossakowski, Andrzej 303
Kott, Jan **107**, **125**, **137**, **143**, **175**, **182**, 306, 309
Kujawski, Aleksander 303
Kujawski, Jerzy 303
Kula, Marcin 9, 295, 318
Kulągowska-Słonimska, Hanna **92**, **115**, **123**, **164**, 303
Kulisiewicz, Tadeusz 331
Kunka, Lech 303
Kuryluk, Karol 292
Kwaśniewska, Barbara **281**, 346

Lambert, Jean-Clarence **273**, 343
Lardera, Berto **174**, 319

Lau **237**
Laurens, Henri **174**, 319
Lean, David 343
Lebenstein, Jan **235**, **244**, **250**, **253**, **280–1**, **283**, 330–1, 340, 346
Le Chapelain, André 293
Lechien, Ivan 346–7, 355 (photograph)
Le Corbusier **277**, 303, 345
Léger, Fernand 313
Leo, Peter **244**, **246**, **248**, 333
Lerendu, Gaston **123**, **134**, **152**, **154**, **175**, 308, 312, 314, 369 (photograph)
Lerendu, father of Gaston **134**
Lerendu, Simone **123**, **143**, **152**, **175**, 308, 314
Lesman, Wiktor Jan *See* Brzechwa, Jan
Leśniewska, Krystyna **37**, 294, 308
Leśniewski, Adam 9, **37**, **123**, 294, 308
Lévêque, Jean-Jacques **273**, 343, 347
Leyk, Anna 9
Lieberman, William S. **264**, 340
Lipiński, Eryk **99**, **262**, 303, 305
Lisowski, Jerzy 346
Listowska, Alicja 346
Listowski, Hieronim 376
Lorentz, Stanisław **175**, 320
Lublin, Lea **269**, 342
Lucheschi 320
Ludwiński, Jerzy 327
Ludwisia **160**
Lustre, Helena **18**, **21**, **40**, **43**, **114**, **127**, **168**, **173**, **190–1**, **197**, **200**, **217**, **222–3**, 289, 324, 327–28
Lustre, Julien **40**, **43**, **127**, **168**, **173**, **185**, **190–1**, **197**, **199**, **200**, **223**, 289, 324, 328
Lustre, Michelle **199**, 324

Łępicki **132**
Łodziana, Tadeusz 348
Łubieńska, Barbara **62**, 298, 300

Maciej **126**
Maillol, Aristide **52**, 298
Mayakovsky, Vladimir **123**, 309
Makarenko, Anton **260**, 338
Malmurowicz, Bolesław 328, 332
Malraux, André **185**, 314, 323
Mantorelle **16**
Marchiori, Giuseppe **257**, 337
Marcin **161**
Marczewska **189–90**
[Marczewski?], brother of Marczewska **189**
Marczyński, Adam 321
Margal, Mariusz **56**, 298
Margul *See* Margala, Mariusz
Marini, Marino **185**, 323
Markowski, Eugeniusz **273**, 343
Marquez-Rodilez, Naya **168**, 317
Martin, Claudine 349
Marysia **222**
Maryško **42**
Maryta **275–7**, **279**, 315
Masaccio **193**
Matisse, Henri **44**, **52**, 296, 313
Matta Echaurren, Roberto **260**, **264**, 340
Maurois, André **67**, 301
Mazurkiewicz, Alfons 323
Mencel, Wiktor **94**, **95**, **105**, 304
Mianowski, Lucjan 331
Michel **230**, **232–3**, 330
Michelson, Michelson's granddaughters 306
Mickiewicz, Adam 305
Mikołajska, Halina **210**, 325
Mikulski, Kazimierz 323
Milhaud, Darius **260**, **263**, 340
Miłosz, Czesław 318–9
Mitzner, Zbigniew 305
Mizerna **132**
Mondrian, Piet **180**, 322
Moniuszko, Stanisław 315
Monsaingeon, André **116**, **174**, 307
Monsaingeon, brother of André **174**
Monsaingeon, wife of André 307
Moore, Henry **185**, **206**, **267**, 323, 328, 341
Morales, Honorio **261**, 339
Morel, Henryk 346
Mossé, Hélène **169**, **175**, **240**, **242**, **255**, 318, 320
Motyka, Lucjan **191**, **196**, **203**, **208**, **255**, 323
Mroszczak, Józef **262**, **280**, 339, 345
Mrozowska **198–9**
[Mrozowski?] brother of Mrozowska **198**
Mrożek, Sławomir **250**, 335
Mukhina, Vera **178**, 321

Neveu, Ginette **123**, **132**, 309
Niclausse, Paul **113**, **174**, 307, 320
Nicoli, Carlo **341**
Nieciuński **168**, **170**, **173**, **175–6**, **201**, 317
Nedoshivin, German **178**, 321
Neizvestny, Ernst **268**, 342
Nowosielski, Jerzy 321, 331
Nowowiejska, Barbara 300

Ofierska, Maria 9
Olszewska, Ewa **42**, 296
Ostaszewska **215**, 326
Ostaszewska, Katarzyna **215**, 326
Ostaszewski **215**, 326
Ostrowski, Kazimierz „Kachu" **121**, **128**, **130**, **132**, **141**, **153**, 303, 307

Pacanowska, Felicja **92**, **95**, 304
Palcr, Zdeněk **97**, 291, 304–5
Pałka, Julian **262**, 328, 339
Panova, Vera **37**, 294
Papa, Giuseppe *See* San Lazzaro, Gualtieri di
Pappé, Julian **95**, 304

Parker, John Carson **22**, **29**, 293
Pągowska, Teresa **187**, **196**, **206**, **281**, 323, 346
Pedrosa, Mario **260**, 339
Penn, Irving **266**, 341
Penrose, Roland **264**, 340
Perry, Beatrice **253**, 336
Pevsner, Antoine **174**, 319
Piasecki, Bolesław **263**, 340
Picart Le Doux, Jean **258**, 338
Picasso, Pablo **25**, **174**, 293, 298, 312–3, 319
Pierre **117**
Pion **232–3**, 320
Pink, Lutka 303
Piwocki, Ksawery 331
Pluchart, François **283**, 347
Płaza, Bogusław **259**, **280**, 338, 346
Pokorný, Karel **42**, 296
Polasińska, Zula **213**, 326
Poleszczuk, Romuald **213**, 326
Poliakoff, Serge 332
Polit, Paweł 6
Pollaiuolo, Antonio and Piero **193**
Pompon, François **178**, 322
Poniż, Duszan 320
Porębski, Mieczysław **132**, **160**, **206**, **239**, **242**, **244**, 303, 311, 316, 331
Pospiszyl, Tomáš 9, 290, 305
Połtawski, Adam **226**, 329
Pronaszko, Zbigniew 321
Przywara, Andrzej 339
Putrament, Jerzy **137**, **143**, 311, 313
Pużyńska, Joanna 292, 329
Pyryev, Ivan 296

Quadrani, Federico 330

Radkowska, Benedicta 309
Radkowska, mother of Jerzy **125**
Radkowski, Jerzy (Georges-Hubert de Radkowski) **125**, 309
Radnitzky, Emmanuel *See* Ray, Man
Radziejowska, Zofia **253**, 335–6
Ragon, Michel **262**, 339
Ramponi **175**
Ray, Man **260**, **264**, 340
Read, Herbert **260**, **264**, 340
Restany, Pierre **250**, **261**, **265**, **271–3**, **275**, **277**, **280–1**, 327, 335, 341–3, 345
Riccio **193**
Richier, Germaine **184**, 322
Robbia, Andrea della **193**
Robbia, Luca della **193**
Robbia, Mattia della **193**
Rodin, Auguste François-René **52**, 297
Roland **102**, **109**, **224**
Romanowski, Tadeusz 303
Rostkowska, Maria Papa **222**, 328
Rostkowski, Ludwik Jr 328
Roszkowska, Teresa 303
Rublič, Ivo **14**, **28**, **43**, **167**, 290
Rudnev, Lev 324
Russak, H. **33**, **105**, 293
Rydel 303
Rypson, Piotr 6, 300, 313, 319

Sadzik, Józef 330, 340
Salanon, René **262**, 339
Salska **16**
San Lazzaro, Gualtieri di **222**, 328
Santelli **274**
Sandauer, Artur **107**, **115**, **261**, 306
Sapieha, Adam Stefan 299
Sartre, Jean-Paul **21**, 293
Scherer-Wirska, Olga **235**, 331
Scholtz, Alina 320
Simenon, Georges **285**, 348
Simoncini, Giorgio 328
Skłodowska-Curie, Maria **25**
Skrowaczewski, Stanisław 303
Słonimski, Piotr 303
Sonnabend, Ileana **281**, 346
Sonnabend, Michael 346
Sosnowska, Joanna 9, 325
Soulages, Pierre **260**, 332
Sowiński, Wilhelm **129–30**, 310
Speyer, A. James **264**, **281**, 340
Speyer, Darthea **264**, **281**, 340, 346
Stadler, Rodolphe 328
Staël, Nicolas de 332
Stajuda, Jerzy **260**, **266**, 338
Stalin, Józef **77**, 302, 324
Stanisławska, Ewa **226–7**, **248–9**, **251**, **254**, **257**, **265**, 300, 341, 355
Stanisławska, Maria **92**, 296
Stanisławska, Olga 9, **283**, **285–6**, 300, 344, 348, 351
Stanisławska-Adamczewska, Teresa **56**, **59**, **62**, 298, 300
Stanisławski, Aleksander **62**, **177**, **187**, **194**, **204**, 298, 300, 321
Stanisławski, Piotr 6–10, **158–9**, **161–4**, **166**, **168**, **170**, **173**, **175–6**, **177–8**, **185**, **187**, **189**, **191**, **193**, **197**, **198–9**, **201**, **203**, **207–10**, **212–7**, **219**, **222–4**, **226**, **228–9**, **230**, **232–6**, **237**, **240–8**, **253–5**, **257–8**, **260–1**, **263–5**, **268**, **270–1**, **273–6**, **279**, **281–6**, 292, 315, 317, 320–1, 329–30, 332–3, 338, 342, 348, 351, 365, 367 (photographs)
Stanisławski, Romuald **34**, **38**, **40**, **48–9**, **54**, **57**, **60**, **62**, **92**, **121–3**, **126–7**, **137**, **155**, **199**, **204**, **232**, **241**, **270**, 295–6, 299, 300, 342
Starzyński, Juliusz **201**, **207**, 311, 321, 325
Stefan, Bedřich **21**, **28**, **42**, **70**, **97**, **121**, 291, 293, 296, 300–1, 304
Stern, Jonasz 323

Stępniowa **160**
Strumiłło, Andrzej **283**, 347
Strumiłło-Olkiewicz, Dobrochna **250**, **252**, **255**, **257**, 335
Stryjeńska, Zofia **141**, 312
Strzemiński, Władysław 347–8
Styczyński, Jan **168**, 317
[Szablińska?] sister of Mietek **21**, **35**
Szabliński, Mieczysław [Mietek] 6, **15**, **21**, **29**, **30**, **35**, **52**, **103**, **110**, **174**, 290
Szancerowa, Gizela **253**, **272–3**, 336, 343
Szapocznikow, Jakub 311, 133
Szapocznikow, Mirosław 291, 294, 297
Szapocznikow, Regina (Ryfka, *née* Auerbach) **15–6**, **21**, **30**, **34–6**, **38–9**, **42**, **44**, **47–8**, **55–6**, **58**, **62**, **66**, **68–9**, **98–9**, **107**, **109**, **114**, **120**, **123–4**, **121**, **127–33**, **140**, **143–4**, **147–8**, **152–3**, **155**, **165**, **175**, **199**, **210**, **215**, **217**, 290–1, 294–5, 297, 306, 311.
Szenwic, Wilhelm *See* Sowiński, Wilhelm
Szewczyk, Agnieszka 6, 9
Szotkowska-Beylin, Katarzyna 9, 10
Szymczak, Zygmunt **253**, 336
Szymczyk, Adam 339
Šetlík, Jiří 304

Taminiaux, Jacques **174**, **185**, 319, 323
Tarasin, Jan 331
Tchorek, Karol **178**, 321
Tchórzewski, Jerzy 323, 326–7
Teisseyre, Stanisław **253**, 332, 336
Tintoretto, Jacopo **192**
Titian **192**
Turowicz, Jerzy 298
Tuwim, Julian **106**, 305

Uzzano, Niccolò da **193**

Vautre **102**
Velimski, Otokar 5
Verne, Jules 329
Veronese, Paolo **193**
Verrocchio, Andrea del **193**
Villon, Jacques **180**, 322
Vincenz, Andrzej **29**, 291, 293

Wagner, Josef 5, 305
Wajda, Andrzej **256**, 337
Walter *See* Borowczyk, Walerian
Warszawska (violinist) 303
Ważyk, Adam **125**, **137**, **151**, 309
Weiss, Jacques **95**, **168**, 304
Wescher, Herta **240**, 332
Wiech *See* Wiechecki, Stefan
Wiechecki, Stefan **38**, 294–5
Wiktorko **132**
Wilczur-Garztecka, Ewa **261**, 339
Wilczur-Garztecki, Juliusz 339
Wilden, Janusz **160**, 316
Wildenstein, Georges 297
Wilski, Wojciech **253**, 336
Wilson, Sarah 292, 322
Wita **174**
Witkiewicz, Stanisław **41**, **67**, 296
Władek **37**
Włodarski, Marek 321
Wogensky, Robert **182**, **258–9**, **263**, 322
Wojciechowski, Aleksander **201**, **207**, **283**, 321, 325
Wouters, Hendrik Emil (Rik) **180**, 322
Woźna, Zofia 331
Wnuk **126**, 310
Wnuk, Alina **40**, **52**, **53**, **59**, **126–7**, 296, 310
Wroński **164**
Wróblewska, Danuta **280**, 345
Wyszyński, Stefan **263**, 340

Zahorska, Beata 332
Zahorska, Michelle 9, **169**, **240**, **255**, 318, 320, 332
Zahorski, Dorian **240**, **242**, 332–3
Zahorski, Lech **163**, **169**, **240**, 303, 316, 318, 332
Zamecznik, Stanisław **201**, **207**, 325, 359 (photograph)
Zanini, W. **265**
Zbrożyna, Barbara 310
Zemsz, Abraham (Abrasza) **170**, **172**, 318–9
Zielonkiewicz, Kazimierz (Kaziel) 303
Zimnoch, Gabriela **39**
Zosia (housekeeper) **160**, **163**, **170**, **175–7**, **191**, **199**, **201–2**, **204**, **209**, **212–3**, **217**, 315, 321, 327

Żmudziński, Tadeusz 303
Żółkiewski, Stefan 292
Żuławski, Jacek **160**, 315

Series editors
Marta Dziewańska
Katarzyna Szotkowska-Beylin

Book editors
Agata Jakubowska
Katarzyna Szotkowska-Beylin

Translated by
Jennifer Croft

Copy-edited and corrected by
Warren Niesłuchowski

Design concept and layout
Ludovic Balland, Typography Cabinet, Basel

Typesetting and lithography
Noviki.net, Kasia Nestorowicz, Marcin Nowicki

Typefaces
Ludwig Pro

Printed by
ARGRAF Sp. z o.o.
ul. Jagiellońska 76, 03-301 Warszawa

Photo credits
All works by Alina Szapocznikow © The Estate of Alina Szapocznikow—Piotr Stanisławski/ACADP, Paris. Photographs from the Ryszard Stanisławski Archive © Olga Stanisławska.
Authors of the photographs:
Roman Cieślewicz, Marek Holzman, Jože Kolosa-Koper, Jerzy Kosiński, Eustachy Kossakowski, Ewa Kozłowska-Tomczyk, Bolesław Malmurowicz, Tadeusz Rolke, Władysław Sławny, Ryszard Stanisławski, Bartosz Stawiarski, Wojciech Zamecznik.

Every effort has been made to contact all copyright holders of the photographs. We shall be pleased to rectify any errors or omissions.

Cover photographs
Front cover: Alina Szapocznikow, 1954, photo by Ryszard Stanisławski
Back cover: Alina Szapocznikow, drawing of Ryszard Stanisławski, 1949

Bookmark
Alina Szapocznikow, photo by Roman Cieślewicz

Acknowledgments
We would like to express our special gratitude to Olga Stanisławska and Piotr Stanisławski, who assured relentless encouragement and involvement in this project.
We would also like to express our thanks to all those who generously provided us with the photographs for the present volume: The Estate of Alina Szapocznikow—Piotr Stanisławski/ACADP, Paris, Olga Stanisławska, Jola Gola, Chantal Petit-Cieślewicz, Anka Ptaszkowska, IRSA Publishing House, Krakow.

Publisher
Museum of Modern Art in Warsaw
Pańska 3
00-124 Warsaw
www.artmuseum.pl

ISBN: 978-83-933818-6-9

Distributed by
The University of Chicago Press
www.press.uchicago.edu

The production of the book was generously supported by Piotr Stanisławski and Hervé Loevenbruck Gallery, Paris.

This publication has been subsidized by Instytut Książki—the ©POLAND Translation Programme

PUBLICATION SUBSIDIZED BY THE POLISH BOOK INSTITUTE
THE ©POLAND TRANSLATION PROGRAM
INSTYTUT KSIĄŻKI
©POLAND

BOOKS

THE MUSEUM UNDER CONSTRUCTION BOOK SERIES

WE ARE BUILDING A MUSEUM OF MODERN ART IN WARSAW WE ARE WRITING A NEW HISTORY OF ART

THE BOOK SERIES IS EDITED BY MARTA DZIEWAŃSKA AND KATARZYNA SZOTKOWSKA-BEYLIN

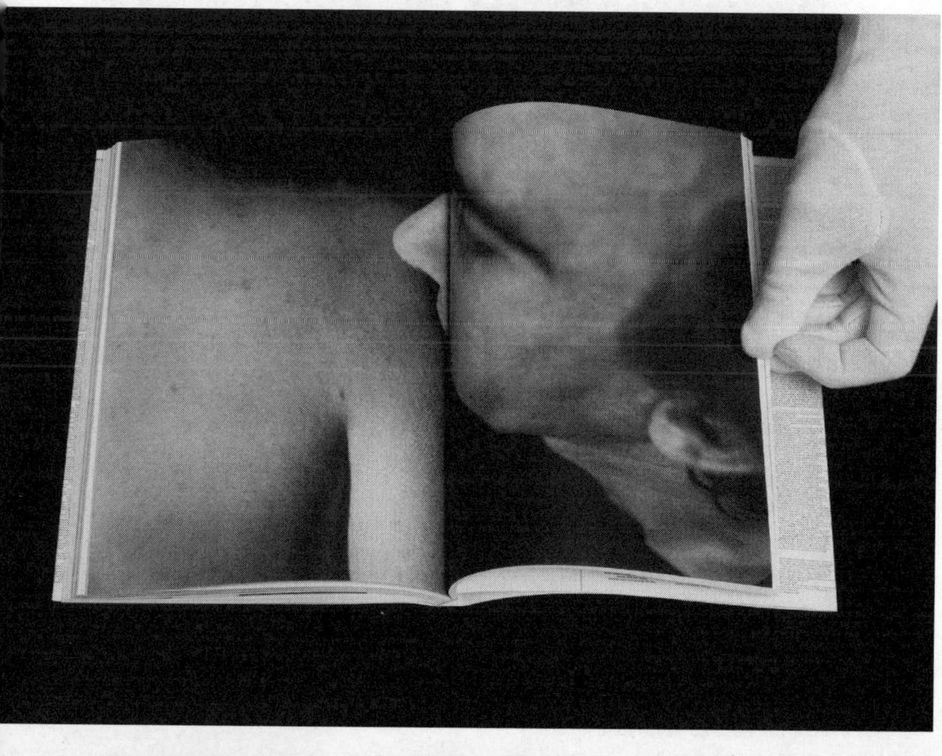

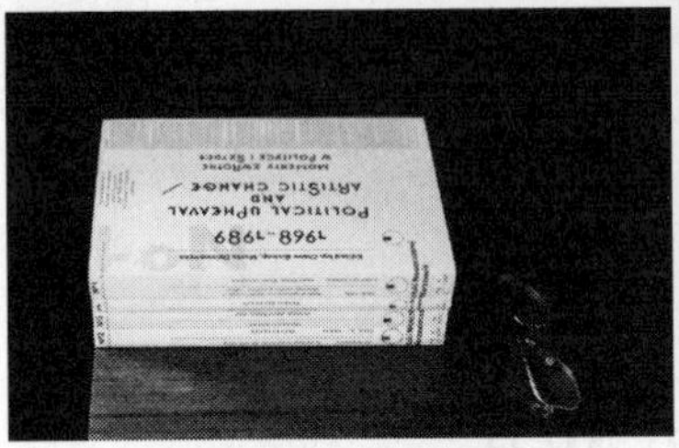

No 1 **1968–1989: POLITICAL UPHEAVAL AND ARTISTIC CHANGE**

Edited by Claire Bishop and Marta Dziewańska

Museum of Modern Art in Warsaw, 2009

The texts assembled in this reader are a selective record of presentations from the seminar "1968–1989," organized at the Museum of Modern Art in Warsaw.

ISBN 978-83-924044-0-8

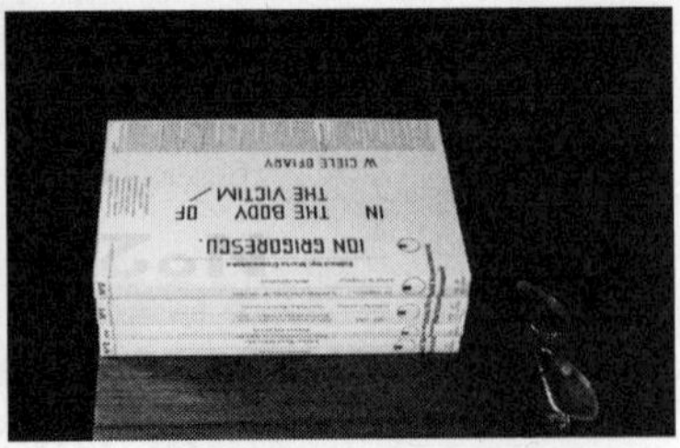

No 2 **ION GRIGORESCU. IN THE BODY OF THE VICTIM**

Edited by Marta Dziewańska

Museum of Modern Art in Warsaw, 2010

This book is an attempt to read the work of one of the most charismatic and original artists from the former Eastern-bloc, who until 1989 worked in relative isolation, and whose art can currently be viewed in relation to similar positions in other parts of the world.

ISBN 978-83-924044-1-5

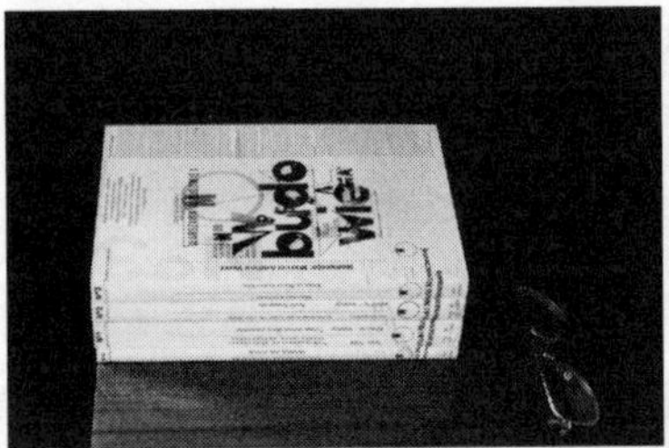

No 3 **WARSZAWA W BUDOWIE 2009**

[Warsaw Under Construction 2009]

Edited by Marcel Andino-Velez

Museum of Modern Art in Warsaw, 2010

The book is a record of the events which took place as part of the first edition of the Warsaw Under Construction festival focused on design, architecture and town planning, an attempt at capturing the spirit and creative energy that had at the time taken over the city.

ISBN 978-83-924044-2-2

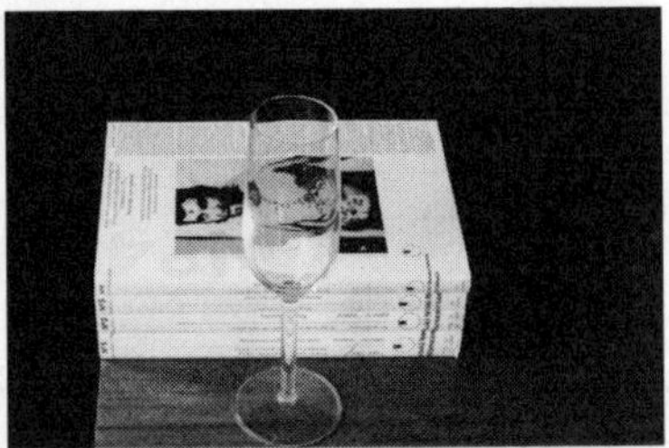

No 4 **AS SOON AS I OPEN MY EYES I SEE A FILM. EXPERIMENT IN THE ART OF YUGOSLAVIA IN THE 1960S AND 1970S**

Edited by Ana Janevski

Museum of Modern Art in Warsaw, 2010

The book is inspired by the first exhibition organized by the Museum of Modern Art in Warsaw. It is a journey to a country which has ceased to exist, but which gave rise to the most important art myth in our part of Europe—the myth of radical art.

ISBN 978-83-924044-3-9

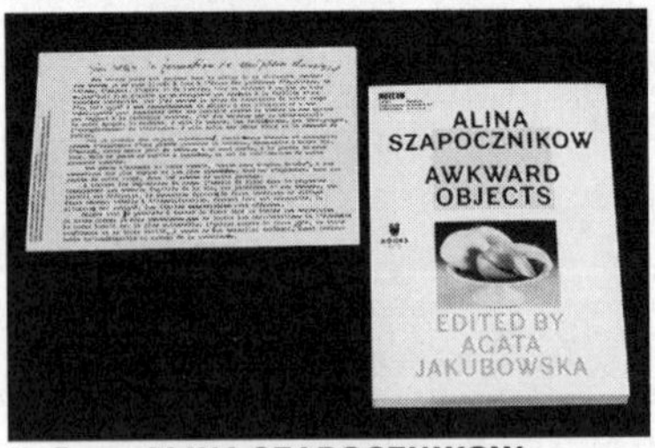

No 5 **ALINA SZAPOCZNIKOW AWKWARD OBJECTS**

Edited by Agata Jakubowska

Museum of Modern Art in Warsaw, 2011

An artist who always put herself in the difficult position of pioneer heading towards the new and unknown, near the end of her life confessed: *As for me, I produce awkward objects*. Here that life and work is addressed by participants in the conference "Alina Szapocznikow: Works. Documents. Interpretations."

ISBN 978-83-924044-6-0